ScribeLife Series

They Will All Know Me

God's Passion and Provision for Sharing Life With You NOW

Tonia Woolever

Here is your God!

See, the Sovereign Lord comes with power,
and He rules with a mighty arm.

See, His reward is with Him, and His
recompense accompanies Him.

He tends His flock like a shepherd:

He gathers the lambs in His arms and
carries them close to His heart;

He gently leads those that have young.

Isaiah 40:9-11, NIV

This has happened more mornings than not since I began seriously writing. I am living the word from Isaiah 50:4 that says, *"He wakens me morning by morning, wakens my ear to listen like one being taught."* I have so loved this, because at every turn when I have gone to bed not clear on what to do next in structuring the book and creating continuity of themes, I awake knowing what to do. We are, again, writing this book together!

Yet this morning I was actually trying to sleep in a little longer, as a cold front came in; heater off, house cold, still pretty sleepy, and wanted to snuggle with warm husband. And the time change last week means it's really very dark still at 6:00 a.m. So I roll over to go back to sleep, and the Lord keeps speaking to my spirit of two things He wants me to write about. Finally I grin at Him and say, *"You really want to go to work on this right now, don't you?"* He grins back at me in His voice, saying, *"You noticed!"*

I look for words to describe this experience. God is not writing the book through me; He is not dictating it to me. Rather, we are a team in just the best way. When He spoke the two concepts to me in a sentence this morning, He was tying into truths that live in me now, that have been developed through years of faithful study, plus treasures whispered to me in prayer and worship, on walks or in couch conversations — treasures we have built together over the years. His faithfulness to give and my faithfulness to receive and be a steward of His gifts, have left a rich deposit in my soul and spirit. So He can say a sentence, sometimes even a word, and I know what to do with it. And because He connects the dots of concepts I had studied separately in detail, but never put together before, God shows Himself to be a brilliant weaver.

For instance, this book on knowing God originally didn't focus on our covenant very much, but now it is totally framed by covenant. Then, He revealed to me that the detailed study I have done and taught on "Entering Rest" should be woven in

1 The Full Message Of This New Life

Go stand in the temple courts ... and tell the people the full message of this new life. (Acts 5:20)

Being a Christian and knowing God are two very different things for too many people.

Does that statement shock you? Or does it seem obvious already?

I am writing this book, adding to the hundreds already out there on Christian living, because as a counselor, teacher and daughter of God, it is clear to me that one can be a Christian — saved and baptized — and still not really know the *person* who is God. As a counselor for over 25 years, it is abundantly clear to me that just about 100% of what people need to become like Christ, live a victorious life, receive healing, joy, peace and love, is to know God in personal experience.

As a Christian working with nearly every denomination that confesses Christ, I have also seen that a great many pastors and churches are focused on teaching people how to be good Christians and church members, instead of teaching them how to know their God — and again, there is a vast difference between these two realities.

The difference is seen between those truly enjoy a relationship with the Lord that actually nourishes the soul, and those who faithfully serve God apart from any sense of His personal presence and comfort. It is seen in Christians who have a continual tug of war with temptation and sin, versus those who are so blessed by walking with God in His ways that not much tempts them anymore. It is the difference between one who genuinely worships God out of a full heart, and the one who just sings worship songs because that's what you do before the sermon. Knowing God in daily life versus just "being saved" is seen in the difference between a Christian for whom the promises in Scripture are fulfilled, and one who can never seem to make them happen, no matter how hard they work at their faith. Taken altogether, the most profound difference is seen in whether a Christian feels entirely satisfied in being a child of God, or is perpetually disappointed.

Knowing God Is Everything

I write this book because many do not know their God, nor have someone teaching them that they can and should. I write this book because knowing God is everything! I write this book because knowing God is actually His idea, being His primary purpose and the greatest blessing offered in the New Covenant of Christ.

I write this book because we have gotten it upside down and backwards: we think we have to become like Christ in order for God to come near. But in fact, God comes near us in order to show us how to become like Christ. Every good father teaches his immature son how to be who he should be. I am a profoundly different woman after 35 years of knowing God, in both character and contentment. That didn't happen from just reading my Bible and going to church; it happened through experiencing God as a real Father, Christ as a living Savior, and the Spirit as a divine, ever-present Friend, Teacher, and Enabler.

I write this book to build your faith in knowing God, to tell you my own experience and how it has changed my life, and to reveal the most important things you need to know to embark on a journey to seek God's heart. I write this book in hopes that once you have read it, you will never again settle for what I call "spectator sport Christianity." I hope you will come away with a real hunger to know the most amazing Person ever, who not only promised us abundant life, but who IS abundant life to us, and in us.

You were not saved to just have your sin forgiven, then left to pray to a distant God whom you cannot know until you die and go to heaven. In a fresh and unbiased reading of the New Testament you will not find any language to support this idea. What you will find is an incredible chorus of voices spurring you on to know God, walk with God, hear God, work with God, rest with God, be comforted by God, and along the way, become like God. Because in the end, YOU, child of God, become like your Father by knowing Him — there is no other way.

Knowing God Begins Now, Not In Heaven

You can know God. You have been brought into a covenant relationship with the Trinity for that very purpose. It doesn't begin after you die. Christianity isn't having only 10% of God now and the other 90% of Him later. Everything the Bible invites you to put your hope in flows out of this relationship — the experience of knowing the real God in real life.

A.W. Tozer said in His timeless classic, "The Pursuit of God":

> *The Bible is not an end in itself, but a means to bring men to an intimate and satisfying knowledge of God, that they may enter into Him, that they may delight in His Presence, may taste and know the inner sweetness of the very God Himself in the core and center of their hearts.*[1]

We have unfortunately, over time, been lulled into accepting the idea that knowing God in any intimate way is only for some heavenly day or for some super-spiritual ones.

---

[1] Page 9, The Pursuit of God by A.W. Tozer, ©1982, WingSpread Publishers, Camp Hill, PA.

Scholars have researched and written of the evolution of Christian life, an evolution in which we steadily moved away from the sheer joy and power of the first century church — who walked and talked with God — to a largely powerless religion of knowing more *about* God than actually knowing God.

The Apostles who first walked with Christ clearly lived and taught that all born again disciples of Christ can and should have a genuine fellowship with God. It is not earned, it is received — from the moment one is saved, baptized in water and filled with the Spirit. To believe otherwise is to put your God-given, blood-bought life on hold until your earth suit dies. It also means God's desire to live through you, expressing Himself to your little part of the world, will have to go largely unfulfilled. He won't love you any less, but you will both lose out, big time.

Jesus Revealed What We Are Made For

The main reason Jesus spent years among men before He went to the cross was to demonstrate the life He was purchasing for us. He showed us what it would be like for a redeemed human being, filled with the Spirit, to share life with the Father. This is why the Lord gave us His Spirit: to make it possible for us to know the Father, Son and Spirit while we yet live on earth. True, His primary motivation is to reveal His glory — but it just so happens that while God does *that* through *your* life, you win the lottery of life more abundant, life more joyful, life that gives life to others. In all this, you get to give God much joy.

God's purpose wasn't just to save us; it was to bring us into the relationship we were created for.

God's purpose wasn't just to save us; it was to bring us into the relationship we were created for in the first place. The limitations of our flesh faculties make it impossible for us to physically see or hear God, but our spirits have no such limitations. For this reason, faith is needed; not just to believe in God, but to enjoy God, in a life that is never boring, never disappoints, and is deeply satisfying.

If you still feel like you are on the outside looking in, if you are bored or frustrated with your experience of being a Christian, if you've been wearing yourself out to confess and "pray in the promises," and if you feel like you are the one who has to hold everything together in this Christianity thing — **you're doing it all wrong!** In order to run the race all the way and win the prize, you must quit living as if you have to do it all on your own and keep yourself talked into it all.

I want to shout it from the rooftops, because I've tested it thoroughly, and it is true: you are called to know God *now*. You can know God now. Every promise God makes is fulfilled in and through this relationship. All comfort, all satisfaction of heart, all ability to forgive, to be wise, to fulfill your creative potential, to live worthy, comes naturally as you live in your true identity as the beloved child and family member of a very present Father, Brother and Friend.

You are called to know God *now*. You *can* know God now. Every promise God makes is fulfilled in and through this relationship.

You might earn a good welcome in heaven because you perform well as a Christian, but you make all of heaven rejoice — and become the 100-fold fruitful Christian — only when you have lived your life on earth according to the full plan of God: seeing, hearing, walking and talking with Him.

God couldn't wait to share life with you. He couldn't wait to show off His best Dad stuff. He couldn't wait to show *you* off to the world you live in, after He teaches you His ways. He couldn't wait to nourish you, then nourish the world through you. He couldn't wait to brag to the devil, *"These are the children of my strength, more powerful than you! They are my people, I am their God, and you are toast."*

From the beginning, you were made to know God in personal experience, not just get a ticket to heaven. It is His idea, His passion, and the joy of Jesus the Christ. I pray that this book will stir absolute faith in God's passion to share life with you now.

2 Making The Case For Knowing God Now

I used to wonder why God would want to share life with little old me. In fact, for a while I studied the Bible in search of Scriptures to shoot the whole idea down, because it seemed too good to be true. Instead, I found ample evidence that indeed, God wants to share life with us, every bit of it. He found many ways to say it in Scripture, and made all the necessary arrangements for it to happen. So I chose to believe, and stepped into faith that the Lord really wants to be involved in life where I live it: on the earth, and in my heart. Somewhere along the way, He opened my eyes to a very important fact about what really motivates Him.

God's Glory Is Revealed In Relationship

As one reads through the Scriptures it becomes evident that God loves to reveal His glory. God's glory is displayed in the heavens, in the majestic mountains, the boundless oceans and the incredible creation all around us; but nowhere is God's glory revealed more than in relationship, where His character is on display. The Scriptures contain many more references to God's glory as it is expressed in how He relates to people and nations, than to His majestic power in nature.

Everything about God's character that is most glorious — how He loves, how He teaches, how He comforts, forgives, and guides; how He saves, helps, restores, encourages, loves — is revealed in the context of relating to another being. These are things that happen between two living souls, and God has made them a matter of covenant promise. He says in multiple ways in Scripture: "*This is who I will be to you. This is how I will treat you. This is how I will love you as we share life together.*" His language is intimate, inviting, and passionate; His actions with mankind throughout history have backed up every word. He wasn't just being poetic and metaphorical.

After a straightforward read through the Bible, one would have to construct quite a fiction to explain away God's clear intentions and passion: to know and be known by His creation. Yet some live believing that this kind of personal experience of God is only for some day far off in another place called heaven.

Think this through with me: in heaven, there is no need for comfort, or the Comforter. In heaven, there is no need for help or encouragement or salvation. All is complete in heaven, where there is no sin, no tribulation, no one wounding our hearts. I hope by the time we finish walking through this book together you will feel how very preposterous that notion is, and come away determined to never settle for anything less than knowing God now, in your everyday life.

In heaven, there is no need for the Comforter.

There is another thing to consider: if we aren't meant to truly know God *before* we go to heaven, why would Jesus warn people He will find it necessary to say to some trying to enter there, *"Depart from me, I never knew you!"* [1] And this spoken to people who were doing His works and teaching His stuff!

We tend to think that the full expression of God's glory was that He redeemed us and gave His beloved Son to open heaven's doors to us. Believe it or not, that awesome act was just the seed of what would become God's greatest glory; a glory He dreamed would fill the whole earth. God's dream is that

[1] Matthew 7:21-23

through His redeemed children, the fullness of His glory will be revealed to all creation:

> *For the earth will be filled with the knowledge of the glory of the Lord as the waters cover the sea. (Habakkuk 2:14)*

The glory He wants to display the most is His character to give abundant life to His people through His steadfast righteousness, boundless goodness, kindness, wisdom and justice. God glories in His character.

Boast Of This One Thing

> *This is what the Lord says: "Let not the wise man boast of his wisdom or the strong man boast of his strength or the rich man boast of his riches, but let him who boasts boast about this: that he understands and knows me, that I am the Lord, who exercises kindness, justice and righteousness on earth, for in these I delight," declares the Lord. (Jeremiah 9:23-24).*

As Christians, we really need to think about why we pursue spiritual growth. What are we after? Is our goal to be spiritually perfect, or is it to know and understand God? While God's admonition through Jeremiah was addressed to people who did not acknowledge Him at all, it is also a warning to all who bear His name. Those who strive for religious perfection while making little effort to actually know God are just as likely to entirely misunderstand Him.

"Let him who boasts boast about this: that he understands and knows me."

Religious perfection is the wrong target, and if you are aiming for the wrong target, you will never hit the right one. You run the risk of being in error, as the Pharisees were. The Apostle Paul was a man of great integrity and religious devotion, but He had the wrong target. He became an expert in the law, but not in knowing God. This resulted in Paul being deceived as to what truly honors and pleases God. He even murdered those who followed Christ, until a personal encounter with Christ set Him on a path of knowing God — the true target.

Those who seek perfection while failing to seek God's heart may end up doing so for their own sake, not for His. It can become what Paul referred to in Philippians 1:17 as *spiritual ambition.* It feels like you're honoring God; but if you do not truly know and understand His core values, you can actually end up dishonoring Him, as Paul did.

Isaiah 27:11 warns that if we do not grow to understand our God, we will not increase in His grace or favor. In other words, God favors those who make it their goal to know and understand Him. The Apostle Peter underscored this when he said, *But grow in the grace and knowledge of our Lord and Savior Jesus Christ.* [2]

Goal: ~~Christian Perfection~~ Knowing God

We don't need to pursue perfection, we need to mature, as all children must. Children don't need to be perfect, but they do need to grow up and find their place in the family. This is especially critical for the Christian who now has God for a Father! This requires faith, and complete reliance on the Holy Spirit. It may also require you to change your whole goal, where knowing God becomes Job One, in place of merely "trying to be a good Christian."

Everything about Christianity will be redefined as you focus on the goal of knowing God. Take, for instance, Jesus' instruction that every disciple who follows Him needs to die to self. The serious Christian typically responds by finding ways to abase and empty himself, quenching all personal desire, ambition and need; but this isn't at all what Jesus meant. Dying

[2] 2 Peter 3:18

to self isn't the actual target, it is only the means to what the Lord is really after. Jesus made it abundantly clear that our primary target is to love God and others with all our might. Pursuing these goals forces us to forget ourselves. While we are busy loving God and others with all our might, self dies while we're not looking — a natural death that does not draw attention to ourselves. It's a great way to go.

When Jesus began to teach and minister publicly, He sounded so very different than all the other teachers, rabbis and religious lawyers (Pharisees) because He didn't hound people about the law. He spoke of the Father and taught them His ways, encouraging people to know the real God instead of focusing on doctrines made up by men. [3]

Jesus exposed the truth: the most devout religious leaders among them did not actually know God, while presenting themselves as God's spokesmen, pronouncing His will and judgments to the people. This ultimately caused them to misrepresent the true heart of God to His people, which greatly angered Jesus. While not believing in God is a sin, *believing the wrong things about God* and expressing them to others may be an even greater one, as this maligns God's character.

The Pharisees displayed less value or faith for knowing God than achieving religious perfection, and taught others to do the same. But then came Jesus. In all of His teaching and miracle working, Jesus brought His Father and the people close to one another, and made everything intensely personal. By His words and actions, He revealed the true and living God to a people desperately hungry for what they did not know they needed: a real experience with a real God in real life. Throughout His public ministry Jesus tried to shift their focus from pursuing the law of Moses to pursuing the real prize: knowing God the Father, and Jesus Christ.

---

[3] Matthew 15:8-9

Knowing God Is The Prize

The whole purpose of living by faith is to know God in personal experience while we live on earth. Remember, the story of humanity began with God and Adam sharing life together in a real garden on earth — God's idea! He planted the garden, He put man there, He came to be with Adam in the cool of the day. He provided all that Adam and Eve needed in the garden and on the Tree of Life. Then Adam sinned against God, which defiled his spirit and rendered him unfit for that happy intimate fellowship with God. This forced God to expel Adam and all his family line from their garden, so man lost the privilege and ability to know the Lord in close relationship.

The whole purpose of living by faith is to know God in personal experience while we live on earth.

Yet this didn't alter God's plans or dampen His desire. God created us for that intimate relationship with Him, and until we have it, He and we can never be satisfied. All mankind was created with a hunger to know the God who created them, whether they are aware of it or not. Those who lived in the days of Jesus, who had a taste of the Father through Him, discovered both their true hunger and the satisfaction of that hunger as they encountered the true God. Proverbs 13:12 says, *"A longing fulfilled is a tree of life."* Through Christ, we have been restored to the Tree of Life, to God Himself.

Jesus not only paid the price to reverse that loss, He has brought us into a vastly superior relationship with the Father, Son and Spirit than Adam ever knew. If you read John Chapters 14 through 17 you'll find that Jesus had a two-fold mission and passion: (1) to reveal the Father's true heart and ways; and (2) make it possible for us to know Him as He does. As He prayed to the Father in John 17:3 He said,

Now this is eternal life: that they may know you, the only true God, and Jesus Christ, whom you have sent.

Did you catch the simplicity of that? Jesus defined "eternal life" as knowing God! It turns out that eternal life is a relationship, a forever relationship with your divine Creator, that begins the moment you are born again of the Spirit, and adopted by the Father as His child!

Eternal life is a forever relationship with your divine Creator that begins the moment you are born again of His Spirit, adopted as the Father's child!

In all that Jesus taught there is no hint that this eternal life begins only after our earth suits die, someday when our souls go to heaven. Instead, Jesus and His apostles taught and wrote extensively on how to put faith in the real persons of the Trinity, to rely upon and fellowship with them now. The Word says, *"...you were called into fellowship with His Son, Jesus Christ our Lord."* (1 Corinthians 1:9) Nowhere does this say or infer, *"After you die."*

He Is Within Reach; We Just Need To See

The realm or kingdom of heaven is not far away; the Lord said it *"is near."* A literal translation from the Greek of this phrase in Matthew 4:17 actually means *it is within reach.* The kingdom of heaven is around us, and in some ways, within us, because the Lord is present in us. The kingdom means "the king's domain" — where He lives and rules. That is us! We don't travel there as if to a far-away place; when our physical bodies die, we ARE there, instantly, because there is nothing left to block our view of the heavenly realm, and Him.

The fact that the heavenly realm is invisible to the human eye is what we allow to trip us up, and the reason we need faith.

Certainly, our way of knowing God will go to the highest possible level when we see Him face-to-face in heaven, but that does not mean we cannot know Him to a great degree now. As we believe, the Holy Spirit enables us to perceive what the Lord is doing and saying. Yet it has been likened to seeing the Lord through a glass darkly, compared to how we see with our natural eyes and ears:

> *For now we see only a reflection as in a mirror; then we shall see face to face. (1 Corinthians 13:12)*

Seeing "darkly" refers to the fact that for now, our perceptions of God — who is invisible to our human eyes — must come through the faculties of our spirit, not our flesh. We are not accustomed to using these facilities, but as we seek to know God, they do become stronger and more familiar.

Our physical eyes and ears tend to impede our ability to perceive the Lord's presence and communication, being so full of all going on around us. Yet our spirits can *see* and *hear* without the help of the body, as seen in the stories of people whose bodies died temporarily and returned to life. Most report that while their bodies were lifeless, they saw the people in the room around their body, and heard what they were saying.

Clearly, with a lifeless body, their physical eyes and ears were not functioning! How did they see and hear? With the faculties of their human spirit. All of us have one of those — a spirit, that is. We all are three-part beings: body, soul and spirit. Some have a spirit still defiled by original sin and separated from God; while those who have found salvation in Jesus Christ have a new spirit that is born of God and joined to Him.

His Veil Of Separation Is Gone Forever

When Christ died, the veil in the temple separating the priesthood from the presence of God was torn top to bottom [4]

---

[4] Matthew 27:51

— God's dramatic message that now — after Jesus sacrificed Himself — nothing would separate God from His people again, at least from His side of the equation. The fact that God did this supernatural act the very moment after Jesus died underscores how very much God's joy and glory is in relating to His people, to share His life with us and participate in ours. That is why Jesus had to suffer a brutal death on the cross: to remove all barriers to His Father's dream and desire.

But let's back up to the night before this happened, on the eve of His departure, where we find more evidence of the Lord's plan for bringing us into a personal experience of knowing Him. At the Passover meal — commonly called "the last supper" — Jesus said to His disciples, *"A new command I give you: love one another as I have loved you."* (John 13:34)

His new command pointed directly to how had He loved them: in close daily relationship, teaching them, serving them, encouraging and counseling them. Jesus personally mentored His disciples in every way, preparing them for the day when He would be able to call them "friend" instead of "servant."

He gave this new command as He was preparing to die and return to heaven. They grieved, for they could not bear to lose Him, but He promised that in His place, the Father would send them the Holy Spirit, who would continue mentoring them just as He had been:

> *And I will ask the Father, and He will give you another advocate to help you and be with you forever— the Spirit of truth. The world cannot accept Him, because it neither sees Him nor knows Him. But you know Him, for He lives with you and will be in you. I will not leave you as orphans... (John 14:16-18)*

Jesus was telling them, *"You aren't losing me, you aren't losing the daily experience of sharing life together. The Holy Spirit, the gift of the Father, will take up where I have begun, and live with you forever."*

Jesus said the Spirit would take His place and continue the relationship He had with His disciples: sharing life and personally mentoring them.

We were made to live a life like the first disciples — up close and personal with the Lord. It is all summarized beautifully in the four chapters of John referred to earlier. If sharing life now was not God's intention, there would be no need to send the Holy Spirit to help us know and walk with God on earth!

The Scripture clearly defines His role in being with us:

- To help us know God as Abba, Daddy, Father.
- To counsel us, revealing the thoughts and wisdom of God to us;
- To comfort us, expressing the Lord's compassion and nurture.
- To make us effective in prayer and conversation with the Lord;
- To teach us how to apply God's truth and righteous ways in daily life; and much more. [5]

The Spirit enables us to enter into the fellowship we have been called to with the Father and the Son. We need the Spirit for everything concerning knowing God on earth. He lives with us to teach us how to live the life that is ours in Christ, as sons and daughters of God. Paul tells us in Galatians 5:25, *"Since we live by the Spirit, let us keep in step with the Spirit."* We are told elsewhere that the Spirit IS the Lord.

---

[5] See Appendix at the end of this book, "The Roles of the Holy Spirit," which lists many other functions of the Spirit and the Scriptures which refer to them.

Jesus' language and God's desires could not be more clear. They are a far cry from a life of reading some daily Scriptures and going to church on Sundays. The exhortation, *"Taste and see that the Lord is good"*[6] is your invitation. It is right to believe *in* God's goodness, but He wants us to TASTE it, to taste of Him. God isn't waiting for your perfection or worthiness before allowing you to come near, or drawing near to you; Jesus built that bridge for us, so we could taste of God now, while we learn to grow up in our salvation. It is the way of all fathers and their beloved children.

We Are God's Witnesses

Finally, we have a very important service to offer our awesome God: that of being a faithful witness to His glory. We don't bring God glory just by going out and witnessing to others *about* Jesus; we bring Him glory by offering Him a place to live — our heart — from which "home" He can express Himself first *to* us, then *through* us to others.

God consistently speaks and acts throughout Scripture as one who reveals His glory to mankind. To those who live as His enemies, God warns He will reveal His glory in a terrible and powerful wrath. To those who love Him, He promises to reveal His glory as a loving, righteous, wise and just Father.[7]

> *"You are my witnesses," declares the Lord, "and my servant whom I have chosen, so that you may know and believe me and understand that I am He." (Isaiah 43:10)*

He also speaks of His redeemed ones as *the people I formed for myself, that they may proclaim my praise.* (Isaiah 43:21)

The Christian is not just meant to be a witness to God's power to save, but also — even more so — to God's profound, righteous and nourishing personality. As God's true children we

---

[6] Psalm 34:8

[7] See Deuteronomy 7:9-10

are to testify to the world — both in words and by the quality of our character and lives — of God's glory as a redeemer AND as a father, AND as a friend, AND as a king. To do this, we first must experience Him in all these ways.

Jesus: The Firstborn Of A People Who Know God

Jesus was the prototype, the "firstborn"[8] of a nation of people who would know and walk with God, personally experiencing the power of His life, witnessing His beauty, wisdom and strength. He was the first human being who walked on earth with the Holy Spirit dwelling within, relying entirely upon the Spirit and the Word of God to develop His intimate relationship with God the Father — just as we must do!

Jesus had to learn to know God the Father, just as we must: through the help of the Holy Spirit.

Jesus was a human like us, so He also had to learn to "see" and "hear" God with the eyes of His spirit. Jesus had to learn to know God the Father by faith, just as we must: through the help of the Holy Spirit. Through faith and obedience, Jesus came to know the Father intimately. He then entered public ministry to do the work of revealing the Father's goodness and demonstrating the Spirit's power. In all He taught and did, Jesus was the most reliable witness the earth had ever seen of God's character and power. In Revelation 3:14, Jesus calls Himself *the faithful and true witness.*

Then Jesus died for us, enabling us to become children of His Father. After three days, the powerful Spirit resurrected Jesus to life. He then hung around earth for about 40 days in His resurrected body, teaching His disciples all they were finally

---

[8] See Colossians 1:18 and Romans 8:29

ready to understand about their new covenant life. He then returned to heaven, and commanded His disciples — for all time — to continue doing just what He did. Your job as a Christian isn't dragging your neighbors and family into church; it is being a living witness to a God who is incredibly good, powerful and personal.

There is only one way to reveal the true God to people, and that is to know Him for yourself. Apart from that, we are likely to offer a false picture of God, as many have done through the ages, to the harm of countless souls. If God is risking His reputation in the world's eyes on how His children portray Him to the world, we need to be sure we have an authentic version, not gained second hand; not a version we only read of in a book, learned about in sermons, or based solely on a church's doctrinal guide.

I hope to convince you in this book that God loves you so much that He wants to know you and be known by you, in all the real ways of knowing. The Bible says that it was because of God's need to satisfy His *"great and wonderful and intense love"*[9] for us that He created a plan to help us be holy and blameless in His sight. Have you ever loved someone so much that you had to do something to act on it? God loves you that way, which is why He sent His Son to us, and then to the cross — to make real relationship possible between a perfect holy God and imperfect human beings.

God loves you so much that He wants to know you and be known by you, in all the real ways of knowing.

Knowing and rejoicing in His creation is God's passion; He's looking for a people for whom knowing and rejoicing in Him will be their passion.

[9] Ephesians 2:4, The Amplified Bible

> *I will bring him near and he will come close to me — for who is he who will devote himself to be close to me? declares the Lord. So you will be my people, and I will be your God. (Jeremiah 30:21-22)*

This is God's plan for building His kingdom, for filling the earth with His glory.

I am a changed person today, but not because I strong-armed myself into better behavior. My transformation is the result of hanging out with my perfect Father and Jesus my hero, the one who chased me down so He could love me to life. Sometimes I weep for joy at His goodness and beauty and kindness to me. Real love and affection grows out of these moments. His goodness is something I could not know from afar, on the other side of fear and reverence alone. Moses said to the Lord when they were together on the mountain, *"Show me your glory."* God's response was, *"I will show you my goodness."*[10]

[10] Exodus 33:18

3 Who Am I To Personally Know God?

When we consider the idea of knowing God, we are assaulted with thoughts of our own inadequacy: *"Who am I to think I could know God?"* The idea is intimidating and daunting. Even if you have total confidence in God's love for you, you may believe it's just too hard to know an invisible God. Until we come to totally trust in what God says about us, our approach to God will always be with an eye on ourselves — our flaws and human limitations — rather than on God.

Who are you? The standard religious answer is, *"Just a sinner saved by grace."* While this statement humbly embraces our state before we were saved, it does not accurately describe who you are now! You were not just saved, you were brought into God's family. Your identity is no longer "sinner," your identity is *beloved covenant child of God.*

Your identity is no longer "sinner," your identity is *beloved covenant child of God.*

You were born with a human soul and spirit that was defiled by the original sin of our ancestor Adam. Because of His sin — because we were all born into his lineage — you were born under the curse of death that came on him as a consequence. Jesus came and offered Himself as a sacrifice in your place, accepting death and removing the curse from you. Having done that, you became eligible to enter into the intimate family and fellowship of God once again, something God desires with all His heart. Here is the point: you were not just saved from sin, you were saved to know God!

How does He make this happen? When you believed, a new spirit was created within you — what Jesus refers to as being "born again:"

> *Very truly I tell you, no one can enter the kingdom of God unless they are born of water and the Spirit. Flesh gives birth to flesh, but the Spirit gives birth to spirit. You should not be surprised at my saying, "You must be born again." (John 3:5-7)*

Not only are you given a new human spirit, God then sends His Holy Spirit to seal you together with Him forever. He forms a bond of peace between you and Him, marking you as belonging to God's family. Children born into a family don't have to earn a place in it.

Children born into a family don't have to earn a place in it.

Christianity was never meant to be just another box you check off in a list of religious choices. Unlike every other religious sect that merely offers a set of impersonal truths for you to follow, Christianity is a relationship with real personalities; a family established by a Father who loves you dearly and wants you to know Him.

We Tend To Do Christianity Backwards

We don't get to become children of God because we deserve it, or because we become spiritually mature enough to merit a place at His table. The truth is quite the opposite: God wanted you in His family. He made a way for that to happen, so that day by day you would know Him, learn from Him, and grow up to be a mature son or daughter that looks and acts like Him.

The relationship between Father and child is primary, meaning it is the first thing that should be established and developed between God and his newly adopted child.

Human logic assures us that we cannot see, hear and know God until we become mature Christians. The truth is that we can ONLY become like Him as we relate to Him; or to put it in modern terms, hang out with the Living God!

Such terms of familiarity with God may seem offensive to you, but I invite you to consider the result of eons of a much more formal concept of relating to God. Just look at the world around you. After centuries of Christianity, if keeping things strictly formal with God was working, we should by now have a worldwide population of wise, loving, powerful and awesome characters who act like Jesus, maintain God's justice, and demonstrate real power over sin and evil in the world. Where is that crowd? I suspect they are biding their time in a life-as-usual existence, waiting for heaven, believing that is where abundant life will *really* begin. I promise you, there is nothing life-as-usual about personally knowing God, and if my abundant life hasn't begun *yet*, I can't even conceive how awesome it will be.

It's time to stop hiding behind formality and press in to the heart of God, who asks us to call Him Father and know Him as Father — really. Yet, some of you will still say, *"I'm not holy enough to press in to God like that."* Apparently this isn't a problem for God, who put a new spirit in you when you were born again, then arranged for His Spirit to become one with your spirit [1] so He could live with you and not just be a God far away.

If you are born again, God has already leaped over the "not holy enough" issue, by giving you His Holy Spirit. Ephesians 1:13-14 says you have been *sealed with the Spirit.* By all means, you should live a life worthy of this divine helper, responding to and honoring His wonderful and gracious presence. Apparently

---

[1] "But whoever is united with the Lord is one with Him in spirit." (1 Corinthians 6:17)

the Spirit doesn't think He is too holy to live right with you, so you should accept the fact that God is not put off by your imperfection. Why? Romans 3:22 explains that *"righteousness is given through faith in Jesus Christ to all who believe."* (Romans 3:22) When you put your faith in Christ, you share in HIS righteousness. It feels crazy, improbable, too good to be true. But as you will soon learn, this is what happens in a covenant.

Backwards thinking says, *"I have to be holy enough to share life with God."* But God says, *"If you share life with me, I will teach you and empower you to be holy."* So it is not all about you and your flaws. God made a covenant promise that He would do everything to make it possible for you and He to share life together. Even the timing of His promise is a signal that when we are at our worst, He still wants us. I say this because of the first time in Scripture where God said:

> *No longer will they teach their neighbor, or say to one another, "Know the Lord," because they will all know me, from the least of them to the greatest, declares the Lord. (Jeremiah 31:34)*

When God first uttered these words, His people were undergoing judgment — being evicted from the Promised Land — for chronically violating their covenant with God under Moses. As they marched into exile from Jerusalem, God had Jeremiah give them this promise! God sent the clear message that in spite of how much they failed He still loved them and was determined to make a way for authentic, life-sharing relationship to happen between them. To make the promise viable, the very next words He spoke were, "*...for I will forgive their iniquity and their sin I will remember no more.*"[2]

"They will all know me, from the least of them to the greatest," declares the Lord.

[2] Jeremiah 31:34b

I will put God's words another way: *"I choose to forgive your sins and wipe the memory of them from between us. I choose to make it possible for you to know me, no matter your station or skills."*

They Will All Know Me

Again, the promise is for *the least of them to the greatest.* So wherever you would put yourself on that scale, the promise of knowing God is for YOU. Jesus actually put a finer point on it when He added a surprising qualification in Luke 18:17: *"Unless you come as little children, you cannot enter the kingdom of God."*

Yet even knowing all these things, many still ask: *"How on earth can I really enter into a relationship with an invisible, all-powerful God? I am flesh and blood, He is Spirit, and I can't see or hear Him!"*

God covered that one in His amazing promise as well. He had a plan, which He described like this: *"I will put my laws in their minds and write them on their hearts."* (Jeremiah 31:33)

Wow! And remember, all of this was first spoken to a people who had been unfaithful to Him for hundreds of years, displaying chronic unfaithfulness, idolatry, selfishness, foolishness, and sinfulness. You can't top that! Whether you are the worst or the least, you're still on the list of those He is calling to know Him.

God knows He is Spirit and you are flesh, and He had a plan to overcome the obstacles facing a personal relationship between you. Jesus revealed it on the night before He went to the cross, saying to His disciples as He shared the Passover meal:

> *"I will ask the Father and He will give you another Counselor to be with you forever — the Spirit of truth ... on that day you will realize that I am in my Father and you are in me and I am in you ... But the Counselor, the Holy Spirit, whom the Father will send in my name, will teach you all things." (John 14:16-20)*

Wow, what language is this? "*...I am in my Father and you are in me and I am in you...*" We are not accustomed to describing relationship this way. But it was a vocabulary that Jesus and His disciples grew up with, familiar to the whole Middle Eastern culture. These words were commonly spoken in a covenant ceremony between two parties who had just entered into a covenant of life-long friendship!

The clearest evidence that Jesus was speaking about a covenant relationship is that at the end of that meal, He held up the 5th cup of wine — reserved for the long-awaited Messiah — and said:

> *This cup is **the new covenant** in my blood, which is poured out for you. (Luke 22:20)*

So Jesus not only promised His followers that the Holy Spirit would come live in them as a constant companion, He announced that what He was about to do would initiate a new covenant for them. He wasn't about to merely *save* them, He was about to make a way for them to enter into a covenant of forever friendship with God, in which they would actually be able to know the Father He loved so very much. The Spirit was being given to them to make it all happen.

Your Salvation Is A Covenant

Has anyone ever told you that your salvation is a covenant? It was God's idea, planned from before time began, and brought to fulfillment through Christ. Very few Christians have been taught the full truth about covenant bonding and covenant love. It is a vast subject, too big to cover in this book; but in the next few chapters I will share the most crucial concepts with you. These truths will change your entire view of the relationship Christ purchased for you with His precious blood.

The primary message of the book of Hebrews is that you are not just saved, you have become a legal child of God through the New Covenant of Jesus Christ. In Chapter 6 the author admonishes us to grow up in our salvation, to *"leave the elementary teachings about Christ and go on to maturity."* But what does maturity look like, according to the author of Hebrews? He implies that it begins when we understand our relationship to God through His covenant promises, and totally trust Him to be faithful to those promises.

This is crucial. We were never meant to exercise our faith by way of performing perfectly towards God, which keeps the focus upon ourselves. The object of our faith is meant to be God: who He is, what He has promised, and what He now calls us to be — His child legally adopted through the New Covenant of Christ.

The author of Hebrews explains that in this covenant, Father, Son and Holy Spirit provide all we need to live holy and fully participate in this family to which we now belong. He makes it clear that our primary job is to *rest in faith* in all that God has promised, and set the full attention and hope of our hearts on God — in the way of all covenant people.

To be a mature Christian is to really believe God is now your father through the New Covenant of Christ, that you are His beloved child, and live accordingly. The author of Hebrews explains this New Covenant in detail, including God's promises to those who come Him through Christ:

> *I will put my laws in their minds and write them on their hearts. I will be their God, and they will be my people. No longer will a man teach His neighbor, or a man His brother, saying, "Know the Lord," because they will all know me, from the least of them to the greatest. For I will forgive their wickedness and will remember their sins no more. (Hebrews 8:10-12)*

Here the author directly quotes the exact promises God made to His people through Jeremiah hundreds of years earlier, making it clear that these words were spoken for the day of salvation!

Going on to maturity begins with placing total trust in God's covenant promise, believing you can actually know and be taught by the Lord. Putting your faith in anything else may well prevent you from ever getting to maturity — at least the kind God is after.

The Purpose Of Faith

The work of faith didn't come to a conclusion when you chose to believe that God exists and that Jesus died for you. Having crossed that threshold, the purpose of faith is to live your life as a response to God's promises and His Presence.

The purpose of faith is to live your life as a response to God's promises and His Presence.

To believe *in* God and yet not trust in His covenant promise, dishonors Him. Furthermore, when the God of all creation gives the life of His beloved Son to make a covenant of love possible between you and Him, it is more than a promise; it is a calling. We been offered the most amazing gift ever, and we need to respond appropriately.

We need to get over the idea that it is presumptuous to believe we can know God. He has, in essence, raised His right hand and sworn an oath that you *will* know Him! To shrink back for fear of imperfection, or believing it is impossible, or for any reason, invites the Lord's displeasure. God said as much through His prophet Habakkuk: [3]

> *"My righteous one will live by faith, and if He shrinks back, I will not be pleased with Him." (Habakkuk 2:4, NASB)*

---

[3] Later quoted in Hebrews 10:38.

That we should "live by faith" is such a familiar concept that it is easy to overlook the main point, which is *the object* of our faith — in *what* or *whom is our faith to be placed?*

To believe that God exists is a first step, and a great comfort in an evil world; to believe that Christ died for us is pure joy and salvation from the evil of the world and in ourselves; but to believe God's promises in the New Covenant is to understand our true place in God's family and kingdom. We should live in faith that God wants to know us and be known by us, in a joyful, reciprocal and eternal relationship through which He reveals His goodness and glory to the nations.

To believe God's promises in the New Covenant is to understand our true place in God's family and kingdom.

Frankly, it is impossible to please God while living just as "a sinner saved by grace." That attitude keeps us in a mentality of unworthiness, and keeps us at a distance. Because we *are* unworthy it seems right to be at a distance from a holy God. But the truth is that God has covered our unworthiness in His love and grace, and in the righteousness of Christ. He paid the ultimate price for us to come close, so if we stay at a distance, we say to God, *"All you did is just not enough for me to get over being puny me while you are so very God."*

I hope and pray the Holy Spirit will open your eyes to the dishonor such an attitude brings to your heavenly Father! Surely it grieves Him to know He has offered you a place at His feast table, and see you settling for a paper lunch bag with a stale sandwich. I agree with the Apostle Paul, praying that you will be given a spirit of wisdom and revelation to know and understand your true place in God's family and in His kingdom. [4] I ask the Spirit to fill you with trust in the fullness

[4] Ephesians 1:17-19

of God's grace in this covenant, so you will never again shrink back. I want you to know in the deepest places of your soul that the answer to the question, *"Who am I to personally know God?"* is this: *"You are His covenant child."*

Covenant child of God is not just a nice term for us to cling to while we wait to be redeemed from earth and go to heaven; it is our new identity, our reality, and our calling.

Balancing Intimacy And Fear Of The Lord

In this book, I will be opening windows to my intimate life with the Lord; a life I believe all Christians can and should experience. I anticipate that if you are a serious Christian, you will be concerned about how intimacy with the Lord works with maintaining a proper fear of the Lord. It is an important question, and I think this is the best place to answer it.

The natural instinct of man has been to shrink back from being too familiar with the Lord as a way of showing proper fear and reverence. There is a right reverential fear of the Lord that we should never lose; but fear that causes us to back away from the intimacy God calls us to is inappropriate for His adopted son or daughter.

A right fear of the Lord is revealed by genuine concern about upholding His values and ways. Failing to do so is what God calls sin. David wrote in Psalm 36:1-2:

> *I have a message from God in my heart concerning the sinfulness of the wicked: There is no fear of God before their eyes. In their own eyes they flatter themselves too much to detect or hate their sin (Psalms 36:1-2)*

The "wicked" (by God's definition) are unconcerned about the Lord's values, ways and judgments. They are so busy with their self-esteem program, needing to feel good about themselves, that they are not focused on the Lord in any real way. Guilt feels really uncomfortable, so they avoid the sensation of conviction at all costs. Living at a distance from God makes this easier.

The fact is that intimacy and fear of the Lord go hand-in-hand. When God's child stays close to Him, awareness of what disappoints or offends Him grows keener; the desire to please Him grows deeper. These things reveal a true fear of the Lord. This doesn't develop in us at a distance, but only as we live up close, knowing God as we can, and as He desires.

Intimacy and fear of the Lord go hand-in-hand.

On the other hand, Psalm 25:14 tells us that the Lord reveals Himself more intimately to the one who fears Him:

> *The Lord confides in those who fear Him; He makes His covenant known to them.*

The Hebrew language is what is known as a "word picture" language. It offers many amazing visuals that reveal a fullness of truth which cannot be conveyed by words alone. Such a picture is hidden in this verse, where the Hebrew word translated as "*confides*" is pictured by two friends on a couch in intimate conversation! I love that. This same word is seen again in Proverbs 3:32, in the word *"intimate"*:

> *For the devious are an abomination to the Lord; But He is intimate with the upright. (NASB)*

Who are the *"upright"*? Those who are in Christ, committed to a life of knowing and understanding Him, honoring Him by walking in His ways.

I say without pride, but with sincerity of heart, that conversations on the couch is my experience with God every week. In fact, I tend to walk with God more faithfully AND more reverently the more I respond to His invitation to intimacy. I believe this is because only in truly tasting of God — experiencing His invisible but very real presence — will love, reverence and a passion to obey naturally increase, in a way that you own it. You don't have to be forced or shamed into it. Instead of a command or rule you must make yourself obey, true fear and worship of the Lord simply grow in you as you grow in knowing God.

Without true fear of God, "knowledge" of Him can be perverted or distorted. Apart from the Holy Spirit's guidance, we all have a tendency to make God in our own image — whatever we need or want Him to be. Genuine, healthy fear of the Lord is expressed by a complete dependence on the Holy Spirit to reveal the Lord to you. He will keep you in the right balance of reverence and intimacy. He will train you, just as He did Jesus. Isaiah prophesied about this centuries before Jesus was born:

> **The Holy Spirit will keep you in the right balance of reverence and intimacy.**

The Spirit of the Lord will rest on Him—the Spirit of wisdom and of understanding, the Spirit of counsel and of might, the Spirit of the knowledge and fear of the Lord — and He will delight in the fear of the Lord. (Isaiah 11:2-3)

Likewise, the Spirit's job is now to establish you in all these things, and it is vital that you rely on Him entirely to do so. To delight in the fear of the Lord — according to the example Jesus set for us — is to live a life of closeness and utter dependence upon the Spirit.

God wants to be known by His creation. He wants to show off His glory as a father, lover, provider, defender and ruler. He delights for us to personally taste of this goodness, so He invites us to approach Him in childlike trust and presume upon His love and grace.

Our relationship with God must always be clothed in the reverence that never ceases to honor Him as Sovereign Creator and Lord. But this reverence does not cancel out our invitation — indeed, our calling — to know Him as the Father He wants to be to us: tender, available, encouraging. There is a scene in the movie "Anna and The King" that perfectly illustrates the unique access a child has to His father, even when that father is a mighty king.

In this story the fierce King of Siam has no trouble executing severe discipline on those who violate the strict protocol of his court, where no one is allowed to enter his presence, speak to him or even look him in the eye without his permission. One day while conducting the kingly business of his court, one of the king's sons comes bursting in the room, runs through all the guards, the court officials and the many subjects bowed low with eyes to the ground, straight to his father. All court business is forgotten as the King scoops his son into his lap and asks with all fatherly tenderness, *"What is it, my son?"*

Yet there are other scenes in the movie in which this same son bows down, face to the ground, honoring the King alongside all the other subjects. He knew there was a time to worship and a time to climb into Dad's lap. I worship the Lord often, and on occasion, I feel such reverence for Him that I prostrate myself before Him on the floor. But I usually have to crawl out of His lap in order to do so.

I believe we have this kind of access to our heavenly Father, the King of all Kings. If we shrink back in fear of the fact that He is Almighty God while we are unworthy and unwelcome subjects, we dishonor His invitation to drawn near Him as beloved children.

The child of the king of Siam feared most that he would disappoint or bring dishonor to his father. Every citizen of the kingdom had that obligation, but it was an entirely different matter for a child of the king. The servants who only knew the king through fear, who had no permission to look into his eyes, could only express their reverence by bowing low and keeping proper distance. The king's children — who had access to the king's heart and a birthright permission to know him more intimately — had a much greater capacity to bring him honor by imitating His character, values and ways.

The only thing we should fear — and we should fear this above all things — is misrepresenting the true heart and character of God. As His redeemed ones we are called to know God in personal experience — for our joy and for His glory. To us He reveals His character and goodness, and counts on us to tell the truth about Him to the world.

The covenant child of God who believes the Lord is truly present, who wants to love and honor Him, will walk in the most natural fear of all: fear of ignoring, dishonoring or disrespecting the King they know as Father. The fear that truly honors the Lord isn't born from a distance.

To Understand Covenant Is To Understand God's Heart

What does it mean to be God's covenant child, and how is it different than simply being God's child? The fuller answer to that question is the subject of the rest of this book. On the surface, covenant has to do with providing security in a relationship; but underneath is a rich treasure of truth that reveals much more than my place in heaven or the kingdom. It reveals my place in God's heart.

Being God's covenant child comes with joy, privilege, intimacy and responsibility. It invites me to step into God's life, not just accept Him into mine.

God has what I like to call *a covenant heart.* By this I mean a heart that is committed to showing unfailing love to the one with whom He is joined. Beloved, that is you!

To understand covenant is to understand God's heart; to realize that above all the wonders of creation and the universe — all of which express the glorious power of God — WE are His glory. Expressing His life to and through us is God's highest

Being God's covenant child comes with joy, privilege, intimacy and responsibility. It invites me to step into God's life, not just accept Him into mine.

joy. He is absolutely committed to us, in a way that I did not comprehend before I learned about covenant. The culture of our times no longer makes us feel secure just because someone says, "I love you."

Loving us in an unfailing way expresses the best of who God is. This is not an offer of mere pity or mercy; it is the passion of God's heart, a lavish love:

> *How great is the love the Father has lavished on us, that we should be called children of God! And that is what we are! (1 John 3:1)*

Romans 5:5 tells us that the Holy Spirit is the one who reveals God's love to us. He has absolutely done this for me. You know what makes me happy every single day? I feel my preciousness to God. I never wonder if He loves me, approves of me, or wants to share life with me. He has convinced me of this, on a journey that began with a wave of powerful, palpable love that He caused to wash over me. The Holy Spirit reinforced this with scriptures like 1 John 3:1, quoted above. Confidence in God's tenacious love has grown in my soul over years of pressing in, knowing God from baby steps to increasing maturity. Understanding the covenant heart of God has given me a boldness I never had before, to press in to a way of knowing Him that has changed my life in every way. It would not be an exaggeration to say that I weep for joy over this reality, fairly often. The joy never fades.

The Lord says personal and tender things to me, fatherly things, instructive things, corrective things. This has continually fed the validation that I am His beloved child, until there is not one ounce of insecurity about that fact left in me. Feeling the Lord's deep love for me, knowing that He treasures me, is very different than drumming up faith in hearing someone else say, "Jesus loves you."

I say that because my journey towards God began when someone kept telling me that very thing. Unwilling to talk myself into believing it, I shook my fist at God and demanded, *"If you're really God, you can make me feel this love."* He did! He does! And today my heart rests in that fact.

I hope it doesn't embarrass you for me to say so, but God adores me. He loves the way I walk about the garden and ponder how to best show off what He has created. He especially loves that I know how much He enjoys sharing life with me. He loves it when I'm in a movie theater and recognize that a certain line of dialogue is actually His voice speaking to the people He longs to bring to Himself.

Jesus paid the ultimate price to bring the Father and I together so we could enjoy one another, and I'm not wasting it! I am no longer anxious; I live at rest in His love. He is also at rest in me, not having to strive with me continually to convince me of His will or His love. I want all this for you. Like Jesus, I want you to experience the joy and life that comes through knowing the Father.

Towards that end, I want to teach you some essentials about the concept of covenant relationship — the Father's chosen means of bringing us into a mutual commitment of love.

Covenant is a relationship concept that has become lost on our modern culture, but it needs to be revived, taught and established in our minds. Indeed, in God's heart, covenant has never left the stage. As you will see, it defines all that we are meant to experience in knowing God. Covenant will forever change how you view God, yourself, and the Word of God. You're going to love it.

4 Your Salvation Is A Covenant

In sharing the annual Passover Supper with His disciples on the night before His crucifixion, Jesus did something new. He lifted one of the traditional cups of wine and said:

> *Drink from it, all of you. This is my blood of the new covenant, which is poured out for many for the forgiveness of sins. (Matthew 26:27-28)*

Christians are familiar with the concept of salvation, and understand that Jesus had to sacrifice His sinless life to redeem us from the penalty and power of sin. However, too few are familiar with the concept of "covenant," unaware of how thoroughly it is woven into the fabric of their Christianity. In light of the fact that Jesus used the terminology of covenant at the most crucial moment of His human life, we need to understand what He is saying.

A covenant is a relationship formed when two parties are bound together for life. It begins with a ceremony in which the two promise in front of witnesses to live a life of complete faithfulness to one another. This is what the Bible refers to repeatedly as "unfailing love." [1]

This is not the emotion of love, but the commitment to love at all costs. David wrote much about God's covenant love in his Psalms: *"I have always been mindful of your unfailing love and have lived in reliance on your faithfulness."* (Psalms 26:3)

---

[1] NIV translation. Rendered as "lovingkindness" in the NKJV and the NASB translations.

Has anyone ever told you that your salvation is actually a covenant, a legal contract between two parties? Taken as a whole, the Scriptures testify to God's passion to have relationship with His creation, from the very first page to the last. In fact, God's relationship to man has always been governed by a covenant.

God's relationship to man has always been governed by a covenant.

Scripture is laced with covenant language — a certain vocabulary of words that signify covenant activity or connection — and the actual word *covenant* appears in Scripture over 270 times. For Christians, the most crucial instance is when Jesus lifted that cup of salvation and said, *"This cup is the new covenant in my blood, which is poured out for you."* (Luke 22:20).

The Prologue, Or Back Story

Here's the back story: the Trinity planned for our New Covenant relationship from before time began! Michael Horton explains in his book *Introducing Covenant Theology*, that there are three primary "overarching covenants," the first being made between the Father, Son and Spirit before creation took place. Scholars call it "the Covenant of Redemption." It is referred to in Scripture as "the eternal covenant," because it exists outside of time, and will endure as long as the Trinity endures — forever.

Mr. Horton explains that while this Covenant, out of which all other covenant activity flows, is not explicitly described in Scripture, it is clearly *revealed* in Scripture. It is, he says,

> *... the eternal decree to elect, redeem, call, justify, sanctify, and glorify a people for the Son. At the same time, this eternal purpose would have remained utterly hidden from*

> *us unless it had actually been realized in our time and space.* [2]

Scripture validates this when it says that we were chosen in Christ *"before the creation of the world"*[3] and that Christ is *"the Lamb that was slain from the creation of the world."*[4]

Ephesians 3:11 speaks of God's *"eternal purpose which He accomplished in Christ Jesus our Lord."*

Hebrews 13:20 describes the blood of Christ as *"the blood of the eternal covenant."*

I like the way Mr. Horton explains this covenant:

> *The Father elects a people in the Son as their mediator, to be brought to saving faith through the Spirit. Thus, this covenant made by the Trinity in eternity already takes the fall of the human race into account.*
>
> *The Father elects a people in the Son through the Spirit. Our salvation, therefore, arises first of all out of the joint solidarity of the divine persons.*
>
> *The joy of giving and receiving experienced by the Father, Son, and Holy Spirit spills over, as it were, into the Creator-creature relationship.*
>
> *In the covenant of redemption, the love of the Father and the Spirit for the Son is demonstrated in the gift of a people who will have Him as their living head.*
>
> *At the same time, the Son's love for the Father and the Spirit is demonstrated in His pledge to redeem that family at the greatest personal cost.*

---

[2] Page 82, Introducing Covenant Theology by Michael Horton, ©2006, Baker Books.

[3] Ephesians 1:4

[4] Revelation 13:8

Those who trust in Christ belong to Christ, are elect in Christ. [5]

In the next few chapters we will trace the major covenants through the Bible, beginning with God's creation covenant with Adam, and ending with the New Covenant of Christ. This latter covenant, which is our "covenant of grace," is the fulfillment of the pact made between the Father, Son and Spirit, their commitment to redeem a people and bring them into their fellowship — presumably to make their joy complete! That, dear reader, is you, together with the rest of the Body of Christ.

A Covenant By Inheritance

The Biblical book of Hebrews contains the most detailed explanation about the new covenant of Christ. Covenants vary in how they are initiated and administrated; some are initiated by mutual agreement of two parties, and others are given as a gift from one party to another. Hebrews 9:16 explains that our new covenant is the latter, left to us like an inheritance after someone dies — in our case, Jesus.

Hebrews describes the new covenant of Christ as His "last will and testament."

The Trinity's will was to offer this covenant relationship to us as a gracious gift, yet it would only be made possible as Christ earned it for us, first by His sinless life and then by His sacrificial death. Hebrews describes the new covenant of Christ as His "last will and testament." (In fact, the use of the word "testament" had its beginning as a covenant term.) What did Jesus leave us as an inheritance? A relationship with the Father, the Spirit and Himself.

---

[5] Pages 78-79. Introducing Covenant Theology by Michael Horton, ©2006, Baker Books.

Jesus was born on the earth as a man like us, but was guided by the Holy Spirit as He grew up. The Spirit introduced Him to His heavenly Father, and helped Him to understand who He was. By the time Jesus entered public ministry, He had four obvious passions: (1) His Trinity family — the Father and the Spirit; (2) the Truth; (3) the people God loved; and (4) the Kingdom. The knowledge that He could by His obedience and sacrifice bring all these together, is the joy that was set before Him as He faced the torture of the cross.

Jesus had complete faith in the Spirit, and knew that if He died for us, He could then live with us, because the Holy Spirit would raise Him from death.

Most of the Bible stories we are familiar with are centered around covenant activity. Once you know what to look for, you will see this covenant activity everywhere. We read of covenants which governed relations between God and man, as well as those which governed man's relations with man, such as marriage or geo-political treaties.

The Bible Is A Covenant Witness For God

After studying covenant in detail for years, it seemed reasonable to assume that when the Spirit guided scholars in choosing which writings to include in the canon of Scripture, His goal included the preservation of the Lord's covenant records. In other words, the canon of Scripture would establish a "legal" basis for the righteous dispensation of God's justice.

The Scriptures as a whole testify to the faithfulness of God, and to the faithfulness or unfaithfulness of men, rulers, cities and nations. The Bible not only testifies to who God is, it validates His righteous judgments based upon covenant commitments.

Genealogies in the Bible — known to bored readers as "the begats" — exist to show the lineage through which covenant promises are kept, handed down and fulfilled on God's part, from Adam to Jesus Christ. These include some who are not of the bloodline, but entered into God's family line because they believed His covenant promises — such as Rahab the prostitute.

Likewise, the histories in the Bible are not by any means exhaustive in recording the activities of men and nations, but they do include anything that pertains to how God and nations fulfill or fail to fulfill their covenant commitments. Thus the Bible as a whole is a witness or testimony to the Lord's faithful governance of His creation, His work to bring mankind into a righteous relationship to Himself, and establishing His right to justice when the requirements of His covenants are broken. The Biblical narratives and records are narrowly focused upon God's covenant history, and upon revealing His character, attributes (power, wisdom, creativity), and His ways.

God has bound Himself to mankind through covenants, and He lives by them.

God has bound Himself to mankind through covenants, and He lives by them. When the Bible teaches us how to live, it is teaching us how to live in covenantal faithfulness; how to have what I like to call *a covenant heart.* A covenant heart is a faithful heart like God's. The highest joy of a covenant heart is to be life-giving to others by loving them faithfully. A covenant heart sets the example for others in how to walk in unfailing love.

Faithfulness is God's supreme value. It is only within a personal, intimate, interactive relationship with the Lord that we are able to be mentored in what faithfulness looks like in all the real moments of life. God wants to teach us how to have a covenant heart like His, and if all His children were to walk in this way, the earth would indeed be filled with the glory of the Lord, as the Lord promised through the prophets.

Why Doesn't The Bible Explain Covenant More Clearly?

The reason all of this is has not been clear to the average Bible reader is that most of us grew up in a Western culture, rather than the covenant cultures more prominently seen in the Middle and Far East cultures, classified as Oriental cultures. The Bible was recorded by an Eastern Oriental people — the Hebrews — in ancient days when covenant was commonly practiced and understood. The scribes, prophets, historians and poets did not stop to explain covenant concepts in their writings because their audience was totally saturated with the concept. For an ancient author to have explained covenant would be like an American explaining the entire game of football to another American whenever they used words like "touchdown" or "quarterback." It simply wasn't necessary for an audience who would naturally recognize the language, activity, values, and demands of covenant.

Evidence of covenant practices has been found in all primitive cultures on every continent; yet these practices have faded for the most part as those cultures have become more modern, more "civilized." The result is that today we have only a vague notion of what covenant is all about.

If you've ever seen a Western movie in which a Native American Indian and a white man cut themselves to become "blood brothers," you witnessed a blood covenant ritual. Though it gave us only a glimpse of what that really meant, we understood that these two parties had chosen to become related by choice, to become blood relatives, in a permanent commitment to one another.

There are several major covenants revealed in the Bible which, taken altogether, reveal God's consistent passion to relate to mankind. The culmination of all is the New Covenant of Christ, the place where we now find ourselves. These covenants clearly communicate God's desire to build *with* us the abundant life which reveals His glory, giving joy to both creator and creation. It is the ultimate circle of life.

How Learning About Covenant Changed My Life

As a "blank slate" Christian, reading the Bible in those first years always stirred up new questions. Among other things, I wanted to understand why God showed favor to certain peoples and nations while severely judging others. I could not believe He was a capricious God, but I didn't understand His behavior at times. And why would God give a law under Moses that required an adulterous woman to be stoned to death, but when Jesus was confronted with such a woman, He set her free, even though He believed in upholding the law?

Also, after a few years as a Christian, I was experiencing an ebb and flow in my faith, once the initial passion and fascination wore off. I sometimes felt uncertain if God actually heard my prayers or if they made a real difference in situations. I tended to self-examine a lot, so it was easy to slip into believing that how well I performed as a Christian might determine how much God would use me or even if He would listen to my prayers. And if I wasn't living up to my expectations, I sometimes avoided praying because I felt like such a hypocrite.

I never doubted my salvation, and always loved how God had won me with His love. I had some great experiences with God, mountaintop moments; yet in daily Christian life I had developed one abiding disappointment: the effort it seemed to require to keep my soul full of the joy, peace, hope and trust promised by the Lord.

At some point I realized I was striving, as if I was the one holding it all together by faith. Somehow that just didn't feel right, especially when Scripture spoke, as it often did, of entering God's rest. I loved reading about that, and wanted it truly; but for the most part, I just wasn't there. It still felt like a lot of work on my part to get to that "rest." I knew something was missing, but I didn't know what — until I learned about covenant.

Covenant changed my whole understanding of what is supposed to be going on between God and His saved ones. Learning about covenant profoundly changed my entire view of Christianity, and brought me into the rest I had not known, until it became a constant in my life. The balance of this book will tell you more about that, but for now, here are a few of the things covenant changed for me.

I don't have to earn fellowship with God, because we are one: He is in me, and I am in Him. Covenant explains it all.

First, covenant settled forever the question about whether my prayers are *always* heard by the Lord. Second, insecurity about God's approval and Presence evaporated when I realized I couldn't lose the Spirit of the Lord or drive Him away even if I failed. I understood for the first time that I belonged in a forever family in which God is my Father and I am His beloved daughter; and that Jesus is not just my Savior, He is my brother. I don't have to earn fellowship with God, because we are one: He is in me, and I am in Him. Covenant explains it all.

Reading my Bible through the first time after studying covenant was amazing. When I saw how tenaciously God had worked in His history with mankind to make a way for us to share life, my focus finally made the tectonic shift from MY self and MY performance and worthiness, to GOD's heart, His character, His unchanging nature. I became convinced of His passion and faithfulness to make a way for me to know Him in my everyday life, now and forever. I rested, really rested, for the first time when this sank in upon me. It has become my passion to introduce these truths to others in my Christian family, so they may also enter the rest that Scripture emphatically calls us to:

> *Therefore, since the promise of entering His rest still stands, let us be careful that none of you be found to have fallen short of it. (Hebrews 4:1)*

When Ron and I first began to study Covenant, there weren't many books to be found on the subject. I am happy to say that has changed. I won't offer a thorough teaching on covenant here, but I want to reveal enough of this vast subject that the light will come on for you as it did for us regarding the true riches of your relationship to God through the New Covenant of Christ. Without this information you cannot fully grasp what Christ has done for you, or understand how covenant-minded the Trinity is!

5 Ancient Covenant History And Ways

Most Christians have been taught how the blood of Christ was completely poured out for our salvation. They understand that Jesus gave Himself up as the sacrifice who died in our place, for the forgiveness of sin — original sin, as most know it. But what really was "the original sin?" The original sin occurred when the first man, Adam, violated the covenant relationship which God initiated between Himself and man.[1] He did this by disobeying God in the one forbidden thing: eating fruit from the tree of knowledge of good and evil.

Have you ever wondered why that event warranted Adam's death, and why that sentence of death rests upon every person born into this world? It is because the stated penalty for violating God's covenant was death. God clearly warned Adam:

> *And the Lord God commanded the man, "You are free to eat from any tree in the garden; but you must not eat from the tree of the knowledge of good and evil, for when you eat from it you will certainly die." (Genesis 2:16-17)*

Because covenants are generational matters, handed down a family line, that death curse was attached to me when I was born, and to you. We are all descendants of the first man, Adam, and all born under the curse of death for the first broken covenant between man and God. I learned these things from a man named H. Clay Trumbull, one of the original students of covenant history.

---

[1] Hosea 6:7

The History Of Covenant In Cultures Of The World

In the late 1800's, H. Clay Trumbull was editor of the Sunday School Times for 28 years, author of 38 books, and known as "a Sunday school teacher's teacher." As a student of both Scripture and world history he began to see a profound connection between primitive world practices and the constant references to covenant in Scripture.

Trumbull's studies led him to conclude that every primitive culture known to man, on every continent in the world, practiced some sort of covenant ritual and relationship. These basic elements were so similar and common as to be astounding in a time where there was no global communication. Trumbull concluded there could be only one explanation for this amazing revelation: that the concept of covenant must have been initiated by the creator of all men, God Himself. His theory is easily validated when one considers the common elements of covenant ceremonies and practices alongside the Bible narratives. Trumbull published his discovery in his book, "The Blood Covenant."

Once you learn to recognize the fairly universal steps, signs and language of blood covenant ceremonies and relationships, it is easy to recognize that what happened between God, Adam and Eve in Eden was a covenant which God initiated with mankind, though it does not explicitly say so in their specific story.

I believe with Trumbull — and now a chorus of others — that God created the concept of covenant relationship as a permanent union entered into by two parties. These parties swear oaths to offer their all to one another, and their pacts result in a shared life that makes them "as one" in the eyes of their community. The choice to enter into covenant with another was a means of offering security to the other party for what is otherwise a matter of faith — one's word, one's verbal promise. In covenant each party agreed to be held accountable for their promises under threat of death at the hands of those who witnessed their sworn oaths — even God Himself.

Trumbull writes in his book, *Blood Covenant*:

> *... in all cases, the idea seems to be, that the life of the one covenanting is, by this covenant, devoted — surrendered as it were — to the one with whom he covenants; and the rite is uniformly accompanied with a solemn and an imprecatory appeal to God as witnessing and guarding the compact.*[2]

The word *imprecatory* means to invoke or call down curses of evil. In ancient covenant ceremonies, a blood oath was made that included a self-invoked curse of death in the event one broke the covenant, giving God or man legal permission to take one's life. Knowing that you have authorized another party to take your life if you are unfaithful to your promises produces quite the motivation to keep them, no matter how difficult the relationship becomes! Our own watered down version of this in our wedding ceremonies has become, "till death do us part."

Of course, the most noble guarantee underlying a covenant was honor, as most men guarded their honor at all cost. In ancient days a man's honor was measured by how he kept his word. But men can be fickle creatures, and honor can be lost to a lust for something else; so the fallback security was death. You be unfaithful, you die.

Of course, God never takes such an oath, since He cannot die; and He is incapable of being unfaithful. So why would He agree to obligate Himself in a covenant binding Him to man? He would do it in part because He is amazingly compassionate, understanding and gracious, wanting to make man feel secure. He did it to offer man an anchor for His faith in the promises of an invisible God, just like men had with other men. And He was entirely willing to be held accountable to His promises.

---

[2] Page 9, "The Blood Covenant - a Primitive Rite and Its Bearings on Scripture" by H. Clay Trumbull, 1975, Impact Christian Books, Inc.

God wasn't just looking for created subjects, He was looking for family: sons and daughters who would have a type of equality with Him. This doesn't mean we are gods, nor does it bring God down to our level, but it does mean we share life with the assurance of belonging, acceptance, permanence, favor. Family members have privileges that outsiders don't share.

God wasn't just looking for created subjects, He was looking for family: sons and daughters who would have a type of equality with Him.

Clearly, God wanted to be bound together with us in a permanent, legally binding and secure relationship. This is the origin of the promise that flowed out of His heart through the pen of Moses, *"I will never leave you, nor forsake you."* This is God's natural character, and it should be ours as well; but history reveals how very much we tend to fail at faithfulness. So entering covenant with man was also a way of bringing men into accountability to God and one another, creating between two parties a law of love and faithfulness that could be enforced by means of a dire penalty: death.

God wanted to be in a life-sharing relationship with His creation, even with the foreknowledge of our weaknesses and needs. With His righteous requirements in view, He gave us the structure we needed as earth-dwellers to live securely with Him and one another, so we could have abundant life. Abundant life is not possible outside the context of a secure, healthy and nourishing relationship. God wanted a permanent union with us that could be experienced as family and friendship.

How astonishing this is! Coming to understand God's covenant heart can forever destroy our wrong concepts of God's motives and attitudes towards us. We were created for the very purpose of knowing and experiencing life with God, becoming like Him in character, behavior and creative glory, and thus filling the earth with His glory. [3]

The progression of God's covenants with man, culminating with the New Covenant of Christ, clearly reveals that all of this life-sharing with God was not just meant for someday in heaven. You never find Jesus offering even a hint to His disciples that the promise of eternal life would only begin after the physical death of our bodies. In fact, a fair reading of His words reveals that the phrase "eternal life" was summed up in one thing to Jesus: knowing God. He said it plainly in His prayer to the Father:

> *Now this is eternal life: that they know you, the only true God, and Jesus Christ, whom you have sent. (John 17:3)*

It is clear from Christ's teachings, plus the experiences and teachings of the apostles, that eternal life begins the moment one is joined to God through Christ, in a relationship so secure it will endure forever.

Ancient Covenant Ways

A covenant was the most solemn and legally binding relationship between two parties. It began with an intent of the heart, such as love, or peace and protection among tribes, or as a business transaction. It was also the common way in which citizens pledged their allegiance to a king or sovereign ruler. Covenants were typically solemnized in a ceremony in front of witnesses, like our modern wedding ceremonies. In fact, ancient covenant rituals are the origin of today's wedding ceremonies, and God identifies marriage as a covenant in Malachi 2:14.

However, the ancient ceremonies differed significantly in one crucial aspect: they were all sealed by a blood oath to accept the sentence (or curse) of death if one violated their promise to keep the covenant. This was clearly understood, and truly

---

[3] Ephesians 1:3-12; 2 Corinthians 3:18

honored by all. A covenant maker typically would invoke such a curse upon himself in front of witnesses, thereby giving his wronged partner (or their surviving relatives, the witnesses or other authorities) permission to take His life. It was considered as legally binding as a law passed by our modern Legislature.

For centuries modern couples have said, "till death do us part" at the end of their marriage vows, signifying theirs was meant to be a permanent relationship which could end honorably only by the death of one of the parties. But today, marriages often end in divorce, and the concept of permanency and accountability to those marriage vows has all but vanished. In fact, people often live together without even making vows to one another so they can easily extricate themselves if the relationship no longer suits their needs. It seems the more modern our cultures become the less we value the kind of honor and faithfulness that might cost us something. Instead of joining themselves to another with the goal of serving the other, people unite in the hope the other will make them happy.

The more modern our cultures become the less we value the kind of honor and faithfulness that might cost us something.

Clearly, man still needs to have something outside himself to help motivate him to do what is right in relationship. We are still weak and fickle in love and allegiances, but in our times, any penalty for being unfaithful has all but disappeared. All of modern society is moving towards giving each other permission to do anything they like, without consequence, because that means I can do anything I like without consequence. It feels like freedom, but it is a snare that destroys character and sets up a society in which hearts are broken again and again, in danger of becoming isolated, crippled, bitter and selfish. After all, if no one else will love me faithfully, it must be up to me, myself, and I to love myself well.

We have become a culture that defaults to loving ourselves first, and we get a pass from the greater part of society for whatever choices we find necessary to keep life good for us. This is life at the expense of others, not life that nourishes others; and ultimately it fails to nourish us as well. This is not the kind of life God designed for His creation, and especially not for His people, who are meant to express His character to the world they live in. We can only become what we have the potential to be in an environment of secure love and connection.

We turn now to a review of the common steps in primitive covenant rituals that will open our eyes to many things our Lord did for us.

The Covenant Gift Of Promise

Commonly, covenant makers exchanged gifts — a garment, a ring, ornament or other meaningful object — as a visible token of one's commitment. In ancient times one often had only one major garment or special adornment, so when exchanged, it would be obvious to everyone in the community that they had entered into covenant with the one who now wore that garment or ornament. This gift said, *"I promise to give myself to you."* The only modern remnant of that practice is the giving of an engagement ring to a bride-to-be.

The Covenant Pledge Of Protection

Typically men exchanged the belts which carried their weapons, or exchanged the weapons themselves. With this came the stated or implied pledge to defend the new partner against every enemy, even at the cost of one's own life. This exchange said, *"I offer you all of my strength and protection. From this day forward your enemies are my enemies."*

Ancient covenant partners could always call on each other in times of threat, and were willing to lay down their lives for each other without hesitation. In fact, it was an honor to do so. In Psalm 35, David implored God to come to his rescue when he was in trouble. He spoke to God as if God was a real person, a real covenant comrade who would come to him and aid him in a battle. The utter confidence David expresses in God's help is not merely based on faith in God being God, but upon the covenant faithfulness that all men honored in David's day. In fact, the most clear example of a covenant ceremony in the Old Testament is seen between David and Jonathan, the son of King Saul:

> *Jonathan became one in spirit with David, and he loved him as himself. ... And Jonathan made a covenant with David because he loved him as himself. Jonathan took off the robe he was wearing and gave it to David, along with his tunic, and even his sword, his bow and his belt. (1 Samuel 18:1-4)*

Substitutionary Sacrifice And The Blood

The most common element in primitive covenant ceremonies was the sacrifice of an animal, usually cut in half so the two parties could walk among the pieces while making their vows. The slain animal represented each person in a two-fold way. First, the covenant maker would point to or lean on the animal and say, *"This animal represents me; I am now dead to my old life. And may this same fate be mine if I ever break this covenant."* Thus each party invoked a death curse upon himself in the event he broke the covenant, making it legal to take his life as an act of justice for breaking the law of friendship.

The blood of the slain animal was often used, either by common drinking or to mark objects or bodies. However, God forbid the drinking of blood. In many instances the two parties would make a cut on their bodies and draw blood, then mingle their blood together. This symbolized the most important point of a covenant, that the two parties will now become *as one.* Leviticus 17:11 says that the life of a man is in his blood; thus sharing blood symbolized sharing life. The covenant makers would then be "blood relatives" in the eyes of their community. For this reason the parties would also either exchange names or link them together publicly.

The Public Covenant Mark Or Sign

Often the covenant makers would rub their cuts together to mingle the blood, and rub something like dirt or fire ash in the cuts to create a permanent and publicly visible scar. This scar or mark served as a reminder in one's body of their covenant obligation to another person. It also showed others that one was united with another person (or tribe), which came in quite handy if you weren't big and strong, and someone wanted to do you mischief. Seeing that a man was in covenant with another was to know that if you hurt them, the covenant partner would not rest until he found you and avenged his friend.

Our modern handshake originated from men grasping one another's hands so each party could see who the other was allied with, by the covenant scars on their palms, wrists or arms. This purpose was served on occasion by tattoos as well, in the form of tribal, sovereign or family symbols.

A covenant scar or mark also served the function of remembrance, reminding its bearer of obligations to their covenant friend. A fascinating example of covenant remembrance is found in the story of David and Saul's grandson Mephibosheth in 2 Samuel Chapter 9. After Jonathan, David's secret covenant friend, has died in battle, David has become king, taking over the throne that once belonged to Jonathan's father Saul. Therefore Mephibosheth (and everyone in Saul's family) have become David's enemies by political necessity, and gone into hiding, for fear of their lives. Then one day, something — likely a covenant mark on David's body — focuses David's attention on the covenant promise he made to

Jonathan. He then asks, *"Is there anyone still left of the house of Saul to whom I can show kindness* (i.e, covenant faithfulness) *for Jonathan's sake?"*[4]

I share this because a key concept in the Bible connected with covenant is that of *remembrance.* God "remembered His covenant with Abraham, with Isaac and with Jacob" in Exodus 2:24. Jesus gave us the Lord's Supper (communion) and said, "Do this in remembrance of me." When you encounter the word "remember" in the Bible it is usually a pointer to a covenant promise or commitment. Scars, marks, stones etched with names, trees carved with symbols, all served as reminders of one's union with and obligations to care for another in sworn friendship. Every covenant had its public mark or symbol.

The word *remember* in the Bible usually points to a covenant promise or commitment.

We receive a "public mark" today when we put on wedding rings, a sign to the community that we belong to another, and a reminder to ourselves to be faithful. Unlike a scar, however, a wedding ring is all too easy to remove.

Covenant Promises: The Focus Of Faith

In every covenant ceremony the purposes and promises of the union were announced. These would be the terms, vows, or stipulations declared in the presence of witnesses. These were the promises of the covenant, the blessings or commitments made by one party to the other. Every covenant — or relationship, for that matter — begins in good faith. You are asking the other party to put faith in you, your character and promises, and you are likewise extending such faith to them. In

[4] 2 Samuel 9:1

ancient days, no one broke a covenant, because to do so would be considered "breaking faith," the highest form of dishonor. To destroy the faith another had placed in you was too dishonorable to go unpunished.

This is the concept God refers to in Malachi Chapter 2 when He is responds to the complaints of the Jewish priests that God is not honoring their sacrifices. They want to know why. God's response: the Jewish priests had *broken faith* with their wives by not treating them right, divorcing them for frivolous reasons, and probably abusing them in some way.

Referring to covenant values, God made it clear that He hates it when we break or destroy the faith that another person has placed in us — especially when it is the result of a vow or promise we made. Repeatedly the Lord says in Malachi, "*Do not break faith!*" This is a core covenant value, and reveals God's heart for relationship and His concern for the well-being of His people.

God hates it when we break (destroy) the faith that another person has placed in us.

In addition to promises, curses would be pronounced as the legal penalties for breaking one's covenant oaths. These were either self-invoked or pronounced by the opposite party. I call them "legal" because these curses carried the same weight in their ancient communities as a law upheld by courts in our modern times.

If you break a law today, the law states clearly what penalty you will suffer for breaking it. You know ahead of time what the enforcing authorities have a legal right to do to you if your guilt is proven. Ancient covenant ceremonies and their curses *were* the legal system that primitive peoples used. This ensured righteous behavior and trust were maintained among its citizens. They didn't lock you up in a jail cell, they just hunted you down and did to you what the curse called for.

David Livingstone witnessed primitive covenant practices in his missionary work in Africa. He recorded in his journals that he never knew of a covenant being violated, because if a man broke his covenant promises or vows, even his own mother or father would hunt him down and deliver him to "the avenger" to carry out his self-invoked death sentence! A covenant vow was considered a lifelong commitment, and one's word was a matter of great honor to oneself, and security to one's family and village.

A covenant relationship was passed down like an inheritance through the generations.

Covenants bound two parties together for the duration of their lives, but were typically also binding upon their descendants. A covenant relationship was passed down like an inheritance through the generations, as each child came to an age of accountability, capable of affirming and upholding the obligations to the relationship. This brings us to the blessings such covenants guaranteed in the first place.

Covenant Friends Share Everything

Everything changed between two parties once a covenant joined them together. From then on, the two parties shared everything: all assets and wealth, as well as all debts and obligations. A covenant partner would give freely if the other had a need, not merely feeling obligated but honored to do so. It was mutually understood that *"What's mine is yours, and what's yours is mine."* Period.

In this sense covenant is a type of equalizer between two unequal parties. Small, vulnerable tribes often made covenants with larger tribes as a matter of security. If a poor person covenanted with a wealthy person, the poor person became wealthy. The privileges and authority that a title or office gave one party could be shared by the other, except in the case where a covenant was the type that bound ordinary citizens together under a sovereign such as a king. In such a case citizens of this kingdom would enjoy the king's protection, but they also might be expected to pay taxes, provide sons to serve in the king's army, and they did certainly not share the king's authority.

The Covenant Meal

Covenant makers would share a celebratory meal together, usually of bread and wine which represented their flesh and blood. They often fed it to one another while declaring, *"I am in you, and you are in me. We are one."* The belief was that if we both eat of the same food, we are sharing life, because the bread we shared today becomes our bone, blood and flesh tomorrow. The shared meal was like a sacrament in that it symbolized an invisible reality — becoming as "one" — with visible elements.

This concept carried over into the everyday sharing of food in ancient Middle Eastern cultures. To them, sharing food was never done lightly, and never with an enemy or outsider! This is one reason why Jews refused to eat with non-Jews in Jesus' time. Sharing a meal with an enemy or outsider could be tantamount to declaring a truce and the end of hostilities. One only shared a table with friends. When David wrote of the Lord, *"You set a table before me in the presence of my enemies; my cup overflows,"* I believe he was referring to a covenant meal, expressing faith in God's absolute commitment to him.

This covenant tradition of a meal had a direct impact on the work of Scottish missionary David Livingstone in Africa, where he took the gospel to both friendly tribes and those that would just as soon eat you for dinner. He would preach the gospel about Jesus Christ, then serve communion. The natives often showed suspicion about Livingstone's "good news" about Jesus, until one day when he set out the bread and the wine of communion; to Livingstone's amazement, the tribe got excited and pressed in to accept what he was offering. He learned from his interpreter that the meal of bread and wine were familiar covenant symbols. Therefore, they believed they were being offered a secure relationship with God, through binding themselves with Jesus the Son — which they were! They were willing to trust Jesus, because they had faith in covenants. No one ever broke covenant in Africa.

The Public Covenant Memorial

Finally, it was common in primitive cultures to establish a memorial as a public "witness" to the covenant. A tree might be planted, or something carved into a tree (perhaps the origin of lovers carving a heart into a tree with their names); a pile of rocks might be erected, or a large stone inscribed with the covenant makers' names. The latter is most commonly seen in Bible stories when covenant activity occurs, which is why you often see "stones" prominently mentioned in otherwise brief narratives that seem insignificant to the Western mind.

We see a stone used as a covenant memorial in Genesis 28 when Jacob is visited by God, who invites him to receive (and honor) the covenant God has with his father Isaac and grandfather Abraham. God reveals the covenant to Jacob in a dream, and when he wakes up, Jacob takes the stone he used for a pillow and sets it up as a memorial. Then he vows to honor the covenant of his father and grandfather with the Lord.

The most famous memorial to a covenant is the stone tablets inscribed with the Ten Commandments, known to ancients as *God's covenant words.* Treaties and covenants

The most famous covenant memorial is the stone tablets inscribed with the Ten Commandments, known to ancients as *God's covenant words.*

between kings and men were commonly inscribed on stone tablets; was what uncommon was for them to be inscribed by the finger of God! Covenant records of this nature are often uncovered in archeological digs.

Covenant Friends

From the day of swearing their oaths, covenant makers called each other *friend,* a word reserved for those in covenant, not a casual moniker for just any social acquaintance, as it is today. After God instituted a covenant with Abraham, He referred to him as "Abraham my friend." When God introduced Himself to Moses and others, He always included Abraham's name, saying: *"I am the God of Abraham."* He wasn't just saying, *"I am the God Abraham believes in,"* He was announcing, *"Abraham and I are covenant friends."*

Covenant friends considered themselves bound together forever. The Biblical phrase that expresses this is, *"I am in you, and you are in me,"* reflecting their view of their *oneness.* While each party retained their own identity, they belonged to one another in a way that would forever redefine what life would look like for both.

A covenant friend was committed to give his all to his friend in whatever way was needed. A right attitude towards your covenant friend would be, *"I live to be faithful to you. My eyes are on you to see how you are, to know if you are safe, cared for, or in need of anything I can provide. My devotion and attention belong to you above all other things and people. We are at peace with one another. I will never withdraw my love and favor. I am, and forever will be, your friend."*

6 The Biblical Thread Of God's Covenants

While Scripture doesn't give us a nice neat linear or obvious teaching about covenant, we can move quickly through the Bible to see if what we have learned bears out its prominence. The point of discovering covenant activity is to witness God's persistence to know and be known by His people; to understand how He stayed close by them in faithfulness, while displaying His full wrath against those who not only were not His covenant friends, but acted as enemies to His people. It also helps one understand why He ultimately punished those who chronically broke faith with Him after suffering long with them.

To understand the heart and faith behind the commitment, it is helpful to look at the familiar language of a typical marriage covenant ceremony:

> *I take you ____, for my lawful (wife or husband), to have and to hold from this day forward; for better, for worse, for richer, for poorer, in sickness and health, until death do us part.*

In the beginning, we assume the best about the person we are binding ourselves to. God knew the worst before He ever made a promise. Mankind, His beloved creation, would give Him the worst; betray Him, ignore Him, commit adultery, misrepresent His character to the world, and worst of all, doubt His goodness and His intentions. And still, He pursued us on a level made necessary by our humanity, so He could bring us into a relationship where we could enjoy His divine love and friendship. It is astounding. Since God will never die, His promises and faithfulness will never end. In Christ we will never experience the death of our being; only our dusty bodies.

With that, let's begin our quick journey through the Bible.

The Creation Covenant With Adam

In the beginning, God put Adam and Eve in the garden He planted, where they shared life with Him. That God came daily to walk with them "in the cool of the day" in Eden is an expression of intimacy and closeness, of knowing and being known. It is friendship and a type of equality that one usually doesn't associate between the creator of the universe and His human creation.

"The cool of the day" points to that time when we rest from our occupations to relax with and enjoy one another. We share stories of our day. We talk over ideas, dreams, goals. We spend time being face-to-face with our intimates, rejoicing in the shared life that enriches us in multiplied ways; solving problems together, creating together.

God didn't have to do this with His creation. He could have given Adam life, given him the earth, and said, "I'll be off in heaven if you need me." Eden tells us that the original Being is incredibly relational, that He created mankind *for* relationship and all the potential that offers, and that He delights in this fellowship. We can be sure that the fellowship of Father, Son and Spirit is rich and full; yet God still made man and wanted relationship with him.

Though the word "covenant" is never seen in the Eden story, the elements are evident. God states His purposes (requirements) for this relationship between His Sovereign Self and His Creation: man is to multiply and fill the earth with God's glory. God promises to provide all man needs through the Tree of Life. They are forbidden to nourish themselves from the tree of knowledge of good and evil. If they break this covenant law, God tells Adam and Eve, *"You shall surely die."*

Here is the death curse. Of course, Adam and Eve did eat from the forbidden tree, and thus broke their covenant with God, bringing themselves — and all their family line — under the curse of death.

It is less clear how God responds after Adam and Eve sin. God does not slay them, which He has a right to do! Instead, He covers their nakedness with animal skins. Clearly, there is only one way to separate an animal from his skin, and that is by taking its life — something Adam and Eve had probably never seen before, being vegetarians.

God either kills or has Adam kill an innocent animal. We can be confident — because of how substitutionary animal sacrifice is taught by God later under Moses — that God surely says to Adam and Eve, *"You deserve to die, but this innocent animal is dying in your place."* God has not overlooked their sin. The animal dies so they can live, while God maintains His covenant right to justice. God then clothes Adam and Eve in the skins of that sacrificed animal, so that instead of experiencing the shame of their new nakedness every day, they are clothed in the provision of God's merciful love.

In performing the first substitutionary sacrifice for mankind, God ensures a continuing relationship to His creation. By giving and teaching this to Adam, God extends a measure of grace to fallen man. As Adam and his descendants sacrifice an animal occasionally to acknowledge the death sentence and show devotion to God, the covenant curse and God's justice will be "stayed" until another day.

How can we know all of this happened when the scripture doesn't clearly say so? Because of what happens next, in Genesis Chapter 4. Here we see Adam and Eve's sons, Cain and Abel, both bringing offerings to God, though the substance of their offerings is very different. Abel brings animal organs, obviously obtained only by killing an animal; God is pleased with his offering. Cain offers God vegetables he has grown; God is not happy with Cain and does not accept His offering. Why would God refuse one and accept the other?

As far as God was concerned, any offering brought to express worship had to come with acknowledgement of the sin and death curse that still stood between Himself and man. Each time you came to God, you came saying, *"I know I deserve to die; please accept this animal's life in place of mine, which belongs to you."* Clearly, someone has taught these brothers to sacrifice an animal and offer its parts to God. It could only have been their father, Adam; who had to have been taught by God Himself, who would have provided the reason.

God has not abandoned His relationship to man, though it is dramatically altered. In giving Adam a substitutionary sacrifice God is graciously continuing the connection with His fallen man through what scholars believe is another covenant — one in which God promises not to slay Adam as He deserves, but to receive an animal offering instead.

Now that man has tasted of knowledge of good and evil, he finds himself with an ever increasing appetite for giving himself whatever he wants, even at the cost of others. This is seen both in Cain's choice to approach God HIS way and to murder his brother when he didn't get what he wanted from God. The next chapters of Genesis reveal that all mankind becomes evil in their lust for self-serving knowledge, save for one.

Now I Know Why I Was Born A Sinner

Until I understood what really took place in Eden, I couldn't see how the "original sin" of Adam and Eve had anything to do with me. When one party makes a covenant with another, all of his children, even those unborn or yet conceived, are included in the covenant's blessings, obligations and penalties. I now understand that all human beings, as descendants of Adam, are born under the curse of death for the original broken covenant between God and man.

The sin of Adam and Eve came with me into this world, and the curse of death hung over my life. It is the same with my children, and their children, until the day when they hear and understand that a sinless man died in their place. Jesus accepted the full wrath of God upon His human flesh to satisfy that curse of death once and for all. God received His justice for the broken covenant.

The sin of Adam and Eve came with me into this world.

Covenant Is The Foundation Of God's Justice

The covenant promise, vow and curse of death are sacred to our Creator. Such things are the foundation of all justice. God will not waver on this, for we are told often in scripture that He loves justice. God the Father had a dilemma, because He could neither destroy the foundation of all justice by waiving the penalty for breaking the original covenant, nor give up His beloved children. Jesus became the answer to His dilemma.

Why Didn't God Just Start Over?

When Adam broke the covenant, God could have ended it there; He could have put Adam and Eve to death according to the covenant law, and just created new people. But if He had, He would still have the same situation that created the problem in the first place: free will. God created mankind in His own image and likeness,[1] with the potential to become good or evil. God desired to build a nation of people like Himself who would use their freedom of choice to become as righteous and good as possible. Apart from free will, morals have no meaning. God's glory is revealed in His choice and commitment to be good instead of evil, to be steadfastly faithful and just as He relates to

[1] Genesis 1:26

His creation. The same thing that makes this possible — free will — also makes evil and lawlessness possible. God's people had to have free will like He has if they were to become true children of glory.

A being without the same free will could never be a worthy family member for God. He did not want a nation of puppets who had no true moral core; He wanted a people who would use their freedom to choose to walk in His likeness and character. Such a nation magnifies God's glory to all creation.

God Covenants With Noah

We next see God covenant with Noah in Genesis Chapter 9. God's heart has broken over how all mankind has become evil; He decides to cleanse the earth with a massive flood. God knows one righteous man with whom He can continue to pursue His dream: Noah. God will build a lineage of men through the righteous stock of Noah. God commissions him to build an ark to house his family and all animal species so they can survive the cleansing flood. After Noah spends 100 years building the ark, God sends the animals to the ark, and the rains come. A year later, when the ark finally rests on dry land again, Noah's first act is to build an altar to God and offer animal sacrifices in worship, just as his ancestor Adam did.

God is pleased. He responds by making a covenant with Noah. He essentially restates the original covenant stipulations He first given to Adam, now assigning stewardship of creation to Noah. It is a new start for a cleansed earth, sealed as covenant between God and Noah and all his descendants. God adds the promise that He will never destroy the earth by water again, and gives a sign of this covenant promise: the rainbow. Every time it rains, when men fear God might be judging the earth with a deluge again, the appearance of a rainbow will remind them of God's promise to never do that again.

Revelation 4:3 tells us that a rainbow encircles God's throne. This is not merely ornamental, it is God's reminder of

His promise to Noah. Each party to a covenant would forever keep or wear an object to remind them of their promises, such as an amulet worn around the neck with promises inscribed on it; or a leather pouch containing the promises etched on some material or stone. God arranged for His own special reminder!

God Covenants With Abraham

The thread of God's covenants continues with a man named Abram, in Genesis Chapter 12. The story of God's covenant with Abram — later named Abraham — will become the crucial link in a Christian's lineage from Adam to the New Covenant of Christ. This is because God makes a promise to Abraham that through his line, all peoples of the earth will be blessed. This promise is fulfilled through Jesus Christ! To prove it, the Holy Spirit put a genealogical record at the opening of the gospel of Matthew, showing the direct line of "Jesus Christ, the son of David, the son of Abraham."

The Apostle Paul further builds the case for this when he explains in his Galatian letter that Jesus "redeemed us in order that the blessing given to Abraham might come to the Gentiles through Christ Jesus..." He also makes other explanatory statements, including this one:

> *"If you belong to Christ, then you are Abraham's seed, and heirs according to the promise." (Galatians 3:29)*

So this potentially obscure Old Testament story in Genesis turns out to be all about us, further verified when Paul says that God *"announced the gospel in advance to Abraham."*[2] We are still in the first book of the Bible, and God's covenant record has already connected us to Jesus Christ, our Savior!

What happens between Abram and God (as told in Genesis Chapters 12 through 22) is our most clear Biblical evidence of the *culture* of covenant. There are slain animals cut in two, and

[2] Galatians 3:8

two elements of fire passing between the pieces in covenant fashion. God promises Abram something amazing: that He will bring forth from him a nation of men too numerous to be counted. This is amazing because not only does Abram have no sons, he and his wife are both aged beyond the ability to naturally have children!

As the story of Abram progresses we see God changing Abram's name to Abraham, a confirmation that they are covenanted together. We see God calling for a covenant mark to be cut on Abraham's body, which is circumcision. Most of all, we see God keeping His covenant promise to give Abram and Sarai a son, from whom will come 12 sons, who will become a nation of people known as Israel — from which Jesus will come!

How Does God Choose A Man?

How does God choose a man from among all men to build a line to His Christ, His Son who will build Him a kingdom? He looks for faith. He has always looked for faith. I learned this from studying Abraham, especially the worst moment of his life.

After years of waiting on God, the promised son Isaac comes. Abraham and Sarah raise him to honor God. One day, God tells Abraham to take this son and offer him as a sacrifice. This shocks me, and it surely must have shocked Abraham at first. Can you imagine a more difficult command of God? Yet Abraham responds to this command fairly quickly, setting out on a three-day journey to where he plans to obey God. We don't know for sure how old Isaac is, but the account of Josephus, a Jewish historian, says Issac was 25 years old, that he understood what Abraham planned to do, and as one who also worshipped and trusted God, he willingly got on the altar and allowed his father to bind him as a sacrifice.[3]

We only learn of Abraham's state of mind during this event when we get to Hebrews Chapter 11 in the New Testament:

---

[3] Pages 43-44, The Works of Josephus, ©1987 by Hendrikson Publishers, Inc.

> *By faith Abraham, when he was tested, offered up Isaac, and he who had received the promises was offering up his only begotten son; it was he to whom it was said, "In Isaac your descendants shall be called." He considered that God is able to raise people even from the dead, from which he also received him back as a type.* (Hebrews 11:17-19 NASB)

Abraham was able to obey God in this most difficult thing because he trusted God's faithfulness without question. God met that faith by staying Abraham's hand the moment he raised it to obey, providing Abraham a ram nearby to offer in Isaac's place. It is important to understand that the greater test here (beyond the test of Abraham's obedience) was whether Abraham had faith in God's faithfulness! God wanted to know, *Do you trust me without question?* Abraham's answer was *Yes*. When Abraham came up with the right answer to this question — proved by his actions, God said, *"This is a righteous man."*

> *Was not our father Abraham considered righteous for what he did when he offered his son Isaac on the altar? You see that his faith and his actions were working together, and his faith was made complete by what he did. And the scripture was fulfilled that says, "Abraham believed God, and it was credited to him as righteousness," and he was called God's friend.* (James 2:21-23)

Abraham's ability to be faithful to God was rooted in his trust in God. Abraham wasn't called "righteous" because He lived a perfect life — he didn't — but because he believed in the faithfulness of his God, without question. And if Josephus is right, Abraham obviously taught his son Isaac to do the same.

Abraham displayed a right covenant heart; that is, a heart willing to do two things: (1) place complete trust in the covenant partner; (2) live completely worthy of the trust also placed in him.

I believe this is how God chooses His people, according to His foreknowledge of how men will respond to Him. He cannot

God called Abraham *righteous* because he had absolute faith in God's faithfulness.

show His glory through men who are never quite sure of Him and don't quite trust Him. Abraham could never have carried out such an act if He doubted God was His true covenant friend and would absolutely keep His word, no matter how doubtful it might look.

God is looking for the person who has a heart to believe Him. Our ability to be faithful to God is rooted in our faith in His absolute faithfulness. (If you think that looks like a verbal circle, you're right. I feel God smiling just now because I wrote that.)

God Covenants With The Nation Of Israel

Hundreds of years after Abraham dies, the entire nation of Israel is in Egypt, now in bondage under Pharoah. They cry out to God for deliverance. Exodus 2:24 says, *God heard their moaning and He remembered His covenant with Abraham...*

Take note: God doesn't save the Israelites just because they cried out to Him; He hears and responds to their cry because they are the descendants of Abraham, His friend. He had given His covenant promise to Abraham and was bound by honor to extend all covenant grace to the descendants of Abraham as He would to Abraham himself.

Using Moses as a mediator and leader, God rescues Abraham's tribe of several million people from Pharoah's slavery. Now free and totally dependent on the Lord in the Sinai Desert, God offers them a covenant to be their sovereign Lord, saying *"I will be your God, and you will be my people."* The people accept and vow to obey Him as their only Lord.

This covenant is known as the Mosaic Covenant (after Moses) and contained stipulations we know as the Ten

Commandments. These commandments are God's righteous laws for loving Him and loving others. God ordains a priesthood to keep relations running smoothly between Himself and the people, and provides a system of sacrificial offerings; some to restore right standing with God or people after committing a trespass; others for celebration, worship or consecration.

God gives Moses a detailed plan for a Tabernacle where all of this can take place, a portable sanctuary to go with them as they travel. God is emphatic that this Tabernacle be an exact replica of His sanctuary in heaven, because God will dwell in it, in camp with His people:

> *Then have them make a sanctuary for me, and I will dwell among them. (Exodus 25:8)*

I have always loved that God wasn't content to just rescue them; He chose to live with them. The ultimate in covenant faithfulness to His friend Abraham was seen in God choosing to be personally present with His people in this Tabernacle. His Spirit would rest above the mercy seat, which served as the cover for the box (ark) God had Moses build to contain the covenant laws, the Ten Commandments.

> **God wasn't content to just rescue Abraham's people; He chose to live with them.**

The Spirit of God was powerfully present as a cloud by day that sheltered them from the hot sun, and as a fire which illuminated the camp and saved them from frigid desert nights.

The Promised Land Gift

When God set the people free from their slavery in Egypt, His plan was to give them the land of Canaan in which to settle. Canaan was then occupied by the descendants of Ham, but God would turn all the lands, houses and cities over to His people. God said that as they advanced into the land, He would wipe out the inhabitants for them.

Why would God do such a thing? Had He no feeling for the inhabitants of Canaan? Did He look at them one day and say, *"I just don't like these people. They burn too much incense to fake gods"*? Why does one nation have favor with God, and another does not? The answer is found in the covenant culture and God's value for faithfulness.

In this case, we can trace God's actions back to Genesis 9:18-27 and Noah. After the great flood, Noah became God's covenant friend. Covenant friends support one another's judgments and decisions. One day Noah's son Ham dishonored him in a way that Noah considered a great betrayal. As a result, Noah pronounced a curse on Ham whereby he (and his descendants) would become slaves to Noah's other sons Shem and Japheth (and their descendants) — who had preserved their father's honor in the same incident. Noah felt this judgment to be just, impoverishing Ham by giving all his territory to the two sons who showed honor and righteous behavior towards him.

Much later, while making covenant with Abraham, God enforces the judgment of His covenant friend Noah by awarding the land of Canaan to Abraham and his descendants. God has foreseen that Canaan will be occupied by Ham's descendants, while Abraham and his line are descended from Shem. Thus God's award of Canaan to His covenant people is first an act of faithfulness to Noah, (carrying out his will and justice over the betrayal of his son Ham) and second, an act of faithfulness to Abraham by covenant promise.

God is motivated in all things by faithfulness and justice in relationship.

God is motivated in all things by being faithful and bringing justice in relationship. God also was rewarding the one who worshipped Him — Abraham — by giving him the land upon which he worshipped God; taking it away from those who worshipped idols (Ham's descendants). It's all one big covenant transaction. God rewards those who worship Him through faith and obedience. In light of this, it is easy to see that Hebrews 11:6 is yet another covenant-infused statement:

> *And without faith it is impossible to please God, because anyone who comes to him must believe that he exists and that he rewards those who earnestly seek him.*

While faith and faithfulness bring joy to God and stir Him to reward it, nothing invites His wrath more quickly than faithlessness and betrayal from those to whom He is related. Noah and God are kindred spirits in this, with the same values towards faithfulness and betrayal. These are covenant values; to understand them is to understand all the major Bible characters, their choices, and their fates.

The Cost Of Faithlessness

After sealing the new covenant with the Hebrew nation of Israel, the Spirit of God leads them to the border of Canaan, and commands them to take the land away from the descendants of Ham. Thrilled to be promised a land of their own, the Israelites are not quite so thrilled to learn they must actually fight for the land. They send in a scouting party to see what they are up against. Finding the land inhabited by big and powerful people, the scouting party comes back and fills the people with such fear that they refuse to go in and take the land.

Even worse, the Hebrews actually accuse God of evil intent, of sending them to their harm, saying, "*We'd have been better off to die in Egypt!*"[4] They went so far as to accuse God of callously sending them out to let them and their children die, revealing that they really didn't believe God at all. It didn't matter to

---

[4] Numbers 14:3

them that God had promised to fight with and for them, to give them success in settling in the land. When faced with the obstacles, what little faith they had in God melted away in fear. In their fear and distrust, they maligned God's character, which is one of the highest forms of covenant betrayal.

In righteous anger, God sentences them to wander around the Sinai wilderness until the generation of unbelievers dies out, which takes 40 years. Yet even after betraying Him through disobedience and assault on His character, the Spirit of God remains with the Israelites according to His promise, traveling with them and faithfully caring for them. He commanded a kind of bread to fall from heaven every morning (called manna), and commanded water to come forth from rocks that flowed like rivers, enough to satisfy this nomadic nation of about two million. When they needed to move (for sanitary reasons, among other things) the Spirit went ahead of them to scout out the best campsites. Their sandals and clothes did not wear out in those 40 years; we are even told their feet did not swell. [5]

Our Greatest Sin Against God: Unbelief

One of the greatest sins we commit is not believing God. When we don't believe what God has said, or worse, believe in His character and motives, the inevitable result is that we bring dishonor to His name and belie His true goodness in the eyes of others. After all God had done for the Hebrew tribes, it is incredible they still did not trust Him and could accuse Him of such evil. Yet this is the result of not knowing God in truth. This is the God who instructed Moses to carry these people in His arms, *as a nurse carries an infant* to the promised land, [6] showing His heart to tenderly care for the people.

At the end of their wilderness wanderings, when the unbelieving generation has died off and the next generation is

[5] Deuteronomy 8:3-4

[6] Numbers 11:12

preparing to enter the Promised Land at last, God reviews their covenant, adding stipulations to govern the possession and stewardship of the land. The blessings and curses, profound and abundant, are clearly stated to them,[7] including the warning that if they violate God's laws they will lose the land by being exiled from it. The people vow to obey God, and God promises to bless them abundantly when they do.

It is important to stop and mark a moment in this whole episode that reveals God's heart to be faithful even when He already knows His people will be unfaithful. The story is told in Deuteronomy 31, where God says, *"I know what they are disposed to do, even before I bring them into the land I promised them on oath."* (Deuteronomy 31:11)

Immediately after God and the people have renewed their covenant vows, God takes Moses and Joshua aside and warns them the people will forsake Him by worshipping idols and demons! He then dictates a song that Moses is to teach the people to sing before they break camp and go into the Promised Land. The song tells the story of how just God is and how unfaithful they will be, forcing Him to turn His face away and become their enemy. The song (found in Deuteronomy 32) reveals both the kindness and the severity of God. It is surely God's hope that as the generations sing this song they will be warned away from their rebellion by knowing in advance the dire consequences that would ensue.

Before the covenant vows have left their lips, God knows how badly they will betray Him. Even so, He honors His commitment to give them the land and be their God until He can no longer watch them put their trust in idols and demons.

The people do break their covenant vows to God in every way, not the least of which was giving their worship and trust to idols. They are ultimately sent into exile to Babylon for 70 years. But God had not judged them quickly; He endured their

---

[7] Deuteronomy Chapter 28

chronic unfaithfulness for several hundred years before seeking justice and giving them over to the consequences of their betrayal. God invented long-suffering. Furthermore, this story ends as all stories do concerning God and His people: with God promising to rescue and redeem them!

God's Covenant Promise Of A Righteous King

When the nation of Israel settled in the promised land, they first lived under God's rule by way of of judges and prophets like Samuel. God revealed His words to these prophets, authorizing them to represent His will and governance to the people. But the people don't like this; they want a "real king" like other nations have. God yields and chooses an excellent specimen in Saul, making him king over Israel. But Saul ultimately shows his heart is to protect his own domain, not to lead the nation in knowing and honoring God. God then finds a better man, one with a heart after His own, a shepherd boy named David.

This brings us to the one remaining Old Testament covenant in our Biblical thread that bears upon our story with God. This is a covenant God makes with David, in which He promises to establish an enduring kingship through him and his family line. It is found in Psalm 89:

> *I have made a covenant with my chosen one, I have sworn to David my servant, "I will establish your line forever and make your throne firm through all generations." (Psalms 89:3-4)*

> *I have found David my servant; with my sacred oil I have anointed him. My hand will sustain him; surely my arm will strengthen him. The enemy will not get the better of him; the wicked will not oppress him. I will crush his foes before him and strike down his adversaries. My faithful love will be with him, and through my name his horn will be exalted. I will set his hand over the sea, his right hand over the rivers. He will call out to me, "You are my Father,*

> *my God, the Rock my Savior." And I will appoint him to be my firstborn, the most exalted of the kings of the earth. I will maintain my love to him forever, and my covenant with him will never fail. I will establish his line forever, his throne as long as the heavens endure. (Psalms 89:20-29)*

Notice the words God uses — *he will call out to me, you are my Father, my God* — as well as the rest of the covenant promises of the relationship they will have. These are a huge insight into God's heart regarding intimacy. Has anyone ever been invited to call God "Father" before now?

David and God were intimates, because David believed in God's righteous heart and in His personal love. David lived from a place of confidence in that love. The story of their relationship and David's many Psalms paint a personal picture of God's unfailing love for a man, and how a believing person experiences and responds to that love. David's words reveal how such love nourishes and emboldens the human heart.

This is the reason God called David a man after His own heart.[8] By believing what God promised, David showed his faith in the real peace between himself and God. When he went into battle he understood that God not only had his back, He encircled David like a rampart, shielding him on all sides.

God's faithfulness made David bold and fearless.

David's Psalms show that resting in God's faithfulness was key to his ability to be bold and fearless. Believing, he beheld God; and seeing, he worshipped, like no other man had before him. King David used his great wealth to establish a choir to sing extravagant praises to God 24/7, and wrote unabashed songs of love to God, preserved for us in Psalms.

---

[8] 1 Samuel 13:14

God's Promise To David: Fulfilled Through Jesus

Back to Psalm 89, and the covenant promise God made to establish David's line in a permanent kingship: God's promises found their ultimate fulfillment in Jesus, later born into David's line. Luke 3:23-38 traces Jesus' lineage from Adam to David to Joseph, showing Jesus to be a descendant of King David and the rightful heir to this promise.

At just the right moment in history, the Father, Son and Spirit carried out their plan for Jesus to enter the human race. God chose Joseph, a descendant of David, to act as the legal father of Jesus; and chose Mary, also a descendant of David, to receive the Holy Spirit's seed and grow this child in her womb. The covenant promise God made to King David was also a prophetic promise to Jesus His Son, who would later hear these words read from the scrolls in the Jewish synagogues:

> *I will appoint you to be my firstborn, the most exalted of the kings of the earth... Your throne will endure before me as long as the heavens endure! (Psalm 89:27-29)*

It is fitting that the human lineage of Jesus the Son of Man ran through a heart like David's: full of integrity as a covenant keeper; full of faith in God's personal love for him; full of joy in knowing God personally. Jesus was the Son of David, indeed.

An in-depth study of these covenants in the Bible is fascinating and worthwhile, with many more layers of detail than I have shared here. My purpose here is not to present a detailed teaching of covenant, but to draw a thread through Scripture that gives you a picture of God's covenant heart. Seeing God's history with man in this way makes it clear just how tenacious God is in loving and knowing us. Now we move on to the ultimate expression of that love.

7 The New Covenant Fulfilled In Christ

We have learned that the gospel as we know it began as God's covenant promise to Abraham, His friend, and was ultimately fulfilled through Jesus Christ. What is this gospel, this good news?

It is not enough to say that we are saved; we must know the effect of that salvation, which is peace between man and God; a peace that no one else can destroy, and which opens the door to His house. We have been saved so we could enter rest with God, having a right relationship restored and guaranteed through Jesus Christ. The good news is that we are now living in the grace and favor of our God.

We have already pointed out what Jesus said at the Passover meal when He shared the cup of wine:

> *This is my blood of the covenant, which is poured out for many for the forgiveness of sins. (Matthew 26:28)*

Jesus gave His sinless life and body as the sacrifice that would finally and forever satisfy the death curse which rests upon all men. He gave God the due justice Him over the original broken covenant. But Jesus' blood also ratified a new covenant relationship which God had promised long ago to Abraham. The writer of Hebrews calls Jesus "the mediator of a new covenant:"

> *But you have come ... to Jesus the mediator of a new covenant, and to the sprinkled blood .... (Hebrews 12:22-24)*

Over hundreds of years, God had proclaimed this new covenant through David and through the prophets Isaiah, Jeremiah, Ezekiel and Hosea.

We've learned about the culture of covenant, seen in both world history and Scripture. Now we shall see how carefully the New Covenant of Christ follows the pattern of covenant traditions, and what it means to those who have joined themselves to Him.

The Exchange Of Gifts

A covenant usually included the exchange of gifts such as garments, which publicly displayed one's pledge to give themselves to another. Was there such an exchange for us with Christ? Yes! Isaiah makes this clear for us in his prophecies:

> *All of us have become like one who is unclean, and all our righteous acts are like filthy rags… (Isaiah 64:6)*
>
> *"In my faithfulness I will reward my people and make an everlasting covenant with them. Their descendants will be known among the nations and their offspring among the peoples. All who see them will acknowledge that they are a people the Lord has blessed."*
>
> *I delight greatly in the Lord; my soul rejoices in my God. For He has clothed me with garments of salvation and arrayed me in a robe of His righteousness… (Isaiah 61:8b-10a)*

Between the cross and the resurrection, Jesus exchanged garments with us. He put on the filthy rags of our sin, and clothed us in His own righteousness. Jesus was the only man who ever lived a completely sinless and righteous life as a human being. He is the Righteous One, and Isaiah prophesied that those who believed in Him would be clothed in His righteousness. We always thought *to believe* simply meant to have faith; now we understand it actually refers to the kind of absolute trust and faith one places in a covenant partner.

When we fully trust in Christ for our salvation, we are looked upon as righteous in the Father's eyes. This not just a kind decision on God's part; it happens because we actually "become one" with Christ in a covenant relationship. From then on we share everything that belongs to Christ, including His righteous standing before God.

As we stand in the Father's presence, we are one with His Son. We share in Christ's authority, favor and grace. We are treated to some degree as equals among the Trinity. Of course, we are not equal to Them; but because we are one with them, we are accorded the honor, fellowship and responsibility of being with Them as a family.

The covenant gift of Christ's righteousness means we wake up every day in good graces with God.

The "robe" of Christ's presence is one we did not earn, but whose hard-earned honors and privileges we may enjoy. We are asked to live worthy of the honor of being clothed with Him, as we should. But make no mistake: this covenant gift means we wake up every day in good graces with God. Yes, there has been an exchange in this covenant transaction: our filthy rags for His righteous robe.

The Strength And Weapons Of Our Covenant Partner

In making covenant, the two parties often exchanged weapons, or the belts which carried their weapons.[1] You may have seen this in movies between cowboys and Indians, or Oriental Samurai warriors. The belt or exchange of weapons came with the vow to use all one's strength in protecting and defending the covenant partner. Essentially it said, *"Your*

---

[1] An example of this is seen in the covenant David and Jonathan made in 1 Samuel 18:1-4.

enemies are my enemies." A covenant partner was willing to lay down his life if necessary to protect his friend.

Did Jesus fulfill this step in any way? Yes! In this covenant, we have not only been given a belt — defined as God's truth — we've been given a whole suit of armor:

> *Therefore put on the full armor of God, so that when the day of evil comes, you may be able to stand your ground, and after you have done everything, to stand. Stand firm then, with the belt of truth buckled round your waist, with the breastplate of righteousness in place, and with your feet fitted with the readiness that comes from the gospel of peace. In addition to all this, take up the shield of faith, with which you can extinguish all the flaming arrows of the evil one. Take the helmet of salvation and the sword of the Spirit, which is the word of God. (Ephesians 6:13-17)*

Jesus described this "belt" as the truth that sets His followers free:

> *Jesus said, "If you hold to my teaching, you are really my disciples. Then you will know the truth, and the truth will set you free." (John 8:31-32)*

How does this truth come to us? Through the primary covenant gift given us from the Father: the Holy Spirit. Jesus called Him *the Spirit of truth* and promised His disciples the Spirit would teach and counsel them just as He had been doing:

> *I will ask the Father, and He will give you another advocate to help you and be with you forever— the Spirit of truth. The world cannot accept Him, because it neither sees Him nor knows Him. But you know Him, for He lives with you and will be in you. (John 14:16-17)*

Our belt, our armor, and all the protective power of God has been given us by means of the Presence of the Holy Spirit — the very same Spirit whose power raised Jesus from death to life.

The Sacrificed Animal

In covenant making an animal was sacrificed. Each party laid his hands on that animal and announced that it represented himself and died in his place. [2] As you know, Jesus didn't get an animal, He sacrificed Himself to satisfy the death sentence we were all born under:

> *How much more, then, will the blood of Christ, who through the eternal Spirit offered himself unblemished to God, cleanse our consciences from acts that lead to death, so that we may serve the living God! For this reason Christ is the mediator of a new covenant, that those who are called may receive the promised eternal inheritance —now that He has died as a ransom to set them free from the sins committed under the first covenant. (Hebrews 9:14-15)*

Jesus became our substitute not only to free us from death, but to enable us to enter covenant with the most holy God.

The Covenant Scars Or Marks

Recall that the two parties cut their flesh to draw blood and mingle it as a symbol of sharing life. They typically made a significant scar from that cut which served as a continual reminder of their covenant promises and obligations, and to show to others — especially potential enemies who would threaten someone alone and vulnerable.

Consider the five wounds Jesus received at His crucifixion: one in each wrist, in each foot, and in His side where He was speared. When Jesus appeared to His disciples after His resurrection, His new body was not all torn and beaten; He appeared to them as His normal self, in a glorified physical form. He walked along the road with them and did not look noticeably different from an ordinary man; He cooked fish and ate with them on the beach. But while the rest of Him showed

---

[2] Leviticus 4:32-33

no sign of the vicious beating He had taken before He was crucified, His body still retained the five scars of His crucifixion. We know this because of Thomas, the disciple who doubted Jesus had been raised from the dead:

> *But [Thomas] said to them, "Unless I see the nail marks in his hands and put my finger where the nails were, and put my hand into his side, I will not believe." A week later his disciples were in the house again, and Thomas was with them. Though the doors were locked, Jesus came and stood among them and said, "Peace be with you!" Then he said to Thomas, "Put your finger here; see my hands. Reach out your hand and put it into my side. Stop doubting and believe." (John 20:25-27)*

Jesus' five scars are covenant scars, now seen in heaven as a testimony that He is one with the people He redeemed.

Thomas had his evidence; but the retained crucifixion scars of Jesus are not just a testimony to Thomas. They exist forever as covenant marks sustained when Jesus laid down His life to guarantee the new covenant. These are covenant scars! Jesus bears those scars in heaven today, as a testimony that He is one with the people He has redeemed of the earth. Those scars are not only a witness to the angelic host, His angels and our angels; they are also visible to His enemy (and ours) Satan, and the fallen angels (demons). All who dwell in the spiritual realm can see these scars. They are a permanent part of Jesus, Son of God and Son of Man; eternal signs of His covenant connection to us.

What about our mark? We've already seen what this is:

> *And you also were included in Christ when you heard the message of truth, the gospel of your salvation. When you believed, you were marked in Him with a seal, the*

promised Holy Spirit, who is a deposit guaranteeing our inheritance until the redemption of those who are God's possession—to the praise of His glory. (Ephesians 1:13-14)

Our mark is actually a person — the Holy Spirit! His union with our reborn human spirit marks us as God's covenant children for all in the spiritual realm to see. The Spirit's mark on us ensures we are continually known by God as covenant family members. We cannot see the Spirit, but all the angelic host sees Him with us, as do God the Father, Jesus the Son, Satan and his fallen angels. In the heavenly realms, there is no question about who you belong to! The Apostle John wrote: *"This is how we know that He lives in us: We know it by the Spirit He gave us."* (1 John 3:24)

Covenant's Result: We Are One, Set Apart With God

Jesus told His disciples at the Passover supper just before His death that one day soon they would understand His statement: *"I am in my Father, and you are in me, and I am in you."* (John 14:20) This is the expression of covenant oneness. Through union with Christ you are now holy — set apart for God, and He for you. You are in Christ, and He is in you through the Spirit. In Christ, you are also in the Father. It's a full circle of life. The Apostle Paul wrote,

But whoever is united with the Lord is one with Him in spirit. (1 Corinthians 6:17)

Oneness is the result a covenant brings to two entities. But what does it really mean? Clearly, we maintain our separate identities, just as those in a marriage covenant do, so it does not mean we are the same. Oneness means that wherever we are and whatever we are doing, we are connected to one another, *indivisible.* This is why we are known by God today: we are joined to Christ, and God cannot ignore the other part of His Son. When the Father sees us, He sees His Son with us.

As we are one with Jesus in covenant, God honors us by treating us the same way He does Jesus. All that God is and does affects your life. And in a similar but lesser fashion, all that you are and do affects God's life, as well as the life of the Body of Christ.

The Apostle Peter wrote of how this looks on God's side of the equation:

> *For the eyes of the Lord are on the righteous and His ears are attentive to their prayer.... (1 Peter 3:12)*[3]

This thrills me, because it tells me that God's attention to my prayers is not based on whether I deserve an audience with Him, or have been "good enough;" it is an act of covenant faithfulness on His part. In Christ, I am "the righteous," as are you. Thus, His face is always turned towards us. He sees us. Always. No matter what.

My personal faith exploded when I began to understand that I needed to view God, myself, and how God is motivated towards people, through the lens of being inside or outside of covenant relationship with Him. Those inside covenant relationship with God are holy to Him, set apart in exclusive relationship. We are His, and He is ours.

To be holy unto God is to be set apart with Him in exclusive relationship.

It is like your marriage covenant, in which you are set apart for your spouse alone. You are holy to your spouse, meaning no one else can have you, since the day you pledged yourself to them at the altar in front of witnesses. This is one of the primary meanings of "holy." To stay holy to another in the context of relationship means you are faithfully theirs and theirs alone. You do not give yourself to another.

---

[3] Peter is quoting David from Psalm 34:15.

To be holy unto God is to be set apart with Him in exclusive relationship. This means you do not worship or rely on any other "god." Holiness certainly includes the concept of purity, but that purity is part of how you express faithfulness. A monk cloistered away may be set apart from the ability to defile himself with the things of the world, but if he lives this drastic life just as a means of achieving sinlessness, rather than as a way of being entirely devoted to God in prayer and fellowship, then he is doing it for himself, not for love.

We Are His Godly Ones By Covenant Connection

In the Old Testament we see references to "His godly ones," or to "the godly man." The Hebrew word often used there is *"hasid,"* which is directly related to *hesed* (the word for covenant faithfulness). *Hasid* is the label applied to those who are set apart to the Lord in covenant commitment, who live by acts of devotion which express that commitment.

The child of God may fail God at times, but even when he does, he does not cease being the Lord's godly one — God's relative by blood covenant. His godly ones are those who belong to Him, like David, who failed at times, even committing grievous sins. God disciplined David, as He does those who are His children by covenant, but never removed His love from David. So while the honor and privilege of being God's child always calls us to live a life of love, a failure does not remove us from the status of being "His godly ones." Human beings think like that. God does not.

Knowing this makes me want to love Him better and be more faithful, which is easier to do when I don't have to live in fear of messing up. It sets me free. In covenant, we are God's *hasid*, His set apart ones.

Taking On A New Name

Did Jesus fulfill the step of a name change? Yes! During His ministry on earth, Jesus referred to Himself in the third person as "The Son of Man." We see this in Matthew 20:28, and about 80 other instances recorded in the New Testament. Jesus did this to identify Himself fully with His covenant people. When He returned to heaven, He took this name with Him, and is now known in heaven not just as the Son of God, but as the son of Man. His name is linked to ours forever.

Of course, Jesus also gave us His own name to wear, and to use. All who belong to the Lord call themselves "Christian" which means "little Christ." But Jesus gave us His name in another sense as well. Teaching His disciples about the realities of His covenant, He said:

> *In that day you will no longer ask me anything. I tell you the truth, my Father will give you whatever you ask in my name. Until now you have not asked for anything in my name. Ask and you will receive, and your joy will be complete. (John 16:23-24).*

Remember, two covenant friends share everything; one could use the other's name to obtain provision or help of any kind. Jesus taught us to petition the Father, using His name, when we are sick, in trouble, or in need of any kind. In Acts 3 we find Peter and John healing a man who had been crippled from the time he was born — a miracle of miracles! They made it clear to all who inquired that this miracle happened through the Name of Jesus, not their own power or authority. This does not mean that the actual name of Jesus does the healing; it means that using His name invokes your covenant connection to the One who does the healing. To call on His name is to call on Him, the faithful One. You have access to His name and permission to use it. When you pray for

Covenant friends share everything.

someone, it's not just little old you trying to summon the power to heal. It is complete faith in *God's* power and faithfulness that draws His response to your prayer. Apostle James instructs us:

> *Is anyone among you sick? Let them call the elders of the church to pray over them and anoint them with oil in the name of the Lord. And the prayer offered in faith will make the sick person well; the Lord will raise them up. If they have sinned, they will be forgiven. Therefore confess your sins to each other and pray for each other so that you may be healed. The prayer of a righteous person is powerful and effective. (James 5:14-16)*

We must view all things through covenant values now. Thus we can see that "*the prayer offered in faith*" refers to the prayer offered because of full faith *in God*, not in your ability to produce a result. Genuine faith never fails to evoke a response from God to do something consistent with His own will. James affirms this when he says "*the prayer of a righteous person is powerful and effective.*" And while we tend to see "righteousness" as only and always a reference to moral perfection, the Holy Spirit primarily uses this word in the context of covenant. In other words, the "*righteous person*" is God's covenant child, who totally believes Him — like Abraham, who believed God and was called righteous because of it. A man who has absolute faith in God's faithfulness is righteous in God's eyes.

Doubting God's faithfulness dishonors Him, and is unworthy of a covenant partner. To pray for someone in Jesus' name without confidence that God will answer is to pray in vain. God responds to faith, not perfection. I have seen people with moral flaws (and even sin in their lives), have God answer their prayers with great miracles, because He honors faith. But don't try this at home, and here's why:

Bringing Honor To His Name

We should live as all ancient faithful covenant people did: conducting our lives with a view to whether we will shame or bring honor to the name of our Friend. In private or public, we must never lose sight of the incredible honor it is to share Jesus' name and be called Christian. We have an obligation to understand and reveal His values and character, because people will judge God by how we treat them and the kind of character we display. It has been aptly said that we are the only Bible that some people will ever read. This is yet another reason we need to know our God in truth, so we can reveal Him as He is, and never assist Satan in his goal to lie to people about God.

Jesus Reveals The Terms Of Our New Covenant

Every covenant ceremony included a formal announcement of the terms and provisions of the covenant: why it was being instituted; what was expected of and promised to each party.

Jesus fulfilled this as He spent hours teaching people about the kingdom of God. He revealed the Father to people, teaching them about His character, His heart, His expectations. He taught people how to be faithful stewards of the amazing grace of a relationship with God. He promised the Father would protect them, care for them, heal and love them. In turn, they needed to live worthy of this honor, put away their old way of life and live as beloved children of God. This required trust and total dependence — demonstrated by personal obedience — living by faith in who God is and what He promises.

As with all covenants, faith is key. A covenant partner who did not trust his partner, maligned that partner by distrust. A covenant of love and friendship has no true strength apart from faith and trust. In fact, all relationships are based upon faith, whether sealed in covenant or not. In covenant, you invite the other person to put faith in your love, and you promise to be steadfast in it. To fail to honor your promise is what God calls "breaking faith," destroying the faith placed in you.

God has invited us to place faith in Him. We can count on Him because faithfulness is one of His highest values. The Lord exercises Himself continually in kindness, justice and righteousness (right relating to others), and it delights Him to do so.[4] God loves to display His glory, and His glory is revealed in being faithful in relationship.

God's glory is His faithfulness in relationship.

We have already pointed out the specific promises of God in the new covenant, first revealed to Jeremiah and later verified by the author of Hebrews. We'll look at those in more depth in the next chapter.

The Memorial Meal To Celebrate The Covenant

The covenant meal used bread and wine as symbols of man's flesh and blood, and celebrated the new shared life. Feeding this meal to one another illustrated the commitment to nourish each other with our whole being.

When Jesus ate the Passover meal with His disciples the night before His crucifixion, He turned it into a covenant meal. The Passover had been observed annually for hundreds of years in obedience to God's command, but this time Jesus held up a cup of the wine and said,

> *This cup is the new covenant in my blood, which is poured out for you. (Luke 22:20).*

Jesus was saying to them, *"All things will change now. This meal will no longer be an occasion to look back at what God did to set you free from your bondage in Egypt; it will become a celebration and memorial of what I am instituting for you: a new covenant."* The Apostle Paul wrote of it this way:

> *The Lord Jesus, on the night He was betrayed, took bread, and when He had given thanks, He broke it and said, "This is my body, which is for you; do this in remembrance of me." In the same way, after supper He took the cup, saying, "This cup is the new covenant in my blood; do this,*

[4] Jeremiah 9:24; Psalm 36:5-6; Micah 7:18.

whenever you drink it, in remembrance of me. (1 Corinthians 11:23-25)

We call this communion, but make no mistake, this is our new covenant meal. It is our memorial of remembrance — as well as a celebration — of what Christ has done, of our secure relationship with Him, what He promises and will faithfully do. It reaffirms our oneness with Him and that we belong at His family table. Like all family meals that bring us face-to-face with loved ones, it also should cause us to examine our faithfulness (or lack of it) regarding Him and others.

Also, we have also been promised a feast in God's heavenly kingdom. This will be a grand covenant celebration for all who joined themselves to God through Christ, throughout history. Jesus said,

I say to you that many will come from the east and the west, and will take their places at the feast with Abraham, Isaac and Jacob in the kingdom of heaven. (Matthew 8:11)

I can't imagine how magnificent that feast will be; but I know I have an invitation and I intend to take my place there with joy!

A Memorial To Our Covenant

Ancient covenants were often memorialized in a public way, such as carving the names of the parties on a stone or a tree. The blood from a sacrifice would be sprinkled or poured or applied on the memorial in some way. We have such a covenant memorial: the cross of Christ! It publicly marks the moment in time when Jesus removed the division between us and God the Father so we could become one with Him. Jesus did not just sprinkle His blood on it; He poured it *all* out for us. The symbol of the cross has endured since that day. Everyone in the civilized world knows what the cross stands for, even if they have no personal faith in Christ.

We also have another permanent memorial: the body of Scripture, our Bible, which testifies to all these things. Only God knows how much blood has been shed so this "book of remembrance" could be in our hands; history shows it has been "sprinkled" with the blood of many to bring the good news to you of God's unfailing love through Messiah.

Covenant Friendship: Committed Righteous Relationship

Jesus carefully observed every aspect of covenant-making with his disciples, including the final step: the pronouncement of friendship. Hours before He went to the cross, following the covenant meal, He said,

I have called you servants, but I no longer call you servants, instead, I now call you friends, for everything that I received from my Father I have given to you. (John 15:14-15)

This is covenant language! In His day the term *friend* was not used casually as it is today; only a covenant partner was called friend. The Apostle James spoke of Abraham as being God's friend.[5] Jesus further underscores the covenant nature of our relationship when He says that as friends, *"everything that I received from my Father I have given to you."* This is why Jesus repeatedly taught His disciples that if they needed anything of God, all they had to do is ask in His name:

> *Ask and it will be given to you; seek and you will find; knock and the door will be opened to you. For everyone who asks receives; the one who seeks finds; and to the one who knocks, the door will be opened. (Matthew 7:7-8)*

This isn't just God being magnanimous; He is inviting us to take Him at His promise to be a faithful covenant friend, willing to sharing all He has — which is everything. We are not

---

[5] James 2:21-23

beggars. We belong to a generous and faithful Father whose joy is to give to His children!

Jesus left no covenant stone unturned in communicating the reality of His new covenant to people of His day. Now we understand more than ever what He purchased for us with His precious blood. I have only shared a portion with you; there is more to learn and treasure about God's covenant heart if you read the Bible with these things in mind.

Let the reader forever understand, your salvation is not a ticket out of hell and into heaven. Your salvation is a covenant through which you enter and abide in the eternal family of God through Christ!

Are You In The Covenant?

Outside of this covenant, you are not in the family of God. Though God created all men in His image, this does not automatically make you His child, or Him your Father. *God only becomes the Father of those who come to Him through Jesus Christ, in the new covenant purchased by the blood of His Son.* This fact is thoroughly presented in the New Testament, and made especially clear in the gospel of John.

Outside of this covenant, you are not in the family of God.

To come into Christ's New Covenant, you must acknowledge your sinful state as a descendant of the first man, Adam, as well as confess your personal sin. Then believe and declare your faith in Christ to save you from the power of that sin. You must believe Christ died in your place to save you, and allow Him to cleanse you. Finally, receive the Spirit who makes your adoption complete and effective! [6]

---

[6] Romans 8:15-16

8 Our Covenant Ceremony And Gift

Two parties entering a covenant always sealed it with a public ceremony in front of witnesses. The New Covenant in Christ also provides such a ceremony, which we call baptism.

The decision to be baptized does not rest with a church or denomination, because they are not entering a covenant of faithfulness, you are. It is a personal matter between you and the Lord. Whether you have been baptized or never taught about it, you need to understand what Scripture says about it to make a right decision. Towards that end, let's revisit some of what we know about the ancient ceremonies and observe how they correlate to water baptism.

Baptism: Our Covenant Ceremony

Most covenant ceremonies took place in front of witnesses from one's community. Likewise, water baptism is done before witnesses. In ancient blood covenants, an animal was sacrificed, and each party swore an oath over the animal's carcass that he would die to his old life and now live a new (shared) life of faithfulness to the other party. We also come to water baptism because a sacrifice has been made in our place. We believe and publicly declare as we are immersed and rise from the water that we are dying with Christ (symbolically) and being resurrected to new life with Him. The Apostle Paul writes:

We were therefore buried with Him through baptism into death in order that, just as Christ was raised from the dead through the glory of the Father, we too may live a new life. (Romans 6:4)

The Apostle Paul employs covenant imagery again when he connects the dots of salvation, baptism and the covenant exchange of garments (the outward, public sign that you belong to another):

So in Christ Jesus you are all children of God through faith, for all of you who were baptized into Christ have clothed yourselves with Christ. (Galatians 3:26-27)

Garments speak of *identity*; being "clothed with Christ" refers to taking a new public identity of being joined to Him. While it may not always be obvious to the earthlings around you that you belong to Christ — though it should be — you can be sure that it is obvious to all who inhabit the invisible realms of heaven — The Trinity, Satan, angels and demons.

People were being baptized in water long before Jesus came on the scene, as a means of showing allegiance to a particular teacher or sect. John was baptizing people in the Jordan River because he had been preaching repentance from sin, and those who came to him to be baptized did so as a commitment to imitate him by living a life that showed true repentance (a changed mind) towards sin.

Immersion in water was a symbolic cleansing and rebirth into a new life. One drew a line between one's former way of life and a new life of obedience to a mentor or sect and their teaching. It carried the flavor of a covenant because one made a commitment to the baptizer and took on a public identity with Him.[1] This is why it astounded John the Baptist when Jesus came to him to be baptized; he knew that he needed to follow Jesus, the Savior, not the other way around:

Then Jesus came from Galilee to the Jordan to be baptized by John. But John tried to deter Him, saying, "I need to be

---

[1] The Apostle Paul had to clarify in Ephesians 4:5 that no matter who baptized a convert he was to follow and obey Christ, not the one who baptized him.

> *baptized by you, and do you come to me?" Jesus replied, "Let it be so now; it is proper for us to do this to fulfill all righteousness." Then John consented. As soon as Jesus was baptized, He went up out of the water. At that moment heaven was opened, and He saw the Spirit of God descending like a dove and alighting on Him. And a voice from heaven said, "This is my Son, whom I love; with Him I am well pleased." (Matthew 3:13-17)*

Why Jesus Had To Be Baptized

It amazed me that Jesus the man, the sinless incarnate Son of God, went to John to be baptized. Both of them knew He had nothing from which to repent. John tried to talk Him out of it, but Jesus insisted it was the right thing to do.

It is clear that Jesus' choice to be baptized thrilled the Father and the Spirit, because they both manifested their presence and expressed their joy as an immediate and visible response to His action. But what did Jesus mean by His statement, and why was baptism proper for Him who had not sinned? I believe there are a couple of reasons for this.

Jesus' choice to be baptized thrilled the Father and the Spirit.

First, it was right for Him to be baptized because the Father desired it; Jesus said in John 8:29 He only did what the Father told Him to do.

Second, it was right because one day Jesus would become *"the firstborn among many brothers and sisters..."*[2] the first of a nation of covenant people, fulfilling the covenant promise God gave to His friend, Abraham. It would be right for the Teacher to set the example for all who would become his disciples.[3]

[2] Romans 8:29

[3] Matthew 28:19-20

Through His public obedience and humility, Jesus demonstrated the choice to abandon one's old life and live a new one for the sake of another. After His death and resurrection men would no longer be baptized to follow this teacher or that rabbi, but only to follow THE Rabbi, The Teacher, Jesus Christ of Nazareth.

Some denominations and churches treat water baptism as unnecessary or optional, but I offer that if we are to be faithful covenant people we should imitate our Lord Jesus, by viewing water baptism as proper to fulfill all righteousness. If it was right for the Master, how much more so for the servant? Furthermore, when Jesus began public ministry, He and His disciples baptized people in water. Finally, remember one of the last things Jesus said to His disciples before returning to heaven:

> *Go into all the world and preach the gospel to all creation. Whoever believes and is baptized will be saved, but whoever does not believe will be condemned. (Mark 16:15-16)*

Understand, Jesus is not saying that baptism saves you; He made it clear in John 5:24 one is saved by believing in Him, period. The Lord taught that the moment a person has his mind opened to his true need of Christ, and responds by trusting in Christ to save him, he *is* saved, and joined to the Lord:

> *Very truly I tell you, whoever hears my word and believes Him who sent me has eternal life and will not be judged but has crossed over from death to life. (John 5:24)*

Jesus spoke as if saving faith in Him and baptism went hand in hand.

Yet it is obvious that this fact did not negate the importance of baptism, because Jesus spoke in Mark 16:16 as if saving faith in Him and baptism should go hand in hand, a kind of package deal for those who would follow Him. This would be a reasonable assumption considering the covenant culture in which He lived, where the private commitment of the heart was announced and sealed in a public way before witnesses.

The Apostle Peter, who was discipled personally by Jesus, also connects baptism and salvation. He invokes covenant language when he speaks of baptism as *the pledge* of a clear conscience towards God:

> *For Christ also suffered once for sins, the righteous for the unrighteous, to bring you to God. He was put to death in the body but made alive in the Spirit. After being made alive, He went and made proclamation to the imprisoned spirits — to those who were disobedient long ago when God waited patiently in the days of Noah while the ark was being built. In it only a few people, eight in all, were saved through water, and this water symbolizes baptism that now saves you also—not the removal of dirt from the body but the pledge of a clear conscience toward God. It saves you by the resurrection of Jesus Christ, who has gone into heaven and is at God's right hand —with angels, authorities and powers in submission to Him. (1 Peter 3:18-22)*

"Pledge" is a synonym for *oath* or *promise*. Peter is saying that one who accepts Christ's sacrifice is not just drawing a line in the sand of his own life and pledging to live better. He is trusting God's pledge that all of his sins are now forgiven, and he can know God with a clear conscience. In this sense, being baptized into Christ carried a very different and much more powerful reality than every other baptism they had ever seen.

Though Peter speaks of *baptism that now saves you*, he makes it clear that *the resurrection of Christ is the actual source and guarantee of your salvation*. The point is, Peter joins Jesus and Paul in clearly assuming a person who puts faith in Christ for salvation will take the step of being publicly baptized.

But water baptism could be important for yet another reason. The Apostle Paul used language that seems to connect the moment of "spiritual circumcision" — the cutting away of the old sin nature — with water baptism:

> *In Him you were also circumcised with a circumcision not performed by human hands. Your whole self ruled by the flesh was put off when you were circumcised by Christ, having been buried with Him in baptism, in which you were also raised with Him through your faith in the working of God, who raised Him from the dead. When you were dead in your sins and in the uncircumcision of your flesh, God made you alive with Christ... (Colossians 2:11-13a)*

Baptism And The Circumcision Of Our Old Nature

Circumcision references the original covenant God made with Abraham, in which He commanded Abraham and every other male descendant to be circumcised as a covenant mark of commitment to Him. A man's obedience to receive that outward mark was crucial in Old Testament days in order to receive all of God's protection and provision. Moses discovered this the hard way. A curious story is told in Exodus Chapter 4, where God threatens to kill Moses right after He commissions him to lead the Israelites out from Pharoah's slavery! This behavior on God's part seems bizarre and completely shocking until one understands covenant realities, which explain it all.

Apparently, Moses had failed to circumcise his firstborn son. God knew that soon He would send a spirit of death to destroy every firstborn son in Egypt, and the spirit of death would only pass safely over all who had eaten the "passover" lamb of God. By God's command, the Hebrew males could not even eat the lamb *unless they had been circumcised, and bore God's covenant mark on their bodies.*

So what looks like an irrational act on God's part was actually His way of forcing Moses to circumcise his son and thus protect him from dying on that night of deliverance!

We do not live under the old law, but the Apostle Paul says in sealing our lives with Christ we are circumcised in an invisible way; a surgery that God performs on our heart and spirit. God's circumcision is crucial. He must remove the old nature that is prone to sin and give us a new heart and a new spirit. God said this through Ezekiel in another reference to the promised New Covenant:

> *I will give you a new heart and put a new spirit in you; I will remove from you your heart of stone and give you a heart of flesh. And I will put my Spirit in you and move you to follow my decrees and be careful to keep my laws. (Ezekiel 36:26-27)*

It is a mystery how and when God does this, but Paul's words clearly link this event to baptism. Remember, the ceremony sealed publicly what the parties had already chosen to do: join themselves together. The outward actions only sealed what was already a matter of faith between them.

Baptism pictures a true covenant ceremony, with both parties active in it.

It would fit into covenant logic that when a new believer steps into this initial public act of commitment to God, God responds by circumcising his or her heart. This pictures a true covenant ceremony, with both parties active in it. The believer commits to God, announcing his full faith in Him to save him and give him new life; God then meets the believer's faith by giving him what only God can: a new heart and spirit with which to receive and live that very life. The believer walks away forever marked and sealed with the Holy Spirit, the old sin nature cut away from him.

Surely God can circumcise a human heart any time He chooses; yet it seems clear from the language used by both Jesus and the Apostles that the decision to join oneself to Christ in the new covenant and being baptized in water were meant to go together in the process of salvation and conversion.

What of the case of the two criminals crucified with Jesus? This simply reveals that baptism is not required to seal one's conversion when a believer's journey to paradise is imminent, and sin can no longer tempt. Those who remain on earth certainly need to have the old nature — helpless against and yielded to the power of sin — cut away from their souls in order to live a righteous life.

There will always be extraordinary circumstances that may prevent water baptism. Since Scripture stops short of saying that a person is not saved if he is not baptized, we should do the same. Even so, it is reasonable to assume that God values water baptism as our public demonstration of faith in Christ and our commitment to live for Him. Such a public acknowledgement of a private decision of the heart (to live for Christ) also brings us into the kind of accountability that helps us be faithful.

I don't presume to know precisely how the glorious mysteries of salvation, circumcision of the heart, and rebirth happen. I only offer my understanding of what Jesus and the Apostles seem to be teaching about how it all comes together. But I will add one personal observation.

In 30 years of discipling and counseling Christians, my husband and I have witnessed something that validated for us the connection of water baptism to the circumcision of the sin nature. As we encountered Christians who struggled often with besetting sins — or even their resolve to trust in and live for Christ — we began to see a commonality: none had been baptized. They might have been sprinkled as infants, but never baptized as consenting adults making a conscious choice to follow Christ. We encouraged such people to be baptized. To our knowledge all who acted on that advice experienced significant victory over sin and temptation thereafter, and found their faith in the Lord strengthened. Something definitely changed for them as they underwent baptism.

The method is up to God; but nothing in Scripture gives us reason to think infant baptism is one of His ways. Infant baptism is a choice your parents make as they dedicate you to God and devote you to His care. It is not a conscious choice on your part to walk with God, which can only be made when you reach the age of personal understanding and accountability. As to whether being sprinkled counts as baptism, that is a matter of conscience between you and the Lord. If your conscience before God is satisfied in this matter, then be at rest in it.

Receive Your Covenant Gift: The Holy Spirit

After Jesus rose from death, He appeared to His disciples for 40 days in His glorified body, to explain and teach them many things they could not understand before. At this time He spoke of another kind of baptism that would take place, recorded in Acts 1:3-5:

> *[Jesus] appeared to them over a period of forty days and spoke about the kingdom of God. On one occasion, while He was eating with them, He gave them this command: "Do not leave Jerusalem, but wait for the gift my Father promised, which you have heard me speak about. For John baptized with water, but in a few days you will be baptized with the Holy Spirit."*

Here Jesus connected the concepts of covenant gift and baptism. He also said they would be "clothed with power" in receiving this gift:

> *I am going to send you what my Father has promised; but stay in the city until you have been clothed with power from on high. (Luke 24:49)*

Jesus told his followers plainly that the Spirit is God's Covenant gift to us, promised to all who would put their faith in Christ! This is the gift of the Holy Spirit, the Third Person of the Trinity. In other words, our covenant gift isn't a thing or a garment, our gift is the Lord Himself, the Holy Spirit!

Our covenant gift isn't a thing or a garment, it is the Lord Himself, the Holy Spirit!

This is the same gift Jesus promised His disciples before His crucifixion. In John 14:16-18 we have a record of Him comforting His confused and grieving disciples shortly before His arrest and execution:

> *And I will ask the Father, and He will give you another advocate to help you and be with you forever — the Spirit of truth. The world cannot accept Him, because it neither sees Him nor knows Him. But you know Him, for He lives with you and will be in you. I will not leave you as orphans...*

Jesus essentially told them, *You aren't losing me, or the way we've been sharing life. The Holy Spirit, the gift of the Father, will take up my role with you, and will be with you forever.*

Two Baptisms

There are two baptisms: one is our public covenant ceremony of repentance and rebirth, a baptism done by men. The other is a baptism done by Jesus in which we receive our covenant gift, the Holy Spirit.

In the book of Acts we see the Apostles being careful to ensure new converts received *both* baptisms. When they encountered converts who had only been baptized in water, they immediately prayed and asked the Lord Jesus to baptize that person in the Spirit. [4] When they likewise encountered believers who had been baptized in the Spirit, but not in water, they immediately baptized the convert in water also. [5]

[4] See Acts 8:15-17 and Acts 18:24-19:7.

[5] See Acts 10:45-48 and Acts 11:15-16.

Sometimes these baptisms happen together. My two baptisms occurred three years apart, because it took a while for me to learn of my need to be baptized in the Spirit.

The Apostles were careful to make sure new converts received *both* baptisms.

Years in ministry have taught me that the ways in which individuals come to repentance and salvation in Christ are very personal and unique. There is no cookie cutter experience, no formula. It's kind of like natural birth: it can be messy, unique and unpredictable, because the Spirit moves as He wishes and as we need. Our task isn't to figure it all out; our task is to be faithful to all that is revealed to us as we begin a life of knowing and loving God.

One thing is absolutely clear: Scripture clearly reveals the importance of both baptisms. In his first public sermon, the Apostle Peter affirmed the need to be baptized in water for forgiveness, and receiving the gift of the Holy Spirit:

> *Repent and be baptized, every one of you, in the name of Jesus Christ for the forgiveness of your sins. And you will receive the gift of the Holy Spirit. The promise is for you and your children and for all who are far off — for all whom the Lord our God will call. (Acts 2:38-29)*

God's desire is that His children mature to the point that they truly bear the image of Christ in character, values and behavior. For this to happen we must be taught, fathered, befriended and mentored — so we may indeed grow up in our salvation. Since this can only happen through the help of the Spirit, you absolutely need to receive Him and be filled with His Presence and Power.

The Father released the Spirit to Jesus, who then baptizes His followers.[6] This usually happens through a Christian (acting

---

[6] Mark 1:8

as Jesus' representative) lays hands on a person and prays for the Lord to baptize them in the Spirit. It can take place anywhere, public or private, church or park or shopping mall. It happened privately for me, on a Saturday church work day, when I sought out a certain woman I could see was filled with the Holy Spirit — because she had a consistent joy in God no one else in the church seemed to have!

I hear stories of people begging God for this gift, even for for weeks, as if God is reluctant to give it. This gift is for all who have sincerely joined themselves to Christ, and there is no evidence in scripture that one has to wait for it or earn it in any way. There is only one "requirement," and that is faith, which the Apostle Paul made clear when he had to set the Galatian Christians straight on this very matter:

> *I would like to learn just one thing from you: Did you receive the Spirit by the works of the law, or by believing what you heard? (Galatians 3:2)*

The woman who prayed for me to be baptized in the Spirit simply asked me to prepare for it by repenting of any unconfessed sin, especially anything connected with witchcraft. I had never thought about that before. Like many kids, I grew up playing around with Ouija boards, attended a couple of seances for fun, and then as a young adult took such a serious interest in astrology that for awhile I studied how to do astrological charts. I confessed and renounced all faith and participation in those things.

Then my friend laid hands on me and asked Jesus to baptize me in the Holy Spirit. I did receive the Spirit, and that by faith, since there were no outward extraordinary signs. There was, however, an immediate and profound change in my spirit: I felt a whole new hunger for God, and a deeper sense of His presence and nearness. With that came joy and renewed confidence in God's love for me. Everything on the inside changed!

In the days and weeks that followed, I couldn't get enough of reading the Bible, His Word. I had studied it before, but now when I read Scripture, I understood more, and had greater faith in the words. For instance, when John 10:27 said we could know the voice of Jesus, and James 1:5-7 said we could receive wisdom from God for anything we needed, I really believed it for the first time. Because of this I began to consistently receive God's counsel in my mind and spirit: in words, pictures, or just knowing. My faith soared.

About ten days later, a foreign and beautiful language flowed out of me as I prayed and praised the Lord. The Scriptures had mentioned this gift, and I wanted everything the Spirit was giving, so I gave Him permission to pray through me as He wished. It was, and is, a beautiful experience, something I enjoy and use often. (The purpose of this gift is more fully explained in my book, "Spirit Life.")

Being baptized in the Spirit changed my life forever. I cannot imagine life without Him now. The Spirit has made possible all knowing and intimacy with the Lord, teaching me how to live this new life. He is my Friend and constant companion.

You cannot know God and fully participate in the new covenant without the Holy Spirit. Period. The abundant life Jesus promised cannot be realized without Him. He is wonderful, and you'll love having Him in your heart and life. Ask for Him, and receive Him, for He is the gift already given by the good Father to those who ask.

Our Covenant Mark Or Seal

Remember the covenant practice of producing a scar from the place of cutting and blood letting, to create a mark or seal in the flesh? We do not receive a mark in our flesh (other than the "cutting away" of our sin nature in circumcision); but the Apostle Paul does refer to our being *sealed* with the Spirit, and thus marked as belonging and being joined to Him:

And you also were included in Christ when you heard the message of truth, the gospel of your salvation. When you believed, you were marked in Him with a seal, the promised Holy Spirit, who is a deposit guaranteeing our inheritance until the redemption of those who are God's possession—to the praise of His glory. (Ephesians 1:13-14)

Being sealed or marked with the Holy Spirit is not to be confused with being baptized in the Spirit. In Paul's day, the reference to being sealed was about the seal imprinted by an authority on document or item, the mark of the author or owner. His reference of being sealed with the Holy Spirit of God refers to your being marked as His, joined by covenant.

If the idea of being sealed with the Holy Spirit versus being baptized or filled with Him is confusing, think of it this way. Married people wear a wedding ring which serves as a type of mark, showing that we belong to another. Our marriage covenant makes us *one in spirit* with our spouse every moment, and the wedding ring is a sign of that union; while the whole point of our union is actually sharing life together — being filled with the life and knowledge of one another. That's why we married!

You need God present in you as Spirit in order to know and walk with Him this side of heaven.

A person can be marked by the Spirit — sealed *with* God — and still not be filled with His presence. We can belong to God and still not enjoy sharing life with Him in a way that is actually shared and empowered. The fact that this is true of far too many precious souls whom Christ has redeemed, is the goad God has used to stir me to write this book. I cannot bear to see people live like orphans in the midst of the most magnificent family ever, out of ignorance about the Holy Spirit's true role. You must have God Himself, fully present in you as Spirit, in order to know and walk with Him this side of heaven. Don't settle for anything less!

9 Orientation: Becoming God's Friend

Being "saved" is nothing less than being brought into the actual covenant family of God. From the day we trust Him with our whole heart, Jesus considers us to be His sons, daughters, brothers and sisters:

Both the one who makes people holy and those who are made holy are of the same family. So Jesus is not ashamed to call them brothers and sisters. He says, "I will declare your name to my brothers and sisters; in the assembly I will sing your praises." (Hebrews 2:11)

And again He says, "Here am I, and the children God has given me." (Hebrews 2:13)

We're family, thanks to an incredible commitment of the Trinity to bring mankind into a relationship with them, so we can all share a life of mutual joy and glory. In Christ, we are brought into God's family, with the same access to the good Father that Jesus had as a man on the earth.

Salvation is not your end goal; it is just the beginning of a whole new identity for you. Not only are you now God's beloved child, you are expected to live like one. Your new identity comes with a new privilege and obligation: being God's friend. Jesus explained this plainly to His disciples just before He laid down His life for them:

Greater love has no one than this: to lay down one's life for one's friends. You are my friends if you do what I command. I no longer call you servants, because a servant does not know His master's business. Instead, I have called you friends, for everything that I learned from my Father I have made known to you. (John 15:13-15)

Being God's child is an irrevocable relationship; being God's friend is what you are meant to be when you grow up in your salvation.

A servant serves as a duty. He may consider it an honor, but he has no share in the heart of the one he serves. A friend has the heart of His friend, and serves him because of love.

Being God's child is an irrevocable relationship, but being God's friend is what you are meant to be when you grow up in your salvation. Living in the full measure and joy of both roles requires nothing less than a revolution in how you think, feel and act. It will require a transformation of your mind in regards to how you see yourself, how you view God, and what your role is in His world.

It's A New World In There

Apostle Paul spoke of this as *the renewing of your mind.* [1] Having gone through one of the greatest revolutions of heart and mind ever, Paul understood the importance of one's mind being renewed in order to live this new life. He had made the journey from Christ being His greatest enemy to Christ being His greatest passion. When Paul prayed this prayer he was also describing how his mind had been renewed:

I keep asking that the God of our Lord Jesus Christ, the glorious Father, may give you the Spirit of wisdom and revelation, so that you may know him better. I pray that the eyes of your heart may be enlightened in order that you may know the hope to which he has called you, the riches of

[1] Romans 12:2

his glorious inheritance in his holy people, and his incomparably great power for us who believe. (Ephesians 1:17-19)

Paul had hated Christ and His followers so deeply — even persecuting and murdering them — that he surely struggled greatly in the beginning with accepting God's amazing love. If you lived a pretty bad life before you came to Christ, you might have that same struggle, as many Christians do. I have a story to share with you.

David And Mephibosheth

This story is told in 2nd Samuel Chapter 9, and takes place after the death of King Saul and his son Jonathan, who would have succeeded his father as king. When Saul and Jonathan perish in battle, David becomes king. In Biblical times, a new king would typically destroy the entire clan of the former king in order to make His throne secure, heading off the possibility that any resentful relatives might try to assassinate him and regain the throne. So when David became king, all of Saul's and Jonathan's relatives went into hiding, including Jonathan's son Mephibosheth, who is so young that when his nurse trips and falls on him during their rush into hiding, it results in his being permanently crippled.

Years pass during which Mephibosheth grows up in hiding, knowing that his father Jonathan and grandfather Saul were killed in a battle that resulted in David becoming king. Mephibosheth can only view King David as his enemy and probably the cause of all his misfortune. After all, as a descendant of Saul and Jonathan, he would have been king some day. Mephibosheth lives his life in fear and hiding, believing that David is a threat to his very existence.

What Mephibosheth doesn't know is that Jonathan and David had made a secret covenant with one another. As sworn friends, they made promises to one another that would have also included their children and all their "seed," their unborn descendants. Covenants and their benefits were handed down as perpetual inheritances.

One day, something — perhaps a covenant mark on David's body — reminds David of his friendship and commitment to Jonathan. He then asks, *"Is there anyone still left of the house of Saul to whom I can show kindness* (i.e., covenant faithfulness) *for Jonathan's sake?"*

David is told about Jonathan's son Mephibosheth. He immediately sends his men to bring Mephibosheth to him. I can only imagine Mephibosheth's terror when David's men arrive at his house, but as a cripple, he cannot flee. He is taken to David, and surely expects the worst — that David is still culling his kingdom of potential enemies.

As he enters David's presence, Mephibosheth is shocked to hear these words:

> *"Don't be afraid," David said to him, "for I will surely show you kindness for the sake of your father Jonathan. I will restore to you all the land that belonged to your grandfather Saul, and you will always eat at my table." Mephibosheth bowed down and said, "What is your servant, that you should notice a dead dog like me?" (2 Samuel 9:7-8)*

Mephibosheth cannot believe what he is hearing; he came in fear of being executed, but instead is being offered a life in the royal palace, eating at the king's table — all because of a covenant he never knew existed between his father and David.

As a cripple, Mephibosheth would have lived in shame as well as fear, unable to provide for a family. But David's faithfulness to Jonathan is going to change it all, as he says to a servant of Saul,

> *"I have given your master's grandson everything that belonged to Saul and His family. You and your sons and your servants are to farm the land for him and bring in the crops, so that your master's grandson may be provided for.*

And Mephibosheth, grandson of your master, will always eat at my table." (2 Samuel 9:7-10)

Mephibosheth's whole life has changed in a moment! It is incredible and wonderful; but it will also require a huge change of attitude in how he sees David, and how he sees himself. He must let go of all hatred and fear of David, and see him now as his faithful benefactor; no longer the enemy, but as family.

The ultimate expression of favor in their culture was to share the family meal and table. David could have just restored Mephibosheth's lands and fortunes — but he treated him exactly as he would have his friend Jonathan, giving him a permanent place at the table. As Mephibosheth sat at David's table, his crippled condition would be covered, and he would be treated like one of David's own sons.

However, Mephibosheth will be expected to show loyalty and friendship to David. It is far easier to give outward loyalty than change the mindset of a lifetime. In the subsequent chapters of 2nd Samuel we see evidence of Mephibosheth's struggle with this, as he later betrays David, then repents and becomes loyal to David once more.

Seeing God As He Really Is

As you walk forward in a life as God's covenant child, the most important thing you can do is abandon all fearful dread and every misconception you've had about God, what He thinks of you, or how He is motivated towards you. He is not a distant and disapproving judge. He is now all to you that He is to Jesus: *Abba,* affectionate Father. You wake up every day beloved of God, accepted by Him.

Who is He? The Lover who desires someone to love; the Giver looking for someone to lavish on; the Wise One eager to share His life-giving counsel; the Creator whose joy and glory is in revealing His goodness. He called for a relationship to His creation that would cause us to blossom into our full potential as we walk with Him.

Who is God? The Lover who desires someone to love; the Giver looking for someone to lavish on; the Wise One eager to share His life-giving counsel; the Creator whose joy and glory is in revealing His goodness.

Learning all of this, seeing the history of what God has done to bring me into His family, healed my heart. My confidence in God's love soared and my faith found a new baseline below which it never goes. Like Abraham, I believe. I do not have faith in myself to be perfect, but I have complete faith in God's unfailing love and faithfulness. My crippled parts are under God's table. He has committed Himself to be my covenant friend, has invited me to become His friend, and provided everything to make it possible.

I want all of that for you. If you see yourself as "the least of these," or like "a dead dog" in the presence of the Lord, you need to repent! You need a total change of mind and heart to see yourself as the Lord sees you, as you now really are. Anything less is not faith; and without faith, you surely cannot please the Lord. Hebrews 11:6 says:

> *And without faith it is impossible to please God, because anyone who comes to Him must believe that He exists and that He rewards those who earnestly seek Him.*

To shrink back from the Lord in a spirit of unworthiness is to spurn the greatest gift ever.

You Must Live As A Forgiven Person

Remember, *God promises in this covenant that He will forgive us of all sin and forget those sins.* Moreover, Hebrews 9:14 says the blood of Christ will somehow cleanse our conscience as well:

> *How much more, then, will the blood of Christ, who through the eternal Spirit offered himself unblemished to God, cleanse our consciences from acts that lead to death, so that we may serve the living God!*

I find this absolutely amazing! I know what it is like to be imprisoned by a guilty conscience. I have lived with a mind so aware of past sins and moral flaws that I could not allow myself to relax into God's love, as I imagined Him seeing me as I saw myself. I have wasted His favor and willingness to bless me. You probably know just how that feels.

Repentance and asking forgiveness cleans our slate with God anytime we repent, no matter how often we fail. He promised!

The reason Jesus told His disciples to keep forgiving someone who sins against them, then repents and asks forgiveness, is because that is exactly what He does with us. Forgiveness and a clean conscience keep clearing the way for us to be restored to the purpose and pleasure of our relationship; it is God's "reset button."

Jesus told His disciples to keep forgiving someone who sins against them because that is exactly what He does with us.

Yet in spite of God's promise, many Christians to find it too hard to really believe this is right and okay. They keep beating themselves up over sin, even after confessing it; going through self-imposed times of penance before giving themselves permission to rest again in God's favor and grace. (How long is your penance timer set for?)

The effect of all this is to disrupt your fellowship with the Lord, the very thing He wants to maintain! Making yourself do penance when the Lord is not calling for it, is not humility, and it is not faith. If your sin has harmed others, it may be necessary to go through a period of reconciliation and regaining trust to restore their broken faith, for which you especially need the Lord's help. But forgiveness from God is quick and complete when you are sincere, and He wants to help you get back up and walking with Him, not make you "do time."

Beginnings: Knowing God As His Child

Another major shift in thinking is made necessary by our human tendency to assume that knowing God is too complicated and too hard. I think this is one reason the Lord uses more than one motif with us — child, brother, friend — because every motif adds an important dimension to the relationship we are invited to enjoy with Him, an added layer of invitation to intimacy. Jesus did not support the idea that knowing God would be difficult; instead, He told His disciples that knowing God begins with abandoning all sophistication and coming to God with a childlike heart:

> *Let the little children come to me, and do not hinder them, for the kingdom of God belongs to such as these. Truly I tell you, anyone who will not receive the kingdom of God like a little child will never enter it. (Mark 10:14-15)*

> *I praise you, Father, Lord of heaven and earth, because you have hidden these things from the wise and learned, and revealed them to little children. Yes, Father, for this is what you were pleased to do. (Luke 10:21)*

I have always struggled with perfectionism and when I first became a Christian that only intensified at first. Then I learned that my highest calling isn't to be perfect; it is to know and understand my Father, and reveal Him to the world. But, you might want to ask, doesn't scripture tell us to "be perfect as your heavenly Father is perfect"? [2] Yes, it does. However, the context of that remark is Jesus teaching His disciples to imitate their Father God like little children imitate their dads!

My highest calling is to know and understand my Father, and reveal Him to the world.

To most Dads, perfection doesn't look like a flawless child; it looks like a child fully engaged with him, eager to learn and be just like Dad. The child is absorbed with hanging out with Dad, watching Dad, learning from Dad, wanting to please Dad. The child isn't overly concerned with how well he is growing up, he just wants to be like Dad. As a child, he enjoys his dependence on a Dad who is always ready to help him.

Sophisticated grownups don't have permission to be totally dependent. The little child comes trusting and submissive and not thinking of himself. The big difference is this: the goal of knowing God makes us God-focused, while the goal of being perfect makes us self-focused. Instead of "What are we gonna do now, Dad?" It's "How am I doing?" Relationship trumps performance in God's eyes.

Though we are encouraged to be perfect, [3] perfection in and of ourselves is not the goal. That produces a burden to be perfect BEFORE we can know the Father. Pursuing perfection makes us full of self-consciousness and self-judgment; it causes us to shrink back until we are good enough.

In fact, the fear that we will never be good enough may keep us from even trying. This is what the Apostle John meant when he said, *"The one who fears is not made perfect in love."* [4] The Lord's desire is for us to *be made perfect in love.* To be

[2] Matthew 5:48

[3] Matthew 5:48: "Be perfect, therefore, as your heavenly Father is perfect."

[4] 1 John 4:18

perfect (in imitation of our heavenly Father) is to love perfectly: being present and being faithful. Fear of our own imperfection always interferes with the perfect giving and receiving of love. This is the fear of those who see God as a harsh taskmaster that is hard to please, not a loving and tender *Abba, Father*.

The goal of knowing God results in the kind of life Jesus led on earth — one of complete dependence upon God. We best enter the relationship to which we have been called through childlike trust. We forget ourselves, we run to Papa. When we go to prayer, we don't fuss around with getting it just right; we sit and talk to Him like the real person He is. We pour out our fears, ask our questions, tell Him we love Him, confess we need help. It honors Father God to ask for His strength. It pleases Father God when you come because you value Him, not out of a need to placate Him or do your duty, and not waiting until you can pray perfect prayers. What parent would like their child to stay away until they were mature enough to come around?

The first step to becoming God's friend is to be His child in every way.

I have grown and known God more easily as His Little One than any other posture before Him. As you go through life leaning into His love and fatherhood, you will naturally grow up in your salvation, coming to a maturity that will bring you both joy, through the same process all children do. The result of this process is that you will come to know your Father's heart. And when you are all grown up, you'll still be His tenderly beloved child. The first step to becoming God's friend is to be His child in every way.

Covenant: The Mutual Accountability Of Two Friends

God has declared Himself to be your Friend, and you must now learn how to think and act like His friend. Covenants produce a type of equality between two parties. When you join your life to another, an ongoing obligation begins in which you owe one another love, honor, devotion and accountability. And while it feels wildly improbable for a holy God to be joined to a flawed, sin-capable human being in the mutual accountability that covenants require, that is exactly what God has done. As Michael Horton observes, *"In the covenant, both the Lord and the Servant are on trial for their faithfulness."*[5]

There is ample language to validate this concept in Scripture, such as Malachi 3:10, where God invites His people to "test" Him in His promise to bless them abundantly when they obey Him in the tithe. God is saying here, *"I promise to bless you extravagantly when you obey me, and you have permission to test me in this."* (Do not peg me as a prosperity teacher; I am not. Through the lens of covenant I know this Scripture is not a formula to force God to bless us, but simply reveals the dynamics of a healthy and mutually faithful relationship.)

Another expression of mutual accountability between people in covenant was the idea of being *face to face* with one another. God invoked this very concept when He promised the Israelites that *"I will be your God and you will be my people,"* and then gave as His covenant stipulation, *"You shall have no other gods before me."* The word "before" in this sentence is the Hebrew word for *face* and/or *presence.* God was saying, *"You shall not be face to face with any other god."*

This idiom is a reference to what one should always have in view as they live life from this new reality: the covenant other. Faithfulness to a covenant friend required always being present for him, facing or seeing him, looking to his welfare and concerns. Jesus has given Himself to you as a Friend, and He asks you to give yourself to Him in like manner.

In covenant, each party must lay down his life in order to be faithful to the other. Jesus already laid down His life for us, but that didn't begin with the cross. It began the moment He

---

[5] Page 22, Introducing Covenant Theology by Michael Horton, ©2006, Baker Books

In covenant each party lays down his life in order to be faithful to the other.

was baptized by John, an act which marked His choice to leave His private life and enter public ministry. He already loved and lived for the Father; now He would die entirely to His former way of living in order to love, teach and redeem His Father's family.

Jesus died to Himself by walking away from the warm circle of family life with His mother, brothers and sisters, and from His work as a carpenter. I identify with the Lord in a small way in this, because over 30 years of ministry, I know what it is like to walk away from the comforts of home and private life to be about the Lord's public work with people. I am a homebody at heart; I enjoy hanging out with my husband, keeping my home, working in my garden. I also love sewing, knitting, and crocheting with the deep satisfaction that comes from creating something with your own hands, something I often imagine Jesus felt in His carpentry work. My favorite depiction of Jesus is Francis Hook's drawing of the Lord doing His carpentry work, planing a piece of wood. It sits before me now as I write at my desk.

There have been long seasons of my life — including now — when I have to walk away from things that give me joy in order to do the work the Lord has given me to do. One day when I was preparing to lead a full weekend women's retreat, an unfinished knitting project sitting in the corner caught my eye. I felt such a longing to curl up with my knitting that weekend, and have no demands on me; to just relax in the peace and joy of working with my hands. It was a selfish, very human moment.

Responding to my thoughts, the Lord said, *"I understand, daughter. One day I had to walk away from my carpentry shop, where I too had joy in the work of my hands. Thank you for feeding my sheep."* I so appreciated His gratitude and compassion, unexpectedly expressed. He understood. He had lived as a man, like us. I loved Him even more for it.

Jesus loved us faithfully with every thought and choice, dying to Himself daily in ways large and small, to preserve the righteousness and sinless perfection that would qualify Him as the perfect sacrifice for us. He walked away from life's pleasures, His rest and every other human desire He might have had, perhaps for a wife and family. He denied Himself all so He could live for our sake. He considered Himself dead to everything that tried to tempt Him away from His goal to faithfully love the Father and love us — all the way to the cross.

Dying To Your Old Life

Likewise, Jesus asks us to take up our cross daily and walk with Him:

> *Whoever wants to be my disciple must deny themselves and take up their cross and follow me. For whoever wants to save their life will lose it, but whoever loses their life for me and for the gospel will save it. (Mark 8:34-35)*

Covenant has taught me to not turn Jesus' words into a Pharisee moment by losing sight of what He is really asking. He is not asking you to deny yourself all satisfaction and pleasure in life, all ambition and accomplishment, as if it is your job to crucify yourself as a lifestyle. Christ did not crucify Himself, and He is not asking you to do so either. You bring no glory to God by impoverishing yourself just for the sheer discipline or humility of it. Believe me, I know, because I tried.

As an immature Christian I tried to die to myself, with the result that I was invariably focused on my own performance — what I call "navel gazing." Trying to die to self on purpose kept my focus very much on me, so self was very much alive. It was ugly, and did not serve Him at all. In His faithfulness, God used a trusted pastor to tell me I was living in false humility. Ouch.

Covenant doesn't work this way, because the supreme value is not dying to self, but living for the other person. We are to carry our cross in the same way Jesus did: as an act of love for the Father and others. You are asked to love God with all your might and love others the way God loves you, as a daily motivation of the heart. And while you are busy loving God and others, your self will die quietly while you're not looking. This is how you lose your life: not as a religious discipline, but as a lifestyle of love and obedience to your Covenant Friend.

While you are busy loving God and others, self dies quietly while you're not looking.

Covenant's highest value is, *"I no longer live for me, I live for you; I live to love you well, at all cost to myself."* People entering a covenant viewed it as a birth into a new life, because they would never again live as they had before. From the day covenant was made they ordered their life around one priority: being faithful to their friend, protecting, serving, providing. Every life choice was made only after considering how it would affect their friend. In essence, they each surrendered their lives to the other.

If you want to know God, who has laid down His life for you, you must likewise lay down your life for Him. You do this by making it your goal to have an obedient heart that is yielded to the Lord. While it requires a lifestyle of sacrifice on your part — saying no to yourself at times in order to say yes to God — the truth is that *your seeds of sacrifice will grow a crop of joy*. How is that? Because to live in covenant is to live a life of reciprocal covenant love. Jesus explains:

> *As the Father has loved me, so have I loved you. Now remain in my love. If you keep my commands, you will remain in my love, just as I have kept my Father's commands and remain in His love. I have told you this so*

> *that my joy may be in you and that your joy may be complete. My command is this: Love each other as I have loved you. Greater love has no one than this:to lay down one's life for one's friends. (John 15:9-13)*

This is the perfect circle of life and love: you lay down your life to love and obey God, and when you do, you both serve Him and position yourself to abide in His love. While you are loving and laying down your life for Him and others, He is loving on you in return. This is the power and fruit of mutual covenant faithfulness.

A Life Established In Love

In God's wisdom, He knew that our relationship to Him had to be first rooted in His love for us, then fully established through a life of mutual love for each another. Apostle Paul prayed for this very thing:

> *I pray that you, being rooted and established in love, may have power, together with all the saints, to grasp how wide and long and high and deep is the love of Christ, and to know this love that surpasses knowledge —that you may be filled to the measure of all the fullness of God. (Ephesians 3:17-19)*

Establishing your relationship in God's amazing love is the Spirit's first task with you. You cannot do this without His powerful help. Here is the plan: as you choose to love and obey God, your knowledge of Him grows until you become filled "*to the measure of all the fullness of God.*"

Our growth begins when we are immersed in the love God has for us, but we cannot become fully mature until we make it our goal to love Him — and other people — with everything we've got. We cannot get to know God in His fullness by any other way. This goal will thrust us into the testing of who we are, making us choose who we will be. The more we choose in these moments to be like Father, the more fully we know Him.

Love The Lord With All Your Might

When Jesus was asked by an expert on Jewish laws to name the greatest commandment, He replied, *"Love the Lord your God with all your heart and with all your soul and with all your mind and with all your strength."* (Mark 12:30)

We have a cultural mindset that places the highest value — where love is concerned — on being captivated by love, rather than seeking to cultivate it. We think we must "fall in love" for it to be authentic, as if love which does not come like this is not true love. But in truth, love that begins by choice and deliberate devotion becomes the deepest and most satisfying, as any happily long-time married couple will verify.

Loving God with all your heart, soul, mind and strength begins with the choice to do so.

The most steadfast kind of love is that which flows out of a heart committed to love. I call this a covenant heart, and God has such a heart. He freely and firmly set His love upon you, and He asks you to respond in kind. He doesn't ask you to love Him out of human emotion; but I assure you that as you know God more — tasting of His goodness — the emotion of love will not only come, it will become like a stream of living water in your soul. Until then, loving God with all your heart, soul, mind and strength begins with the choice to do so.

The commitment to love is the first step in forming that life-giving cycle. We commit to love God, and demonstrate it by obeying His teaching and commands, and setting our desire upon Him. As we do, He makes Himself known to us, giving us a taste of His goodness. Experiencing His goodness then inspires real affection and admiration. As this cycle continues, real love for God grows until somewhere it stops being a commitment and becomes the thing that shapes your whole being and frames your whole life.

Love is what transforms us; first God's love for us, then our love for Him. Between these two "bookends of love" we are changed into the image of Christ. I wrote in depth about this subject and my personal journey of transformation with the Lord in another book in this Series entitled *Rooted & Established In Love*, and also in the book *The Woman God Designed.*

The Choice And Value To Know Him

The Lord's covenant promises reveal His passion to know you and be known by you, regardless of whether you are weak or mighty, learned or uneducated, have committed five huge sins or a hundred and five little ones. By His promise, grace and power, you can know God.

If knowing God is our great covenant promise, then our greatest obligation is to honor His gracious offer by cultivating the value and choice to know Him! Indeed, our greatest failure in this covenant will be failing to pursue knowing Him, a fact reflected in Jesus' warning in Matthew 7:21-23:

> *Not everyone who says to me, "Lord, Lord," will enter the kingdom of heaven, but only the one who does the will of my Father who is in heaven. Many will say to me on that day, "Lord, Lord, did we not prophesy in your name and in your name drive out demons and in your name perform many miracles?" Then I will tell them plainly, "I never knew you. Away from me, you evildoers!"*

This is a warning we should all take seriously. To be offered the incredible privilege of knowing God, then fail to value and act upon it is the ultimate in unfaithfulness. I will not presume to parse out what Jesus defines as "knowing" Him, but I will say, don't risk it! With all God has provided, we have no excuse. We can know God; we must seek Him with this one goal in mind.

I meet many Christians who take great effort to do Christianity right: praying, studying their Bibles, attending church, giving time and money, serving others. People often say things to us like, *"Pray that I will be more obedient." "Pray that I will have more faith." "I wish I could understand the Bible more."* But rarely do I hear anyone say, *"Pray that I will know God more."*

My husband is fond of asking people in a meeting, *"How many of you want to get closer to God?"* Naturally, most everyone raises a hand; but it's a trick question, because he then informs them that in fact they are all as close to God as they have chosen to be.

We choose what and whom we will "know": Facebook, football, hobbies, characters in novels and movies, fields of study. We know and devote ourselves to whatever we truly value, and it is no great effort on our part when real desire is motivating us. No one forces us to want what we want; we choose.

God has rescued us from the bondage of sin and darkness, but He will not make us want Him. He doesn't even make us be good, or make us listen to Him; He doesn't force us to do anything! Though He can and does act sovereignly on the hearts of men at times to accomplish His larger divine purposes (as He did with Saul on the Damascus Road), most of us are left in our freedom to do as we wish while He patiently waits for us to reach for Him. He is not hiding from you, but He is waiting to be sought after. David charged his son Solomon as he prepared to turn the kingship over to him:

> *And you, my son Solomon, acknowledge the God of your father, and serve Him with wholehearted devotion and with a willing mind, for the Lord searches every heart and understands every desire and every thought. If you seek Him, He will be found by you... (1 Chronicles 28:9)*

God promises that if you treat a relationship with Him as the great treasure it is, and set your desire upon Him, to love and obey Him, He will make Himself at home in you and reveal Himself to you! Jesus said as much in John 14:21:

The one who loves me will be loved by my Father, and I too will love them and show myself to them.

God promises that if you treat a relationship with Him as the great treasure it is, and set your desire upon Him, to love and obey Him, He will make Himself at home in you and reveal Himself to you!

It's Okay To Seek Help In Desiring God

I realized one day that I did not have a natural desire to know God. I *wanted* to want more of Him, but my habitual choices kept revealing just how wimpy that desire was. I couldn't make myself want God in the way He deserved, and I was weak in saying no to the things I really did want. I felt terribly guilty. Then it occurred to me that this might be something the Holy Spirit would help me with. Surely, I reasoned, He would be glad to help me do exactly what God wanted — change my heart and my natural desires.

I confessed my lack of desire for God to Him, and my inability to make my heart change. Knowing God would not violate my free will, I gave the Spirit permission to change my desires and take away the passions that were stealing my time and devotion away from Him.

To my great joy, the Lord answered that prayer! It wasn't instant, but it didn't take ages either. The Spirit worked this change, not by zapping me and making me different, but by working with me. When choices arose, He reminded me of my prayer, helped me pause and consider what I really wanted. Then as I set my desire on God He gave me strength to let go of the lesser thing. In this process my desire for God grew stronger and my passions for lesser things faded. For example, I once built my spare time around sewing. One day I noticed my sewing machine was dusty. I smiled, and felt God smile with me.

If you are strong enough to set your desire upon the Lord, good for you! But if you are weak in that way as I was, don't give up. Desiring and knowing God are too important, and I'm confident there are few prayers the Holy Spirit would love to answer more.

10 What God Has Provided To Know Him

There is nothing outside of us that can keep us from growing in our knowledge of God. The only thing which can hinder is our own laziness, lack of faith or desire. Knowing God is easier than we think it will be, but it does require time and devotion. We tend to keep giving ourselves to pursuits that yield quicker, more accessible pleasure. I also think we are still intimidated by the very idea of knowing God.

We have the covenant, we have the invitation, and God has provided everything we need to grow in our knowledge of Him. There are two primary ways we grow in knowing God: by studying His Word, the Scriptures; and by interacting with the Holy Spirit, who enables and teaches us how to live this new life. Through the Holy Spirit's Presence we have within us the power and ability to know God, to fellowship with the Father and with the Son.

There is nothing outside of us that can keep us from growing in our knowledge of God.

The Tabernacle Of The Spirit

When God commanded Moses in Exodus 25:8 to build a tabernacle for Him so He could dwell in the midst of His people, He gave a very specific set of directions for its construction and use. The Tabernacle of Moses, as it is known, is an exact replica of the tabernacle or sanctuary of God in heaven. Even more amazing, God used this tabernacle to give us a perfect illustration of His chosen dwelling place on the earth: the heart of His redeemed ones! Once we are united with Christ in covenant, we become "citizens of heaven," [1] and in this sense our earthly life now becomes our "wilderness" — the place we journey through on our way home. But all the way there, our heart serves as God's chosen sanctuary on earth. God gave this visual so we couldn't miss the reality of what His Presence in us would provide.

Totally ordinary on the outside with only an animal hide as the visible covering, inside this tabernacle was lined with pure gold. It had a table piled with 12 giant loaves of bread God called "the bread of the Presence," (or "face bread," *lechem paniym*). God ordered this bread to be to be freshly baked and replaced every week so as to be kept on the table continually. There was also a lamp stand of pure gold, hammered into a repeating pattern that totaled 66 ornamental elements, and which held seven golden oil lamps. This seven-fold lamp provided the only light in the room. God commanded the priesthood to keep the lamps burning continually. There was a golden altar placed immediately in front of where God's presence would dwell, where the priesthood could pray to Him.

An ornate veil hung between that prayer altar and the Ark of the Covenant. This ark was a special box which held the "testimony" of the covenant between God and the Israelite nation — the Ten Commandments. The ark had a gold cover God called "*a mercy seat*," which He designated as His throne on earth.

When Moses had built, anointed and dedicated this tabernacle to God, the Lord's Spirit came and remained above that mercy seat, and His faithful presence dwelled with Israel. Only the priesthood could share this tabernacle with God. They could only enter after being sanctified (cleansed and made holy

---

[1] Philippians 3:20

to go into God's presence) by the blood of an innocent animal sacrificed, and washing in pure water.

I love this detailed picture God created and recorded in Scripture, because it visualizes and validates His intentions as He dwells within by His Spirit in our portable shared "home away from home." Like the tabernacle, I look totally ordinary on the outside, and one would never guess the treasure hidden inside the "animal skin." I am only able to share this place with the Lord's Presence because I have been washed and sanctified through the blood of an innocent man, the Lamb of God.

Inside, where life takes place between us, God's complete faithfulness and availability to me in covenant is revealed in every part. I am nourished by the continual bread of His Presence. His Spirit illuminates His written Word (the 66 books of the Bible), and in the light of His truth I can see how I should relate to Him. I have continual access to His throne of authority through prayer. *When I go to Him, I am always met with mercy.*

God has gone to enormous lengths to bring us to this life: covenants, pictures, prophets, stories, the total sacrifice of Himself. Jesus did everything because He delighted in the Father, and the Father delighted in you. Jesus wanted His Father to have His heart's desire, to share life with His creation. He wanted you to know the Father as He does.

God's plan is to nourish us in a relationship with His indwelling Presence.

He has set His table with the bread of His presence; He has illuminated the way with His word, and He is listening, attentive to our prayers. God's plan is to nourish us in a relationship with His indwelling Presence. Our task is to keep showing up for that, redirecting our wandering hearts and wayward appetites.

We must hear the voice of the Lord in order to know Him. We must study His written Word as a witness to that voice, and to know His ways. Our final key to knowing God is taking our place in the Body of Christ, His redeemed community. God has made us to need one another in order to know Him most fully. Let us explore these things more fully.

11 Knowing God Through His Word

If you learn to trust and receive the Word of God as His life-giving truth, you will partake of a priceless treasure. You may not always be comfortable with what God's Word says, but if you have faith that it is flawless [1] and divinely inspired [2] — as you should — then you must accept its authority to govern your life and instruct your mind.

There are layers of truth in Scripture, some shallow, some deep. There are things we cannot comprehend when we first begin to know God that we will easily grasp as we mature. When you receive and treasure the seeds of God's truth in Scripture that you can understand, God will open your mind and spirit to understand even more. He will cause the truth you value and live by to become wisdom that lives and moves with you through the moments of life, like a reliable companion who makes life better in every way. When you treasure the Word of God you greatly increase your ability to know God Himself.

The Word of God says, *Blessed is the man who fears the Lord, who finds great delight in His commands.* [3] If you are going to honestly live by faith, you must live as if you believe that every truth and command of God will lead to the fulfillment of His promise to give you abundant life. If God is love — and He is!

---

[1] Psalm 18:30

[2] 2 Timothy 3:16

[3] Psalm 112:1

— then all He commands and counsels is an expression of that love.

Most Christians I meet have never read the entire Bible once, much less a few times. Many have tasted less than 25% of Scripture — usually the 23rd Psalm, the four gospels, some of the New Testament letters, and maybe Genesis and Revelation. Typically it will be what they have encountered in VBS, Sunday School or a Sunday sermon.

I hear all these excuses: *"I don't understand it. I can't relate to it. I have trouble reading."* Christian book stores are now chock full of translations that are easy to read. And quite frankly, to say that you can't relate to the Bible is like admitting you really don't care to know more about God. To many, Bible reading is a bore or a chore, and I suspect the Church at large has not driven home the truth of how life-giving the Bible really is.

Occasionally those I teach express amazement at the things I show them in the Word of God, and marvel at my "gift." Yes, I have been given a teaching gift by the Spirit; but the fact is, it is not my gift that is amazing, it is the Word of God! Anyone with a sincere desire to know and honor God through studying His Word will have access to the same amazing knowledge when he or she has the Holy Spirit as a guide.

While men like David have shown us that one can know God apart from a Bible, book or church conference (if they have the Holy Spirit for their teacher), we do have this amazing, incredible treasure in God's Word. It is a powerful gift for which men lost their lives; a stunning miracle of unified thought written through dozens of men over many centuries, all guided by the same Holy Spirit.

After 35 years of studying the Bible, I am amazed nearly every day at how the Lord brings new treasures out of scriptures I've read dozens of times. Why would the Holy Spirit let me read something 10 or 15 times that seems ordinary, then suddenly make it relevant and extraordinary to me? There have been several reasons. Sometimes it is because the Lord had to build a platform of understanding through other Scriptures or teachers before I could see the full meaning. Sometimes the Lord is building a new teaching for me, so He *quickens* (highlights) certain Scriptures that become a theme. Other times Scriptures stand out because Spirit Teacher is loading my mind and spirit for something I will face tomorrow — in my own life, or in a counseling situation with another. Finally, the Lord and I have what I call *meeting places* in His Word. These are Scriptures He uses to touch me deeply, making them intensely personal between us. I have many marked in my Bible, some with dates. While they probably would mean little to anyone else, they are like snapshots in a scrapbook of our life together, evoking memories of special seasons with God.

It wasn't always this way with Bible reading, but the Spirit has made His Word a place we meet together, not just a book I am trying to work my way through as quickly as possible. Since I received the Spirit, Bible reading is a continual delight to me, a daily reminder that I am in covenant with a very alive God, who is not silent, not too hard to hear, not reluctant to show me things, and who is more interested in teaching me than judging me.

The Spirit has made His Word a place we meet together, not just a book.

The Bible is far too vast and deep for us to comprehend all at once, and we were never meant to grasp it all in a single read. I confess I have opened to read with the thought, *"I've read this so many times already... what can I find I don't already know?"*

Of course, that is the wrong question! The right question is, *"Lord, what do you want to teach me here today?"* God's Word is a living word because its author — the Holy Spirit — is still breathing life through it as you read it. As the author, He alone can truly reveal — illuminate — the Scriptures to us. To read the Bible is to fellowship with the Holy Spirit. When I pick it up to read I almost always have an immediate sense of the Lord's nearness. (Of course, He is always near, but I don't always have a sense of it.)

We all tend to read the Bible through our "personal filters" — opinions, teachings or life experiences that limit how we view and interpret things. Church or denominational doctrines can be such a filter, as well as the teachings of people or celebrities we admire. Disappointments with authority figures like parents, pastors — even God Himself — can skew our understanding, as well as the values of our culture. Something as simple as "common sense" can be a filter through which we interpret Scripture. Even our God-given gifts can be a filter, such as the gift of mercy. For instance, some have taken the message that "God is love" and used it to whitewash certain behaviors that God looks upon as serious sin.

Filters like these do not serve us well in perceiving God's truth because they can actually blind us to that truth. You only need one filter when you study the Bible: seeking to know the God who wrote it. Don't do as those without the Spirit do — deciding who God is or isn't out of your own knowledge, imagination or needs. Your life in Christ will be a continual exercise in yielding to Him; nowhere is this more important than yielding to His revealed truth. His truth colliding with yours will produce nothing less than a revolution, but in this battle, when He wins, you win.

You only need one filter when you study the Bible: seeking to know the God who wrote it.

Where Scripture is clear, let no one convince you it does not mean what it simply says. Always be mindful of the Lord's wisdom for establishing truth: by agreement of two or three witnesses. Man has been known to construct doctrines based upon a single verse that is unsupported anywhere else in scripture; this is not God's way.

Anything important enough for you to live by will have more than one witness to it in His Word. We should read under the Spirit's guidance, in the fear of the Lord and with a heart to honor what He reveals.

Take your unresolved questions to the Holy Spirit, as well as to mature and balanced pastors or Bible teachers. However, you will find that when you read the whole of Scripture, it becomes its own best interpreter; and seeming contradictions are usually cleared up when the whole picture is seen together.

Read Scripture to seek knowing the heart of God, to know what He loves, what He hates, what He delights in, what makes Him angry. God is a person; His is the original heart. Read to discover, not to find proof points for your favorite doctrines. Let God be who He reveals Himself to be, not a version you can be comfortable with. Finally, read to discover who you are to God, who you are in Christ.

When I don't understand what I am reading, I pray: *"Spirit, please give me understanding."* After all, the voice of Wisdom pleads with us:

> *Get wisdom. Though it cost all you have, get understanding. Cherish her, and she will exalt you; embrace her, and she will honor you. (Proverbs 4:7-8)*

Seeking to understand the Word honors the Holy Spirit. It is the faithful covenant response of one who wants to know and worship rather than question, who is ready to trust. God loves to help the one who is ignorant, who may have trouble learning, yet wants to know Him. He stoops down to help the one who looks up from His Bible and says, *"Teach me. Show me who you are."* I know. I am one of those.

The transformation of my mind, character and behavior began in earnest when I chose to accept God's Word as infallible truth. When I accepted its authority to tell me what to think and what to value, it changed my life, in ways I never dreamed it could. This began with my decision to test God's Word from a position of faith.

As I tested God's word by assuming it was true and obeying it, God proved to me that obeying Him always resulted in a fresh experience of His goodness, even if it didn't look like it would at first. God passed all my tests; it wasn't long before God was no longer on trial with me. It was settled in my heart: I could believe His word; I could trust God's promises. I would say with David, *Your promises have been thoroughly tested, and your servant loves them.* (Psalms 119:140)

The Word of God is waiting to change you, help you know God, and lead you to life.

The Word of God will not transform those who hold no value for it or do not trust it; it is just another book on a shelf. The Word of God is waiting to change you, help you know God, and lead you to life.

Bible Reading Plan - A Good Beginning

The Bible is not too hard to understand! Find a translation you like, start a reading plan, set aside just 30 minutes a day and be faithful to it. Keep a notebook handy to jot down things which stir your heart, because often these are your Spirit Teacher highlighting something for you to ponder more deeply that you're going to need. Read the whole Bible, and when you finish, read it again. (The Spirit told me years ago He was calling me to *nag* people about reading their Bibles. So here I am, fulfilling one of my holy callings....)

I confess to a prejudice against using devotional books. Many Christians read one every day *instead of* reading the Bible. Reading a daily devotional as your only study is like living on appetizers and never having the main course and your veggies — not to mention dessert!

A few years ago I discovered one exception to my disdain for daily devotionals: Sarah Young's *Jesus Calling.* Her excellent devotional is simply a compilation of journal entries from her quiet times with the Lord, each accompanied by two or three Scriptures validating what she learned from Him. Her devotional underscores the personal interaction Christians are meant to have with the Lord, and makes the reader thirsty for the same. But even though I highly recommend her devotional, I still beg you to read it *alongside* your Bible, not in place of it!

My first pastor taught me an outstanding plan of reading through the Psalms and Proverbs every month as a morning devotional. There are 150 Psalms, so I read five each day: the first day of the month I read Psalms 1 through 5; the 2nd day, Psalms 6 through 10, and so on. I read one chapter of Proverbs each day. The Psalms give us a vocabulary for worship and thanksgiving. They include honest journals of the interactions — even conversations and rants — between God and His people. Thus the Psalms teach us how to talk to God when we are joyful or in despair; when in doubt or fear; even when we offend God or are offended at God. It's real stuff for real life. Psalms teach us about God's unfailing love.

The Proverbs give practical wisdom for daily life on every timeless topic common to man. It has relationship advice: how to be a great husband, wife, parent, child, neighbor, employer or employee. There is wise financial advice. There are lessons which connect foolishness, sin and evil to their consequences, that serve as warnings. Proverbs help you apply God's values to real life in practical ways. I've never found a better devotional than reading Psalms and Proverbs each morning.

You should also spend some of daily reading time working through the rest of your Bible, beginning with the four Gospels about the Lord. My favorite is John's gospel, as it uniquely reveals the intimacy between Jesus and His Father; and the deep love and compassion Jesus had for people. It also shows the clear connection between the Holy Spirit and our promised life. I also encourage you to read through the first five books of the Bible as soon as possible (Genesis through Deuteronomy). These five books — the Pentateuch, believed to be written by Moses — lay a great foundation in story form for all the crucial truth and history the Holy Spirit reveals elsewhere.

You can read quite a bit in 30-45 minutes each day, and nothing will nourish you more. I've written a Bible study aid called *"Finding the Heart of God In Every Book Of the Bible."* It shows readers that the heart of God is revealed even in places like Numbers, Nahum, Amos, or Habakkuk. Some facet of God's heart is revealed in every book of the Bible, which altogether provides a portrait of God. Just as you cannot see the beauty of a painting by viewing only a few parts of it, you cannot fully see and understand God's heart and truths by only reading a few favorite Scriptures over and over again.

Watch Out For Hesed: God's Unfailing Covenant Love

As you read the Old Testament, especially Psalms, and if you use King James, Revised Standard or New American Standard, you will frequently encounter the words *mercy, kindness*, or *lovingkindness* when newer translations like the New International Version use the phrase *unfailing love* to translate the Hebrew word *hesed.* No matter how it is translated, you need to know that *hesed* is the word the Hebrews used to refer to *the faithful love covenant pledged to another.*

Word usage changes over time. In our modern culture, the words *kindness* and *mercy* simply do not connect us to the idea of unfailing love. Yet as you read your Bible, it is important to understand that faithful covenant friendship, pledged for life, is exactly what is being referenced when you encounter *lovingkindness, kindness,* or on occasion, the word *mercy.*

When the Pharisees criticized Jesus for eating with tax collectors and sinners, He responded with, *"Go and learn what this means: 'I desire mercy, not sacrifice.'"* (Matthew 9:13) He was quoting from Hosea, where *"mercy"* is *"hesed,"* the Hebrew word for faithful covenant love.

In the Greek (the original New Testament language) the word *mercy* in Matthew 9:13 (and most places in the New Testament) is translated from *eleos,* which Greek dictionaries say is also used to refer to covenant kindness and faithfulness. So what we mean by the word *mercy* and how the ancients used it are not the same! We use this word to refer to being gracious or just overlooking an offense. The Scripture can only use it as the ancients did, as written in their times and for their culture.

Because my first Bible was the New International Version (NIV), my initial years of Bible study were saturated with the phrase *unfailing love.* This gave me great confidence in God's love, though I knew nothing of covenant in those days. So at first I was very disappointed when I picked up other older translations and found no mention of *unfailing love.* After researching *hesed* and learning about covenant, I understood. The older translations weren't in error, of course; they were simply being faithful to the original euphemisms of "kindness" and "mercy" used for covenant commitment by the ancients.

Jesus said, "These are the very Scriptures that testify about me, yet you refuse to come to me to have life."

I use several translations now, and find value in them all. I'm not trying to promote or discourage use of any one translation; I just want you to know what *hesed* means when the Holy Spirit breathed it into the Word of God! I found it very helpful to make a list of every reference to *hesed* in the Old Testament, which I keep in the back of all my Bibles. I have included this list in an Appendix at the end of this book for your use.

The Bible Prepares You For Your Real Destination

Jesus once pointed out to the Pharisees,

You study the Scriptures diligently because you think that in them you have eternal life. These are the very Scriptures that testify about me, yet you refuse to come to me to have life. (John 5:39-40).

I believe you should read all of God's Word, and keep reading it, because it tells you what God is like and what knowing God should look like. However, God never meant the Scriptures to be the main thing you rely upon for life. He alone wants that privilege! He alone can give you the life He promises in His Word.

How do we go to Jesus for life? Until we join Him in heaven, we do this with the help of the Holy Spirit. Jesus said,

"Whoever believes in me, as Scripture has said, rivers of living water will flow from within them." By this he meant the Spirit, whom those who believed in him were later to receive. (John 7:38-39)

We cannot live without water, which is why the Lord often used it as a metaphor for the flow of His life to us. When Jesus spoke of living water He was referring to the Spirit that would be sent to the redeemed people of God after His resurrection.

God has always wanted to be the *living water* to His people. He said through the prophet Jeremiah,

My people have committed two sins: they have forsaken me, the spring of living water, and have dug their own cisterns, broken cisterns that cannot hold water. (Jeremiah 2:13)

The choice is clear: keep trying to fill up your own leaky cisterns, or connect with the continuous flow of life that refreshes, renews and nourishes you from the Spirit. In the next chapter we'll learn more.

12 Knowing God The Holy Spirit

The purpose of reading your Bible is to absorb all God has revealed about Himself, but it is not meant to be a substitute for knowing the Living Person who is God. The Scriptures provide a basis by which to recognize God's voice, because they familiarize you with God's language, values, goals and personality. The Bible doesn't tell you many things, like where to attend college, which career to follow, who to marry. This is the kind of personal guidance only the Lord can give.

The Bible tells you everything you need to know about how to walk and talk with God, but it doesn't personally counsel you as to how to live your own unique life, with your gifts, your calling, your flaws, your relationships, your challenges. Only the voice of the Living God can guide you in this. So while reading your Bible is Christianity 101, developing an interactive relationship with the Holy Spirit, the Wonderful Counselor, is your Master's program.

Reading your Bible is Christianity 101; developing an interactive relationship with the Holy Spirit is your Master's program.

You need the living, breathing word of God. A.W. Tozer says in His classic book, *The Pursuit of God*:

"...God is forever seeking to speak himself out to His creation. He fills the world with His speaking voice." [1]

Tozer goes on to describe how faulty our thinking has been:

"A silent God suddenly began to speak in a book and when the book was finished lapsed back into silence again forever. Now we read the book as the record of what God said when He was for a brief time in a speaking mood. With notions like that in our heads how can we believe? The facts are that God is not silent, has never been silent. It is the nature of God to speak..." [2]

The wonderful counselor, comforter, teacher and guide who is the Living Spirit — joined with you in covenant — speaks. He reveals the mind and thoughts of God the Father and Jesus Christ, as the Apostle Paul states in 1 Corinthians 2:7-16:

We declare God's wisdom, a mystery that has been hidden and that God destined for our glory before time began... as it is written: "What no eye has seen, what no ear has heard, and what no human mind has conceived" — the things God has prepared for those who love Him — these are the things God has revealed to us by His Spirit.

The Spirit searches all things, even the deep things of God. For who knows a person's thoughts except their own spirit within them? In the same way no one knows the thoughts of God except the Spirit of God.

What we have received is not the spirit of the world, but the Spirit who is from God, so that we may understand what God has freely given us.

This is what we speak, not in words taught us by human wisdom but in words taught by the Spirit, explaining spiritual realities with Spirit-taught words.

---

[1] Page 69, The Pursuit of God by A.W. Tozer, © 2006, WingSpread Publishers.

[2] Ibid, page 77.

> *The person without the Spirit does not accept the things that come from the Spirit of God but considers them foolishness, and cannot understand them because they are discerned only through the Spirit.*
>
> *The person with the Spirit makes judgments about all things, but such a person is not subject to merely human judgments, for, "Who has known the mind of the Lord so as to instruct Him?" But we have the mind of Christ.*

There can be no hidden meaning when Paul says the Spirit makes known to us the thoughts of God! Furthermore, there is no hint that this gift — the presence and person of the Holy Spirit— is only for a later time when we enter heaven. We will not need Him when we are with the Lord there. Nowhere does it say the Spirit was a special gift only given in the days of the original apostles and prophets. This would contradict God's covenant promise that *"They will all know me, from the least of them to the greatest."*[3]

There can be no hidden meaning when Paul says the Spirit makes known to us the thoughts of God.

The Apostle Paul uses language that is clear, unequivocal, and inclusive when he says we need the wisdom and thoughts of the Spirit *now* to do Christ's work on earth.

The phrase *the person without the spirit* is most accurately rendered *the natural man* in the King James Version. Paul is revealing that the natural soul of any man (saved or unsaved) does not have the capacity to comprehend spiritual things. After we were saved from the curse of death, we were born again; meaning a new human spirit was birthed in us that has the capacity to relate to God, who is Spirit. Yet having the *capacity*

---

[3] Hebrews 8:10-12

to relate is not the same as having the ability to carry it out. Think of it like a house wired for electricity, which has the capacity to power appliances and turn on the lights, but unless you connect with a source that generates power, you'll still be sitting in the dark. The Holy Spirit is the source of that light, the one who both empowers us to relate to God and who teaches us how to do it.

One of the most important purposes of the New Testament is to show us how to relate to the Holy Spirit as our guide and counselor. In writing 2 Corinthians 2:14, when Paul says, *"the person without the Spirit does not accept the things that come from the Spirit of God,"* the Greek words he used refer to *one who fails to reach out for something and take hold of it.* The Spirit is always holding out what we need. In order to relate to Him we must learn to quit relying on our natural (flesh) senses to perceive His activity and develop the sensitivity available through our own spirit instead. It takes practice, but it is not too hard; it simply begins with faith in His presence, and responding to that presence.

Knowing God's voice is absolutely key to knowing Him in the fullest measure while you walk this earth.

We Must Hear God's Voice To Know Him

Knowing God's personal voice to you is absolutely KEY to knowing Him in the fullest measure while you walk this earth. There is no other way to the abundant life He promises. This is why Paul worded his letter as he did. I love how he says we are given the Spirit and the mind of Christ "...so that we may understand what He has freely given us." *Freely given us*. We do not belong to a stingy God!

Jesus said unequivocally, *"My sheep know my voice."*[4] He later affirmed this in John 14:27 when He said, *"The Counselor [the Holy Spirit]...will teach you about all things."*

The counsel of the Lord belongs to His covenant children. In fact, Jesus said that Father God even reveals His truths to little children:

> *I praise you, Father, Lord of heaven and earth, because you have hidden these things from the wise and learned, and revealed them to little children. (Matthew 11:25)*

Little children are the immature, the very young, the complete newbies. If Jesus says God reveals His thoughts to such as these, no believer should excuse himself from qualification.

Disbelief, the fear of presumption and hearing the wrong spirit cause people to shrink back from believing they can hear God. I understand, and I have faced these myself. But these things must be overcome because they are some primary ways the enemy steals God's life from the believer. The devil steals life from the unbeliever by keeping him from trusting in Christ. But once he loses that effort, he works on a believer to steal the life God is offering, using doubt and fear — about oneself and about God.

It is true that if you do not know the character, motives and ways of God, you can be deceived in what you hear, which is one reason you must study the Scriptures. However, the Holy Spirit has convinced me (through Scriptures combined with His personal guidance) that God is willing to risk the errors that come with inexperience so you can get to know Him, and mature in your faith.

In fact, if you don't hear God's voice you may never mature in your faith; and even if you manage to do so, you'll miss out on the joy of experiencing the benefits of personally knowing

---

[4] John 10:27

God as Abba, Father. When He promised you righteousness, peace and joy,[5] His plan wasn't to watch you from heaven's doorway as you figured out how to give yourself those things by memorizing scripture and "standing" on His word. His plan is to build those things in you as you walk and talk with Him all the way to heaven.

When our marriage became very broken after three years, the Spirit taught my husband and I how to really love one another. We both loved the Lord and each other, but had brought so much baggage into the marriage and so many worldly expectations that our relationship became unbearable. We both actually quit, said we were done, and slammed the door on our relationship. But the Holy Spirit spoke to each of us individually and said, *"Go back and try it my way."* Individually and together, the Spirit counseled us in the unique ways that our wounds and flaws required, at home, where "the rubber meets the road." He led us through forgiveness and, one by one, healed the wounds we had inflicted. As we listened and trusted Him, the Spirit literally taught us how to love and serve one another the right way, and while He was at it, He birthed genuine new love in our hearts for each other. It was quite amazing, and we have now been together 35 years. The Lord used that season to teach us what a Wonderful Counselor the Spirit truly is.

I want to add that we also went to a counselor who offered some valuable help; so please don't think I am advising against human counselors in favor of the Holy Spirit. What I am saying is that the Holy Spirit is right with you every moment, and offers the kind of help no human counselor could provide. While the human counselor gave us good ideas and helped us identify areas we needed to work on, at the end of the day, the Holy Spirit truly saved and renewed both our hearts, our minds, our love and our marriage. A human counselor has no power do that. No one knows you like the Lord does.

---

[5] Romans 14:17

The Lord's desire is to comfort you personally (just as He did for Ron and me in our marriage, and still does); to encourage you just the right way in the moment you need it. And there is nothing like "Daddy compliments." I treasure mine, which He has spontaneously given:

"I'm proud of you!"

"I like what you just did."

"Thank you for writing my words."

From the time Jesus ascended to heaven and the Holy Spirit was released from heaven, men have been hearing His voice. Jesus promised His disciples at the end of His earthly life with them:

> *On that day you will realize that I am in my Father, and you are in me, and I am in you. Whoever has my commands and keeps them is the one who loves me. (John 14:20-21)*

> *All this I have spoken while still with you. But the Advocate, the Holy Spirit, whom the Father will send in my name, will teach you all things and will remind you of everything I have said to you. (John 14:25-26)*

There is a subtle but important sequence of truth here. First, Jesus reminds His disciples of the new covenant reality they will soon find themselves enjoying, a relationship where *"you are in me and I am in you."* He then explains the requirements of their covenant friendship: to love Him faithfully by obeying His commands. This begs the question, how will they receive His commands, since Jesus is returning to the Father? The answer is, through the Holy Spirit:

> *But when He, the Spirit of truth, comes, He will guide you into all the truth. He will not speak on His own; He will speak only what He hears, and He will tell you what is yet to come. He will glorify me because it is from me that He will receive what He will make known to you. All that*

belongs to the Father is mine. That is why I said the Spirit will receive from me what He will make known to you. (John 16:13-15)

First, this statement is not merely a description of the Holy Spirit's ministry; it is a statement about *birthright.* Jesus has already told His disciples that they will soon "become as one" with Him in the covenant sense. Now He reminds them that as the Son of God, His birthright is intimacy with the Father and access to all that belongs to the Father. A birthright is what you receive just because you are fortunate enough to be born into the family.

Jesus is trying to adjust the mindset of His disciples, from being servants to family members. Nothing will be held back once they are born again into God's family. Their birthright will

We cannot effectively love Christ with all our might (the definition of covenant faithfulness) unless we know and understand His will for us and walk with Him in it.

be the same as that of Jesus: intimacy with the Father, and access to all that comes with Him. The Holy Spirit's role is to establish you in this birthright, and help you live worthy of it.

We cannot effectively love Christ with all our might (the definition of covenant faithfulness) unless we know and understand His will for us and walk with Him in it. Jesus told His disciples that as He ministered, taught and healed people, He did only what He saw the Father doing, and said only what the Father taught Him to say.

This is our model. It was not a unique experience for Christ just because He was the Son of God, because He said we would do all He did and even greater things! We will only be able to do that the same way He did: through the power and guidance of the Holy Spirit. He was the conduit between God the Father and His mortal Son while He lived in His earth suit like ours. Remember, Jesus was called *the firstborn* of the born-again redeemed community, and we are the rest of the clan!

"He Will Guide You Into All The Truth."

There is truth for all men, and then there is personal truth for you — concerning your relationships, what you should do with your life, how the Lord wants to live and express His life in and through you. These things are unique in each person. In order to know God and live a life of obedience and faithfulness, you must exercise your faith to hear God's voice and personal counsel. There is no other way.

God is not calling us to a life of checking in with Him on every step we take — that would be unnatural and make you a puppet of God. He is not doing puppets, He is raising sons and daughters. As you begin to read the Bible and seek God's counsel in the beginning, you will have to seek His guidance more at first than you will later on, just like a small child needs a lot more instruction than the teenager and the young adult. As you get to know God, you will come to know what He wants of you often without asking. The longer I live with my husband, the more I have internalized what his will and ways are concerning his leadership of our family. Learning to walk with the Spirit and know your God are meant to be a natural process similar to what happens in your earthly growing up, only it involves the invisible God.

"The Lord Almighty is the one who moves mountains and reveals His thoughts to man." Amos 4:13

Even now, some of you may have a hard time believing that the Almighty Creator of the universe wants to be your own personal counselor and friend, and feel cautious about embracing such familiarity. I invite you to consider what the Spirit said about "the Lord Almighty" through the Prophet Amos: that He is the one *"who moves mountains AND reveals His thoughts to man."* (Amos 4:13)

Consider this: all the authors of the Old Testament heard God speak to them, or or had God make His thoughts known to them, by the Spirit. If not for this, we would have no Bible! This was before the New Covenant. The writings of the prophets are filled with messages that God communicated to men, humans like you and me. When you read Isaiah or Jeremiah especially, it becomes abundantly clear that the Spirit communicated both God's emotions and His words to these mortal men. True, it was a function mostly reserved for the office of prophet in ancient days, not something everyone experienced. My point is the same God and Spirit who communicated to unredeemed men and women (before Christ) will especially do so with His redeemed covenant children!

Even when people believe God can and will speak to man, they may struggle with the assumption that it is a privilege to be earned by achieving a certain level of spirituality. Actually, it's true: you do need spirituality, but all you need comes when the Holy Spirit is joined to your spirit. The Spirit gives you all the spirituality you need.

The Apostle James affirmed God's willingness to talk to His people:

> *If any of you lacks wisdom, he should ask God, who gives generously to all without finding fault, and it will be given to him. But when he asks, he must believe and not doubt, because he who doubts is like a wave of the sea, blown and tossed by the wind. That man should not think he will receive anything from the Lord; (James 1:5-7)*

The Lord generously shares His wisdom with me, and I love Him for it. In fact, I often experience that thing the Lord said about responding to prayers that haven't yet made it to our lips:

Before they call, I will answer; while they are still speaking, I will hear. (Isaiah 65:24)

Communication Is The Essence Of Relationship

Here is the first scripture given to me when I came to Jesus in 1979:

Peace I leave with you; my peace I give you. I do not give to you as the world gives. Do not let your hearts be troubled and do not be afraid. (John 14:27)

I put much faith in these words as I came to the Lord broken and tormented. As my introduction to God's word, this verse has always been special. If I became anxious, I would read this and pray for the Lord to give me peace. He was faithful to answer this prayer, but if I was awfully anxious, I often struggled to stay in that peace. This is what it was like before I believed I could hear the voice of the Lord.

A profound shift occurred when I began asking the Spirit to counsel me about what was causing my anxiety. His counsel would shine much light on whatever I was thinking — about myself, someone else or a situation. In hearing His counsel, more often than not, anxiety evaporated and peace came. His peace stopped being something I had to ask for, talk myself into or work to keep; it became the natural result of hearing His truth, which always brought rest and right judgment.

I quickly learned that what I thought I knew and how I judged situations, others and myself, wasn't always right. Asking the Spirit to counsel me about things gave new meaning to Proverbs 3:5-7:

Trust in the Lord with all your heart and do not lean on your own understanding. In all your ways acknowledge Him, and He will make your paths straight. Do not be wise in your own eyes; fear the Lord and turn away from evil. (NASB)

In this verse "acknowledge" is the Hebrew word *yada*, which appears hundreds of times in the Old Testament; it means *to know*. In other words, *in all your ways, know God* — interact with Him, talk with Him about it, get His advice and counsel, let Him show you what's what. This will change your life. It has certainly changed mine.

In All Your Ways, Know God

Until we understood that we can and should know God in the whole of our lives, we once thought knowing God mostly happened when we went to church or a prayer meeting.

God wants you to know Him where the rubber meets the road — in all your ways.

No, God wants you to know Him where the rubber meets the road — your living room, your bedroom, at the mall, on the job, and at your kitchen sink, when you're not sure how on earth to really love and get along with that person you married.

"*In all your ways...*" I have ways; you have ways: ways of being anxious, or impatient, or controlling, or lazy, or independent, or stubborn. The list is endless. It is clear to me that the things which steal my peace most often is ... my own ways!

The reason God wants us to know Him right in the middle of being the way we are is so He can help us to stop being the thief in our own lives. He'd rather help us change than have to keep rescuing us. While He will always be faithful to walk with us through the consequences of our ways, that is not His best.

God's best is to lead us directly to righteousness and abundant life. The concept of having righteousness through Christ not only refers to the favor we have with God because of Jesus' righteousness; it also refers to our ability *to walk in righteousness* because we are walking with God, in His counsel. In Psalm 32:8 the voice of the Lord says,

> *I will instruct you and teach you in the way you should go;*
> *I will counsel you with my loving eye on you.*

The Voice Of The Beloved

Communication is crucial to every healthy relationship. I once had a dog named Lady, who adored me. She had to be with me every minute, following me from room to room all day. The Lord used Lady as an illustration of unwavering devotion. Sadly, Lady went deaf when she was 14 years old. When she could no longer hear me, our relationship changed dramatically, as she became much less responsive and increasingly agitated. In her hearing days I could soothe her with my voice when she was stressed, such as when I gave her a bath or took her to the vet; but once she lost her hearing I could no longer comfort her that way. She became increasingly fearful and uncooperative, unable to hear my commands and therefore obey; so I had to put a leash on her and pull her around to get her to do certain things. I felt sadness and frustration with her then, and understood for the first time how important the sound of my voice had been to the quality of our relationship. It is no different with us and God.

What happened with Lady reminds me of the very next verse in Psalm 32:9, where the Lord goes on to say, *Do not be like the horse or the mule, which have no understanding but must be controlled by bit and bridle or they will not come to you.*

You Hear God's Voice With The Ears Of Your Spirit

In Scripture God speaks of His people having *eyes to see* and *ears to hear.*[6] While these idioms refer to the choice to pay attention and the desire to understand, they can also refer to the

---

[6] Ezekiel 12:2

faculties of your human spirit. Your spirit, made of the same essence as God's, can see and hear. Think back on every story you've heard of people who died in an operating room, and were later revived; who consistently tell of hearing and seeing everyone in the room, including their own body! The body was dead, so their flesh eyes and ears were not working at the time.

You do not hear God with your natural ears, but with the ears of your spirit. Likewise, you see God with the eyes of your spirit, not with your flesh eyes.

When I hear God's "voice," His words come much like my own thoughts; but usually it is very clear that they are not. For instance, I just don't usually think to myself, *"I love you, daughter."* His thoughts feel as natural as my own. Sometimes they come as an idea, a picture, or just *knowing.*

I won't teach you in detail about hearing God here; we have done that in our ScribeLife Series book, *Can I Really Hear God?* which covers all major scriptures on the subject and provides pointers on how to discern His voice. It also answers questions on what might hinder you in hearing the Lord. Meanwhile, in the back of this book is an appendix, "My Sheep Listen to My Voice," a quick study on what the Bible says about personally hearing the Lord.

When you step into hearing God's voice you must commit to trust and respond in faith to what you hear, and leave the results up to God. Though caution and discernment are always in order, don't live in fear of hearing wrong. When God sees you put your faith in hearing Him, He adds His grace to your efforts, and will help you hear Him. The more you step into this, the more He will make His voice known in you.

Jesus said in Mark Chapter 4:

> *Consider what you hear. With the measure you use, it will be measured to you—and even more. Whoever has will be given more; whoever does not have, even what they have will be taken from them. (Mark 4:24-25)*

A person who values what God says will cling to His words and thoughts as a treasure, guarding and using them. This value is found in the phrase, "keep my words" used in Proverbs:

> *My son, keep my words and store up my commands within you. Keep my commands and you will live; guard my teachings as the apple of your eye. Bind them on your fingers; write them on the tablet of your heart.(Proverbs 7:1-3)*

> *Take hold of my words with all your heart; keep my commands, and you will live. Get wisdom, get understanding; do not forget my words or turn away from them. (Proverbs 4:4-5)*

Jesus said in John 8:51, "*Truly, truly, I say to you, if anyone keeps My word he will never see death.*" (NASB)

The word "keeps" in this verse means *to guard and protect.* When God's child seeks His counsel and uses the measure he receives — in other words, *keeps* God's word — God gives a greater measure. It is the same with any living being: we don't keep talking to someone who shows little interest or response, but we'll pour our heart out to the one who cares. The Spirit of Wisdom — the Spirit of Christ[7] — said in Proverbs 1:23, *"If you had responded to my rebuke, I would have poured out my heart to you and made my thoughts known to you."*

It is not perfect hearing that God is looking for; it is a heart to know Him, demonstrated by wanting to hear Him and treasuring what He says. I've had far more missteps in my efforts to know God through *not* listening for His voice than I ever have when I do listen. Just like a child is born into the family with the capacity to hear and speak, yet must develop those abilities, we must learn to hear God in the same way.

You were made to live a life in fellowship with the Lord. In his excellent book "Experiencing the Power of the Holy Spirit," Pastor Lloyd Ogilvie writes that *"Praying constantly is making all*

---

[7] Colossians 2:2-3

of life a companionship with the Lord."[8] He joins a chorus of voices in this assertion, including the Apostle John. When the Apostle John wrote, *"Our fellowship is with the Father and with His Son"* in 1 John 1:3, he used the Greek word *koinonia,* which refers to companionship and conversation between two friends — those conversations on the couch again! God is *your* friend, and longs for the day when you desire to walk with Him as His friend.

God is *your* friend, and longs for the day when you desire to walk with Him as His friend.

Living Face To Face With God

Once you are in Christ, in covenant with the Father, Son and Spirit, the purpose of your faith is to live your life face to face with God, as a response to His Presence. In his mind's eye, when David looked out upon his world, he didn't just see the people and problems that faced him; God was there in every moment and scene, loving him, giving him strength, imparting wisdom. King David expressed this reality when he wrote, *"I have set the Lord continually before me," (Psalm 16:8, NASB)* and *"I shall walk before the Lord in the land of the living."* (Psalm 116:9) The word "before" in both these verses is the same Hebrew word *paniym* we saw earlier (regarding the Tabernacle), which means *"presence, face to face, in front of, before."*

David's faith was activated in the most appropriate way after God made him a covenant promise and anointed him with the Holy Spirit. In Psalm 116:9 David speaks of his faith in God's covenant Presence, saying in essence, *"God, I know your face is turned towards me, attentive to all my needs, and that I walk in your Presence."* In Psalm 16:8 David acknowledges his

---

[8] Page 147, "Experiencing the Power of the Holy Spirit," ©1994, 2001 by Lloyd John Ogilvie, Harvest House Publishers.

covenant obligation to God, saying in essence, *"I will live with my face turned towards you, attentive to all you require of me."* David understood and honored covenant reciprocation.

When you see an Old Testament reference to God's face being turned towards someone or away from them, it is referring to a covenant reality. One's face is always turned to their covenant friend in faithfulness — seeing, knowing, attentive to any need they may have of us.

God said David had a heart after His. One reason for this is that, unlike most other men, David didn't shrink back from God as a harsh taskmaster who couldn't be approached. He understood God could still be God AND step into a relationship with a human man as another man would. David understood that the value and character of God was to nourish and befriend His people through covenant relationship as men do. He "got" God, and God loved it. Like David, you will honor God best by living in full trust that He is present with you by His Spirit, and responding accordingly.

It is the "responding" part that most Christians lack... because this takes faith beyond just believing that God exists. A Christian can believe they belong to Christ and even be filled with His Spirit, and still live a life that mostly ignores God's Presence. God accused His people of this very thing through the prophet Isaiah:

> *All day long I have held out my hands to an obstinate people, who walk in ways not good, pursuing their own imaginations — a people who continually provoke me to my very face..." (Isaiah 65:2-3)*

Ponder His words with me: *"... who continually provoke me to my very face..."* In other words, *"Everything they do, they do right in front of me, as if I weren't there."* Living by faith in God's presence makes everything personal, because sharing life with a Person is very different than following a set of rules. You can

You can ignore rules, but you cannot ignore a person, especially someone you call "Lord."

ignore rules, but you cannot ignore a person — especially someone you call "Lord." [9]

When the Apostle Paul admonishes us in Ephesians 5:17 to *"be filled with the Spirit,"* he is not just speaking of a believer's initial baptism in the Spirit, but of *being continually filled with the Spirit.* This is not mysterious or difficult, in the sense Paul uses. We are all "filled" with whatever is continually in front of us — in our thoughts, what we give attention to, what we plan life around.

In the fall, football fans are full of all that goes with the season, scheduling life around games to cheer on their team. Gardeners are full of gardening, focused on what needs attention, nurturing seedlings, watching things grow, pulling weeds. Being filled with the Spirit is just like this, like anything that naturally fills your heart and keeps your attention. Paul is simply saying, *do this on purpose with the Holy Spirit.*

Knowing God grows as we develop a sensitivity to His presence. If through ignorance or laziness we fail to cultivate this relationship, we do so to our own great loss, missing out on the Lord's comfort, wisdom and companionship.

Jesus went to the cross in faith and joy that His suffering would purchase all of this for you. Don't waste His faith or His suffering by living as an orphan!

Your Imagination: God's Gift To Help You See

God's invisibility is a challenge, but He has given us a faculty to help with that: the ability to imagine. In my first years

---

[9] The 59th Chapter of Isaiah contains a devastating description of the life lived with one's back turned to God, as well as the ripple effect of that life on the world it touches.

I struggled with praying to this invisible God, until I tried something that dramatically changed prayer for me. I put a chair next to me, and imagined Jesus sitting in it. Immediately, the way I talked to God changed! I stopped fumbling for words, became less formal, speaking more honestly and naturally to my Lord, as I would with my closest friend.

Increasingly, prayer became a conversation with my Spirit Friend, as I realized the most basic courtesy I would show a human friend in conversation belonged to the Lord even more. I would never sit down with a friend, say what I wanted to say, then get up and walk away! So I began to wait on the Lord with pen and paper at hand, especially once I began to seek His counsel about things that mattered to either Him or me. I now have journals full of things the Lord has said to me: encouragement, instructions, wisdom, comfort, even jokes; and they don't include the things the Lord says to me in the car, the garden, the mall, or while I'm cooking supper. [10]

Activating my imagination with faith turned my prayer life around. Furthermore, it signaled to the Holy Spirit that I believed in His Presence and was ready to respond accordingly, and honor Him with attentiveness.

The Lord and I don't talk all the time; His is mostly a comforting quiet Presence. Christians make a mistake in thinking if something is from the Lord it will be strong or loud or dramatic. God has never written on my bedroom wall, but He hasn't had to resort to that; He's already got my attention.

Awareness of the Spirit comes as faint impressions in which I sense His moods, feel His love, patience, disappointment, or joy. I've grown more sensitive to Him over the years of being attentive. It is similar to how I sense my husband after all our years together. He can be across the room and I can usually

---

[10] This is why I instantly loved Sarah Young's devotional book *Jesus Calling*; I recognized a kindred spirit who listens to the Lord, is personally taught by Him, and judges all she hears by the written Word of God.

sense his mood or know how he is reacting to something, even if I can't see his face. He is familiar to me now.

My primary purpose is to inspire you to know the real God in real life.

I have heard the Lord laugh. I have experienced the Lord being mischievous with me, making me smile. I never instigate these moments, or imagine them into being, because I want the real thing.

Certainly, not every fleeting thought, idea, or emotion is the Lord, but I now believe many more are than we recognize. You grow in relating to the Spirit of the Lord just as you grew from infant to young child, to teenager and then adulthood, interacting with your parents in evolving ways as you shared life while growing up. The Holy Spirit is always ready and willing to help you, so relax and trust Him.

There is much more to learn about this, which is the subject of another book called "*Spirit Life.*" Meanwhile, my primary purpose in this book is to inspire you to know the real God in real life.

Studying Scripture With The Spirit

As I began to have faith that I could hear God's voice, desire also grew to step into being taught by God, according to His covenant promise. I wanted that. So while I proceeded with the goal of reading through the Bible, I also began to ask the Spirit what *He* wanted me to read.

As I sought the Spirit's guidance in studying the Bible, I enjoyed the timeliness His guidance brought to the real issues I faced in life. I often needed exactly what I had been studying in the next challenge of my life — sometimes in the very next hour — whether in counseling, parenting my children, getting along with my husband, or preparing a lesson for a women's class. The Lord saw to it that I was prepared.

As I would read His Word I would be aware of God teaching me, showing me things I had not seen before. It's hard to describe; I simply would just "know" things I'd not figured out on my own, things so deep or wise or beyond finding out that I would sit there staring at my Bible in amazement. Yet this was no accident, because I asked the Lord for it, having learned from Psalm 119:18 to pray, *"Open my eyes that I may see wonderful things in your law."* God answers prayer, especially from a hungry heart.

I was especially amazed at how He wove the truths of the Bible together. Difficult-to-understand passages would become more clear as the Spirit would bring to mind something I had read elsewhere in the Bible which illuminated the Scripture now in front of me. The Spirit has a way of cross-referencing and connecting things that I could have never discovered by just using a concordance or doing a topical study. It was after I read the Bible through the first time in this manner that I saw how beautifully the Bible interprets itself.

I am not suggesting that one should isolate and never be taught by others. We need one another for balance and accountability; I've had plenty of this in my life, by design. Yet many miss the joy of allowing the Spirit to personally teach them through the book He wrote.

My faith in the Spirit's guidance and my ability to perceive it soared as I continued in this way. But I must admit my faith was tested when the Spirit told me (one day at a time) for six months to read the same three books: Ephesians, Philippians, and 1st John. It doesn't take long to read them; there are only 15 chapters between them, just 12 pages in my Bible.

As the days passed and I kept getting the same assignment, I began to slow down. I would read a section, then ponder what I had read. I then began to write a few words to capture, in my own words, things the Spirit seemed to be highlighting, recording them in a study journal. I ended up with notebooks full of things which have found their way into teaching outlines for seminars, retreats and books — like this one.

This experience was a school the Holy Spirit put me through that forever changed the way I read and studied the Scriptures. Lingering over and meditating on Scripture enabled me to absorb it. It gave the Spirit opportunity to teach me, allowing His truth to take root in my mind and live there. For ages after I'd internalized a particular truth, it would bubble up in my spirit miles down the road and intersect my life in significant ways, in perfect moments.

To this day I have memorized very little Scripture — I'm terrible at it — but its truths are written on my heart. They served me well when the Lord began calling on me to teach publicly. I didn't know in those "days of testing" that the Spirit was preparing me for ministry as a Bible teacher, writer and mentor, laying a foundation for what He would motivate me to teach for the rest of my life.

The Spirit is so amazing and faithful! He has given me great joy in the work He has equipped me to do in teaching and writing. I want that for you, in whatever the Lord is stirring you to do. The Spirit has a program of study tailored just for you; He will guide and teach you day by day. Through His living Word and His Spirit, God will transform your mind and equip you for the life and work He has prepared just for you.

13 Knowing God Together With The Body

God placed all things under His feet and appointed Him to be head over everything for the church, which is His body, the fullness of Him who fills everything in every way. (Ephesians 1:22-23)

After taking you on a journey of building your intimate life with the Lord, you might wonder if I believe you don't need anyone but you and the Spirit. That is far from the truth! In fact, over the years of walking with the Spirit, I have come to see more clearly than ever my need of the Body, and their need for me. Furthermore, I have a tender affection for the Body of Christ that the Spirit has built in me. I love the Body, I need the Body, I honor the Body. The Body is, as the Apostle Paul says, *the fullness of Him.*

You are not only in covenant with the Lord, you have become part of a family of all those who are in Christ. This is God's desire and plan. Offering your gifts to the Body is an act of covenant faithfulness to God *and* to your brothers and sisters in Christ. Connecting with the community of faith on a regular basis is part of God's plan for you to know Him, in ways that you cannot do alone. We all know Him in part, and as we add our parts to one another, the Lord is revealed much more fully to us and to the world that needs Him. Luke described this when He said of the first church,

They devoted themselves to the apostles' teaching and to fellowship, to the breaking of bread and to prayer. Everyone was filled with awe at the many wonders and

> *signs performed by the apostles. All the believers were together and had everything in common. They sold property and possessions to give to anyone who had need.*
>
> *Every day they continued to meet together in the temple courts. They broke bread in their homes and ate together with glad and sincere hearts, praising God and enjoying the favor of all the people. And the Lord added to their number daily those who were being saved. (Acts 2:42-47)*

The Body is meant to provide the teaching and mentoring every Christian needs to grow in a healthy, balanced way. In addition, the community of faith provides a fuller experience of joy, worship and fellowship around the Lord we love.

We share the Lord's covenant communion meal together. We strengthen one another with our personal witness (testimony) to what the Lord is doing in our lives. We worship together, celebrating and loving on the Lord in thanksgiving and songs of adoration. The Lord responds to this by releasing even more of His Presence upon our worshipping spirits.

Though this happens when I worship the Lord in private, it is greatly magnified in corporate worship in a way I believe permeates the atmosphere in our community. I believe that a soul sitting at home in my town can be stirred by the Spirit of the Lord because God's people have worshipped together, even if that soul doesn't know God. I can't prove this, but I know two things for certain: God's Presence always changes the place where He is, and His Presence is always magnified in response to the Body's collective prayer and worship.

We Can Know God Better Together

We can know the Lord together in ways that we cannot know Him all alone. I am so encouraged and inspired by the Lord in others, who shine light on what the Lord is showing me, helping me to know if I am discerning the Spirit's guidance rightly. The Body needs what the Lord has revealed of Himself in me, and I need what the Lord has revealed in them. The Lord established "a safety" for those who would be the leaders and administrators of His truth and justice, which we find in both Old and New Testament verses. Everything should be validated by two or three witnesses, including truth. [1] This guards against both false doctrines or cults and false accusations against others.

The community offers safety against deception and the schemes of the enemy — the thief about which Jesus warned us, who wants to steal our life. We know from the beginning of man's history that deception is one of the primary ways the thief tries to steal God's life from us — lying to us about God, about ourselves, about others.

Isolation makes us vulnerable, as illustrated by the event in Luke 8:29, where Jesus set a demon-possessed man free who had been living naked in the tombs, tormented by a demon who, Luke wrote, *drove him into solitary places.* Demons (evil spirits) can use isolation to take advantage of us, to separate us from the strength of our larger family of faith. (We do not need to go about focused on demons, nor afraid of them; but neither should we deny or ignore their existence. Jesus paid attention to them and set the example in helping people become free of their influence or afflictions.)

Isolation Is Not Good For Us

Isolation can take many forms. When depressed, I have reacted as most do, instinctively pulling away from others. That only deepens the depression, and if prolonged, can lead to mental illness. Fortunately, people who love me surrounded me and refused to leave me in isolation, and I recovered.

As counselors we have seen how isolation can keep an abused wife in danger. Pastors isolated in a leadership bubble can easily fall into pornography or extramarital affairs for lack of

---

[1] See Deuteronomy 17:6 and 19:15; Matthew 18:16; 1 Corinthians 13:1, and 1 Timothy 5:19.

close relationships with peers. When the faith community lives in accountability and transparency with one another, we are all less vulnerable to temptation and abuse.

Transparency And Accountability

A covenant heart values accountability, which community provides.

God's goal is to build a heart like His in His children, which I call *a covenant heart.* A covenant heart values accountability, which community provides as we work out our faith among those we know and who know us up close. A covenant heart lives in awareness of their obligation to love and give themselves to others, and is willing to be held accountable for the moral values they espouse. In community we also learn how to perceive and honor the Spirit at work in other ordinary people like us. We learn how to yield to one another as we follow the guidance of Christ together.

Developing And Using Our Spiritual Gifts

In the community of faith, our spiritual gifts can be developed in a way not possible in isolation. The gifts of the Spirit are drawn out more readily in a healthy faith community, where I find both courage and correction. As we grow in the use of our gifts, we can become those the Lord uses to express His love and goodness to the world. My experience is that being with others who are full of the Spirit stirs up His gifts in me.

It may be tempting to stay home and listen to TV preachers as a replacement for church; but this is unwise if you have no other fellowship with the larger body of Christ. My husband and I do not attend a formal church service every single week, but we do regularly participate in Body life, either a church or a home group.

Covenant faithfulness to the Lord requires us to extend our hearts to the Body as we would to the Lord Himself. The Lord aligns Himself with others in regards to your faithfulness, as He made clear in His instruction to Moses:

> *Any man or woman who wrongs another in any way and so is unfaithful to the Lord is guilty and must confess the sin they have committed. (Numbers 5:5-7).*

In other words, not showing up for those in your faith family — and the community you live in — is not showing up for the Lord. He says He is close to the broken-hearted, the weak, the vulnerable, the needy, the orphan, and the widow. If someone out there needs something from the Lord, you should be willing to show up if He calls you and offer what He is offering. This is yet another way of knowing the Lord that you cannot experience in isolation: serving people.

The Lord's Presence Magnified In His Body

I am nourished when I spend time with brothers and sisters in Christ. They strengthen and encourage me as we worship, pray, eat, and learn together. On occasion I have been unable to break free of something that had taken hold of me — a sickness of heart or body — and gone to be with the Body to ask for prayer. I began to notice that often I didn't even have to ask for prayer; just going into their midst seemed to spontaneously restore my joy and wellbeing. The magnified presence of the Spirit in His assembled community is more powerful than you know, even when they are not being deliberate about it.

As you walk with the Holy Spirit, your own spirit grows, along with His Presence in you. We underestimate the power of God's presence within us, how it can touch others just because we show up with Him in us — at church, at the mall, at work. For instance, knowing God has given me a peaceful spirit, not easily disturbed. People often say to me, *"I feel more peaceful when you are here."* I believe what people are sensing is the peace that normally saturates my spirit, combined with the peace in the Lord Himself. Likewise, I am blessed by the Spirit's presence in others. This is what is called *the anointing*, a rather mystical word for the active Presence of the Lord in His people. My husband and I pray for each other daily, but sometimes we need the strength or anointing found in the assembled Body. I suspect God allows this in His sovereign grace so we will learn our need of one another.

The Body plays a crucial role in nurturing and funding missionaries in their work of spreading the gospel to unreached peoples and in ministries of helps. Just as important is the service the Body provides in covering missionaries in prayer on the mission field. Missions are a mandate from the Lord, and missionaries can't go forth without the Body's support. It is hard for a lone ranger to effectively do the Lord's mission work.

Just as it is wise to ask for the Spirit's guidance in all the rest of your life and study, it is good to ask where and how the Lord wants you to plug in to fellowship with the Body. It can be a church, home group or prayer group, where the Spirit knows you can partake of all the blessings the Body provides.

The Spirit has given me a love for the Body, but also understanding of what she is meant to be. The pastor-centric Church as it exists today in various denominations tends to mass produce Christians who know church life instead of knowing God. I'd love to see the Church look more like the original model: family-centric, strong in community, sharing and accountability. The Body needs to mentor those who are saved through Christ in knowing God and walking with the Holy Spirit. I long for the earth to be full of transformed, joyful, powerful disciples of Christ.

You need the Body of Christ, and the Body of Christ needs you.

Find true Biblical disciple life where you can. You need the true Body of Christ, and the Body needs you!

14 Life With My Spirit Friend

I came to God completely broken, turning to Him as many do: the last resort. I grew up determined to avoid getting sucked into religion, and was totally focused on enjoying life to the fullest. If there was a God, I was pretty sure He would ruin my party. I carefully guarded my freedom from any form of religion or restraint.

But the day came when I saw that not only was I not having a party, I hated who I had become. The choices I had made with my precious freedom had harmed not only my life, but the lives of others. I was lost, depressed, and newly divorced. I wanted to die, but didn't have the nerve to hurt myself. I took a new job, where I was befriended by one of those cheerful Christians who would often say, "Jesus loves you." I was so lonesome for a friend. She made me laugh, so I hung out with her, but I wasn't buying the line. I was determined to never let anyone talk me into believing in God. I sure wasn't going to talk myself into believing God loved me, even if He did exist.

One day I came to the end of myself. I couldn't stop crying, and none of my close friends answered the phone. I had never been so alone in my life. I was so desperate that for the first time I could remember, I wanted God to be real. Lying in a fetal position on the floor, in a puddle of tears, I raised a fist at the God I wasn't sure was there, and issued this challenge: *"If you're really God, then you can make me feel this love everyone says you have for me! I'm not going to talk myself into it!"*

Within 24 hours God answered that prayer, in the most personal way. He caused His love to flow over me in a way so real and powerful that I could never have imagined it on my own. I can still vividly remember how it felt. How that answered my hungry heart! I decided to believe in this invisible God who could and would make me feel His love.

I had not read one word of the Bible, but after this I hungrily read the Scriptures. I wanted to know everything about this God and the life I was hearing about. The Lord won me with His love, and for a while I was in love with Jesus. I came to Him starved, and He fed my hungry heart.

Yet, after the first couple of years I became dissatisfied with how life was going between the Lord and me. I still loved God for what He had done, and was very grateful for His grace and forgiveness. I was a changed woman with a different life and priorities; but all that still did not add up to the joyful and powerful life I was reading about. The Bible described our new life in Christ as personal, powerful, outwardly fruitful and inwardly satisfying. My life bore too little resemblance to that, and what I did possess seemed increasingly like a product of my own effort and striving. It certainly didn't feel like what God called it in the book of Hebrews: "*entering rest.*"

Reading the Scriptures had given me a huge appetite. *I couldn't bear to believe God would promise something repeatedly as just a way of being encouraging and poetic, without it being real.* I was hungry for the life Jesus promised, the healing and renewal that Isaiah foretold would come through Him, and the satisfaction of heart David wrote of in his Psalms. The Bible made me hope that God would be very personal with me, give me direct guidance, and actually satisfy my heart.

The suspicion that I was settling for way less than what God seemed to be offering nagged at me, but I didn't know how to get there. It became like that first day when I refused to talk myself into believing in God's love: I wanted God's real presence and power, not something I produced and had to prop up all the time. I already knew I was weak in sustaining anything for very long. I didn't want a Christian life that was no more powerful than I felt on any given day. And when I read

Jesus' words, *"Love the Lord your God with all your heart, soul, mind and strength,"* I felt like a complete hypocrite. I didn't love God like that, and didn't know how!

I began to read books and listen to teaching by those who also had this hunger for God, who *were* experiencing the life promised in Scripture. I saw a common denominator; it was the Holy Spirit. I began to pay more attention to what the Bible said about Him. Hope began to grow that God had not left me to struggle under my own power to find the life He promised; that He planned all along to provide it through the Spirit of Christ. I realized I needed to know the Spirit in a way I did not; so I was baptized in the Spirit (as I described in Chapter 8).

Mine was not an outwardly dramatic experience, but inside, everything changed! The first thing that changed was a new love for the Lord stirred in me — that love I had been unable to feel. The second thing was an unexplainable but deep joy settled in my spirit, as well as peace. I was hungry to know God; I was hungry to read my Bible. When I did read my Bible, it came alive in new ways as I understood things I had not before.

As I stayed filled with the Spirit, life with God grew to look like all I hoped for, and more.

As I stayed filled with the Spirit (by paying attention to Him), other changes began to come until little by little, life with God grew to look like all I hoped for, and more. How did Paul put it? *Above and beyond all I could ask or imagine.* [1]

I knew the Spirit would help me love and serve God better; that He would give me strength and help, but I had no idea how rich a life shared with Him could be. When I surrendered to Christ's love, I had been looking for a hero all my life. I wanted someone strong, faithful,

[1] Ephesians 3:20

wise and good, who would cherish and protect me, and never let me down. I found Him! He may be invisible to me right now, but He is more real to me than anyone I know.

It is too bad that much of the Church has made the Holy Spirit all about gifts and tongues and supernatural manifestations. Jesus presented the Spirit to His disciples as the One through whom they could know the Father, and experience the faithful flow of God's life. Jesus certainly demonstrated the human life lived in the power of the Spirit — healing the sick, setting people free from demonic torment, displaying wisdom — yet His teaching about the Spirit focused on His role as teacher, guide and nourisher of God's people. His mighty power is displayed in all these things, not just dramatic miracles.

The Fruit Of The Spirit

But the Holy Spirit produces this kind of fruit in our lives: love, joy, peace, patience, kindness, goodness, faithfulness, gentleness, and self-control. (Galatians 5:22-23, NLT)

I began my faith life thinking this verse was a list of how I should be and act because I was saved. It was the big Christian "to-do" and "to-be" list. The bad news: I just couldn't make myself be and do all of these in a steadfast way. The good news: it's called *fruit* because these things naturally grow in a person as they pursue a lifestyle of knowing the Lord.

This fruit doesn't just refer to what YOU become, it describes the character of the Spirit of Christ Himself. Sharing life with Someone who is steadfastly patient, faithful, gentle and kind is an absolute joy and nourishment to the soul. The Lord's unchangeable nature is restful and soothing. While I am thrilled to report that my character has dramatically improved since I met Jesus Christ, the greatest thrill has been living with a divine Person whose character is all of the things that Paul describes, and never changes. And by some miracle of love and God's amazing grace, I get to live with THAT guy, every day!

A warning as we go forward: you will wonder at times, is she talking about the Father, the Son, or the Holy Spirit? The answer is yes! I am only now becoming aware of distinctions between how Father, Son and Spirit relate to me. Mostly I don't try to figure it out, though I have begun to notice a difference in their pet names for me. I assume if I need to know exactly who I am interacting with, they will let me know. So forgive me if I don't parse it all out for you. They are all, equally, *The Lord.* Generally I assume I am interacting with the Spirit who abides in me, but at times I become aware it is Father God or Jesus.

Life With My Spirit Friend

It wasn't easy in the beginning, because I kept getting in the way. I kept trying to be — religious. By that I mean, trying to focus on holding God in proper reverence, fearful of being too presumptuous with this Holy, Almighty God. I was very self-consciousness of my flaws, and didn't know how to make myself "see" and "hear" God.

The Spirit gradually helped me understand that the main problem was my failure to take the Lord at His word. I had not fully trusted in His invitation to come freely to Him as a beloved child who didn't need to figure it all out. So I threw caution to the wind and my religious restrictions out the window. I just went for it, and took the Lord's promises out for a spin. I actually felt the Spirit smile as I began to truly relax into this relationship.

When I quit trying to figure out how to see and hear God in the natural human way, and just believed in His Presence and voice, the ability to see and hear Him just came. The Spirit changed everything for me as I learned to respond to His friendly presence and perceive His voice of guidance, through the faculties of my spirit.

I awaken every day to my ever-present Friend, and say good morning to Him. The last thing I do before going to sleep is thank Him for the day together, and tell Him how much I love

Him. I don't think of the Lord or interact with Him every minute of the day, any more than the husband I love dearly. In both cases, we just naturally move in and out of one another's awareness and activity. The Spirit's main way of being with me is gentle, peaceful, and quietly present.

He Is A Person!

God has become a real person to me, and I'm on a continual journey of getting to know Him as one. I find the personality of God to be embracing, supportive, warm, loving, tender, fun, compassionate, mischievous, smart, joyful, creative, understanding, long suffering, generous and gracious. In a word, He is good. The sheer goodness of God has stunned me again and again as I have pressed into knowing Him. David wrote in Psalm 31 that God's goodness is actually stored up and reserved for those who fear Him and take refuge in Him. *It is true. It is true! It is wonderfully, faithfully true.*

It is appropriate to worship God because He is God, the Almighty Creator of the Universe. I want to worship Him when I see majestic mountains, whimsical wildflowers and the vast, powerful ocean. But what pulls worship right out of me these days is the sheer goodness of God. In a world where people increasingly use their freedom to be as selfish and rad and bad as they want to be, knowing Someone who is unwaveringly good is a feast for my soul. I am still amazed that He belongs to me, and I belong to Him. The word "goodness" in that list of the fruit of the Spirit once felt way less exciting than love, peace or joy... but the longer I know the Lord, the more life I get under my belt, the more magnificent that quality becomes to me.

Knowing Someone who is unwaveringly good is a feast for my soul.

It still seems odd to me that Jesus once corrected a man who addressed Him as "good teacher," but I do now understand why He then said, *"There is no one good but God alone."*[2] As a flesh and blood man on the earth like us, I imagine Jesus was also astounded by the sheer goodness of the God and Father He had come to know with the Spirit's help; so much so that even Jesus felt unworthy to share that label.

He Really Is Counselor, Comforter And Friend

Knowing the Lord is like sharing life with the most gentle and wise companion. Someone smarter than me is always present, happy to guide my way; always ready with wisdom when I don't know what to do. He cares about everything that concerns me, whether I need insight as I counsel a wounded soul; wisdom about buying that outfit I suddenly can't live without; or solving a computer issue. (The first time I realized God knew about computers, I laughed out loud. I'd been treating Him like a senior citizen who couldn't possibly know anything about these new-fangled things.)

I try to live by the Word that says, *"Find out what the Lord's will is"* in Ephesians 5:17. I want to live an obedient life, and there are times when I am faced with a hard thing to obey. Amazingly, God never manipulates or pressures me. In fact, God never makes us do anything; if He did, we would all be obedient and good all the time! He is patient, leaving me in my freedom, waiting for me to choose who I will be, and what I will do.

My choice to do what is right in His eyes is always met with His power to carry it out.

When I do choose to obey the Lord in the hard thing, He never fails to step up with the strength I need to do it. My choice to do

[2] Luke 18:19

what is right in His eyes is always met with His power to carry it out. Our covenant faithfulness to one another always meets in the middle: my choice, His power.

The Spirit's Energy At Work

One day the Teacher quickened me to Paul's words in Philippians 2:13, "*... it is God who works in you to will and to act according to His good purpose.*" Looking up "works" in the Greek, I learned it is the word *energeo*, which of course means "energy." The Spirit is all-powerful, and this word *energeo* is the same one Paul used of the Spirit's work when He raised Christ from the dead!

We've always known the Spirit is powerful, but the idea of the Spirit's *energy* working in me in day-to-day life is easier to relate to. Remember: in covenant, the more powerful partner lends his strength to the weaker. When that "partner" is the all-powerful Spirit of God, we tend to expect His strength to show up as big boom booms, not a quiet, natural-feeling energy like our own. But it does.

For years Ron and I traveled much in the U.S. and some overseas countries, training pastors and teaching seminars on Covenant, Spirit Life and Grace. Typically we spent four weeks at a time in a place like Zambia, beginning with a schedule of a few main events in various venues. As soon as we would arrive and began working with pastors, every single day would fill up with back-to-back counseling, smaller events such as meetings with local pastors, and even all-day conferences. As middle-aged people in a foreign land, we knew the Spirit was helping us, because we always had the energy and inspiration to do everything asked of us. Apart from that, we didn't feel any special "power" from the Lord; we just felt like normal.

At the end of one trip, the Lord let us know just how much His energy had been sustaining us. Having been in transit from Zambia to London to the U.S. for 28 hours straight, we were happy to wake up in our own beds. We knew we'd be a bit weary from traveling halfway around the world after weeks of exertion, but as we got out of bed we were so weak we could barely move — all day. We wondered if we had picked up a virus in transit. Then the Lord said to us, *"There is nothing wrong with you; now that you are done I've lifted the special anointing that has sustained you all through the trip."*

He was allowing us to realize just how much we had been working in the energy of the Spirit through our strenuous month of ministry. What seemed to be "naturally us" had been "supernaturally Him" all the time, physically, mentally and spiritually. It was a personal confirmation of Luke's words in Acts 17:28, that *in Him we live and move and have our being.*

This showed me two things: first, God's awesome power in me is metered down to an everyday energy that feels very natural, like my own energy. I would not know the Spirit's energy is at work in me if the Word of God had not told me. Second, Philippians 2:13 says the Spirit's energy is quietly working to stir up desire in me for the very thing God wants of me, or that is right for the hour I find myself in.

To think that God was actually stirring HIS desires in MY heart was a huge step forward into knowing God for me. It corrected a misconception that had been instilled in me by well-meaning preachers who warned us to be suspicious of all personal desires, usually quoting Jeremiah 17:9 that *"the heart is deceitful above all things, and beyond cure."*

That Scripture quickly came to mind when the Spirit lit my lamp over Philippians 2:13. Conflict!! So I asked the Lord, *"Is my heart deceitful and my desires not to be trusted, as this Scripture says?"* The Spirit answered, *"This is not true of the redeemed heart in which I am known."* Of course the heart in which God *is known* is not deceitful! I love it when He spreads truth on my baloney sandwich.

It makes sense that the Spirit is always trying to direct us into His will. I saw that a more natural way of walking with the Lord would happen if I began with the assumption that a desire stirring in me was probably from the Lord until proven otherwise. As I relaxed into this, life with the Lord took on a new ease of working together.

I've learned that if I can't get something off of my mind, it's probably on His. Furthermore, the Lord doesn't have to wrestle with my self-mistrust as He guides my heart. As I walked in this way more and more, I gradually became more bold and confident in expressing the Lord's thoughts, love and ministry to others. The Lord and I are a better team now, and the joy factor in our partnership is big — all because He revealed how He is always at work in me, even when I'm just minding my own business. In fact, the lines are getting increasingly blurred between His business and my business, and that's a good thing.

When I decided to get over my self-consciousness and self-doubts, and stop shrinking back from what I sensed the Spirit was stirring me to do, the flow of God's life grew from a trickle to a steady stream that nourishes me and those I encounter. For example, when I enter a room, if I am drawn to a particular person I assume the Lord wants to touch them in some way. I may not know what it is, but if I go to them and engage, the Lord will make it clear. Usually He will bring a question to mind that draws the person out about something important to them, or about which He wants to encourage them. So I do.

What happens is that as the Lord directs my attention, He creates a meeting between Himself and another person. He positions me to hear what He already knew, and allows me to feel His own heart and desire towards that soul. If I feel compassion for them I know it is His compassion. The attention I give them is the Lord expressing His love, however small, by noticing and uplifting them. This is not robotic; it is not a duty or me engaging in "ministry." I actually feel the love for them the Lord feels. I *want* to give something to them; I *want* to uplift them. The feelings are as strong as if they've come out of my own heart. The difference is that now, knowing God and knowing me, I know where those feelings originate: His

Spirit, dwelling in mine. In the end, we feel His feelings together, and my task is to act upon them in a way that the Lord gets to express His heart to another. I believe this is the compassion Jesus knew that motivated Him so deeply towards people. The Spirit stirred the Father's passions in Jesus. The same Spirit is stirring in you, no matter how little or long you have known Him.

If you knew the timid soul I once was, you would know this is not arrogance talking, but confidence and boldness that have come from hanging out with the Spirit of Jesus. After all, it was His idea to entrust ordinary souls with His Kingdom. He began with those twelve flawed, selfish, brash, ignorant, hungry, scared, fickle dreamers, and poured His life into them. He fed them the bread of His life, and they became bread to those in their world as the Spirit's energy flowed up out of their trusting hearts.

The Lord is continually trying to express Himself through us. Trying analyze this hinders the flow of His life in me. Trying to manage what God is doing is not nearly as productive as simply trusting Him, and even *trusting myself in Him*. If He is willing to risk it in me, then I should be as well. That said, I never presume I am perceiving Him perfectly; but neither am I anxious about it. The only way I could learn to walk with the Spirit was to get over the continual fear of getting it wrong. God's gracious Presence tends to swallow up fear and anxiety.

The Tender And Intimate Love Of The Lord

I once heard a speaker ask the question, "Does your life show that Jesus can be trusted?" Her question has inspired me for years, motivating me to live with my whole being thrust upon the Lord, to see what He would do with it. I expected life to be blessed as I learned to know God. I expected to become more like Christ. I expected some peace and joy. What I did not expect was God's tender and intimate ways with me, His gentle and affectionate personality.

When I first began to experience His tender love, it startled me. I even wondered, has my imagination gone too far? Could the creator of the universe really be so familiar and friendly and funny and affectionate? But the next time I experienced it, and the time after that, and the time after that, I just wept at the joy of feeling so deeply loved, so tenderly cared for.

As I began to enjoy God, I moved from a determination to know Him to a real delight in Him. He makes me laugh. He teases me. I have sensed Him holding me as I cried. When I understand what He is feeling or thinking, and share the moment with Him, I sense He loves it when I "get" Him. These are the little things that become big things in my heart, reinforcing my faith that I share life with a living, wonderful Person.

As I write this book, we have a history now, and His tender mercies no longer surprise me, except when they come at a time when I have failed Him in some way. This never ceases to amaze me. The Lord has ways of phrasing things that are part of our personal vocabulary, just as one has with human intimates. My journals — my book of life shared with God — are full of messages from the Lord: wonderful, wise, personal things. This is a special treasure, hearing things from the Lord that belong to just you and Him, never before heard or shared with another. I encourage you to go find your own love language with the Lord, and write your own book of life with Him.

Perhaps you are wondering: is this Scriptural? Where does the Bible promise this kind of intimate experience with the Lord? The answer is found in one of God's favorite words for covenant relationship: *rest.* Understanding the concept of rest as God uses the word not only validates this intimacy, it reveals the overall quality of life one experiences in knowing the Lord.

Dwelling Together In Intimacy

Moses used the word *rest* in Deuteronomy 33:12 as he spoke the Lord's birthright blessing over the tribe of Benjamin:

Let the beloved of the Lord rest secure in Him, for He shields Him all day long, and the one the Lord loves rests between His shoulders.

This reminds me of John leaning intimately against the bosom of Jesus as they reclined at the meal table. I sometimes rest between His shoulders, laying my head on His chest, near His heart. Moses' words gave me permission. As we will learn in the next chapter, rest belongs to the one the Lord loves.

The word translated as *rest* in this verse is the Hebrew word *shakan.* It is also used when God tells Moses in the Sinai desert:

Then have them make a sanctuary for me, and I will dwell [shakan] *among them. (Exodus 25:8)*

Shakan has the basic meaning of dwelling with another in committed relationship, but also has the idea of *revealing.* It's like the difference between college roommates and a married couple. Roommates just share a house, while married couples reveal themselves entirely to one another.

God was announcing His commitment to dwell in the midst of the people so He could reveal Himself (His glory) to them. In fact, the word *shakan* is where the word *shekinah* comes from, as in "the skekinah glory" of God. It speaks of the Presence of God which produces a visible change in the atmosphere.

We are now the dwelling place of God on earth! In fact, the Apostle Paul quotes Exodus 25:8 when he writes:

For we are the temple of the living God. As God has said: "I will live with them and walk among them, and I will be their God, and they will be my people." (2nd Corinthians 6:16)

In the beginning it truly amazed me to realize the God who created the universe actually wanted to reveal Himself uniquely to me — and to every child of His grace. But amazement has faded into something more like, "Of course!" as I have experienced the fellowship of the Father, Son and Spirit, who have given me a real taste of their grace, goodness and glory.

The Counselor At Midnight

Living with the Spirit is like having the best marriage counselor on call at all times — as I shared earlier in the story of our marriage. In addition to the wisdom the Spirit provides through His written Word, He is available to personally counsel us 24/7, which is really handy if you're having a fight with hubby just before bedtime. (The book I've written for women, *"The Woman God Designed,"* is full of stories of how the Lord personally mentored me in being a good wife and mother.)

The Spirit taught me to make Jesus' command in John 13:34 my goal: *"Love others as I have loved you."* The Spirit has personally modeled love for me as I have known Him, so I have experienced what it is like to be loved in the best possible way. I've been so nourished by the love of Jesus that I want to give the same to my husband and others.

It is easier to give what you have personally received than try to follow a set of instructions. I have been loved; now I know how to love, and I have His ever-present help. This is part of God's plan to fill the earth with His glory, in every nook and cranny of the world, in every nook and cranny of your heart.

His Graciousness Covers My Weaknesses

I wish I could say knowing God has made me and my life perfect. This is what one tends to expect from walking with God, but that's not my story. I don't share all these things with you because I'm qualified by a perfect life. If I have any "qualification" to write as I do, it is that I am an ordinary human being who fails at times, and knows what it is like to share life with a God who isn't put off by that. God really does love to show off His strength in my weakness; it's a great partnership!

I still wrestle with people, including my beloved husband, over the normal issues of life. I still struggle with tendencies like selfishness and procrastination; I'm tempted to connive to get my way more often than I like to admit. I have vanities; I have follies, like unfinished projects that languish while I start new ones. This book is getting finished a month past deadline because I couldn't tear myself away from the garden when spring began springing. My husband could tell you other things about me, both ordinary and maddening, such as a tendency to multitask when I'm supposed to be hanging out with him.

God seems amazingly undaunted by these things, showing God-sized patience, never controlling or manipulating. One of the things I marvel about the Lord is He doesn't make me change. He shows me wisdom in His Word, but leaves me in my freedom to be as stubborn or foolish as I like until I go to Him of my own volition and say, *"Lord, I want to change in this, please help me!"*

Believe it or not, I am far less consistent in my devotion to my Lord and Friend than He deserves. When I fail the Lord in some way, I tend to expect judgment and rebuke because I know I deserve it, yet He always meets me with patience, grace and understanding. I once heard a nationally known preacher say God's mercy had been a bigger test to Him than anything else about Him. I agree. We naturally expect judgment from a perfect, holy God. The Lord's mercy always challenges my tendency to beat myself up. One day while I was in that mode He said to me, *"I'm not joining you in that."*

I definitely feel the Lord's disappointment and disapproval when I fall short of His glory, but only as a doting father who wants to help me be better. He will show me where I went wrong, open my eyes to the result of my bad choices, and comfort me in failure.

It took me quite a while to relax into God's mercy and grace, especially where it concerns what I call my "besetting sins" — my habitual ways of being that fall short of His righteousness. It is always right to confess and ask forgiveness when we fail; but going back to God for the same thing over and over feels like an abuse of His grace. I'm sure it *is* an abuse of His grace. Again, He who told us to forgive "seven times seventy"[3] does this Himself! There is no hypocrisy in Him, and He is full of graciousness. The more I know God, the more I see how deeply gracious He truly is.

The more I know God, the more I see how deeply gracious He truly is.

Still, this does not make me relax regarding sin and disobedience. On the contrary: His kindness not only leads me to repentance, it increases my desire to please Him. Being treated this way inspires me to be a better daughter more than shame or guilt ever has.

When you live by faith that the Spirit is your ever-present Friend who witnesses all you do, say and think, it makes you more aware of the differences between your private and public behavior. It is easy to put on our best behavior in the presence of parents and others, while letting ourselves slack a bit in private (or with those whose opinions of us don't matter quite as much.) Integrity is being the same with everyone, or no one else around. Knowing the one you want to impress the most is always right with you tends to help you live on your best behavior all the time. That's the effect it has had on me.

I confess that I wonder at times if I fear the Lord enough as *Almighty God.* But there again, I trust the Spirit will lead me in that way, revealing truth about such things, because I've asked Him to do so. For now, He seems okay with being the Father I adore so much I can't bear to disappoint Him, or cause Him to be ashamed or grieved because of my thoughts or behavior.

---

[3] In other words, don't even bother to count, just keep forgiving! See Matthew 18:21-22.

Love Never Fails

Fearing God looks entirely different *outside* of covenant with Him, than it does from the *inside.* Outside, one is facing the impersonal Judge who enforces justice. Inside, one faces the Father who is raising you in love, teaching you good character, and mentoring you in the ways of justice and righteousness. Because you are His child, you live in His favor and good graces. But the flip side of this reality is that in knowing God, sin becomes much more personal, because we have moved from following rules to following a Person. It is easier to break a rule than disappoint someone you love.

It is easier to break a rule than disappoint someone you love.

Jesus once said to His disciples, *"The prince of this world is coming, but he has no hold on me. The world must learn that I love the Father and do exactly what He tells me."* Notice that Jesus connected His love for the Father with His ability to be strong against temptation. I believe this is one reason Paul elevated love above faith and hope, because *"love never fails."* We will do things out of love that we might not do for any other reason.

There have been times when the Lord has asked something of me that greatly tested my trust in Him. The first was when He told me to go back to my husband when I had given up on our marriage and my love had died; another was when the Lord insisted that I give up smoking, after waiting five years for me to quit on my own. I knew each time that I still had the freedom to choose otherwise; but by then I had read the Bible enough to understand that disobeying the Lord would be like saying to Him, *"I really don't love you."*[4]

---

[4] John 14:15-24. Jesus says those who love Him obey Him; those who don't, do not love Him!

Somewhere in knowing God, my desire to love Him faithfully took me to a level of obedience I had not known before. This is, of course, God's plan. The goal of loving God multiplies His opportunities to transform me and my life into the image of His Son. When I came to love God for real, His hook was in my heart, and He knew it. He didn't have to pull out the law anymore; He merely had to tug on my heart.

I must pause and say that while I know the Lord much better than 20 years ago, I am sure I have only a glimpse of Him, perhaps five percent of what is knowable![5] This is impossible to measure; but the point of this book is that however little or much I know of the Lord has already given me abundant life.

I'm sure there is much more of Him to know if I would press in even more than I do. So I haven't arrived in knowing God; I'm just the one who is about nine miles ahead of some on a 200 mile trek, sending back wisdom for the journey just ahead. Knowing God has become the treasure I seek, have found, and keep finding. The more I find, the more I want.

Knowing God has become the treasure I seek, have found, and keep finding.

My purpose here has been to share what my unique life is like with the Spirit. There is much more to learn about sharing life with the Spirit, which is the subject of another book in this series called *Spirit Life*. However, there is an Appendix at the end of this book listing the most prominent Scriptures concerning the Spirit's roles in a disciple's life, entitled "The Roles of The Holy Spirit." I encourage you to make a little study of it and ponder the truths He reveals.

[5] 1 Corinthians 13:12

15 A Life God Calls Rest

The New Testament book of Hebrews is unique among the 66 books of the Bible. The author — who remains unknown — wrote to an audience of Jewish converts in order to convince them of the absolute supremacy and sufficiency of Jesus Christ to bring them into a new covenant of God's grace. The author thoroughly contrasts the Old Covenant of Law the Jews had always lived under with the New Covenant of Christ, to prove that Jesus the Christ is superior to the prophets, to angels, to Moses, and the priestly line of Aaron. He explains that the Jews cannot return to or continue the Old Covenant system they followed under Moses; that they must now look only to Jesus Christ. The atoning death, resurrection and ascension of Jesus Christ, he says, have opened the way into the true, heavenly sanctuary of God's presence.

Hebrews explains the New Covenant of Christ in greater detail than any other Bible book. It quotes the New Covenant promises twice, in Chapters 8 and 10. One day as I read this book the Spirit riveted my attention to the author's passionate plea in Chapters 3 and 4 for God's people to "enter God's rest."

I knew from my studies that *rest* was a reference to the Sabbath rest God commanded His people to observe by the cessation of all work on the seventh day of each week. It fascinated me that in the midst of telling God's people to abandon the Old Covenant law for the New Covenant of grace, the author begs the reader to enter this rest with God:

There remains, then, a Sabbath-rest for the people of God; for anyone who enters God's rest also rests from their works, just as God did from His. Let us, therefore, make every effort to enter that rest, so that no one will perish by following their example of disobedience. (Hebrews 4:9-11)

The author sounds an alarm, pointing back to a terrible event under Moses where the people rebelled against God by refusing to take the land He had given them. The author does not mince words as he pleads, "*....make every effort to enter that rest, so that no one will perish by following their example...*" The author wants his readers to learn from the mistakes the Hebrews made so long ago, which cost them everything God was offering.

Apparently the Sabbath rest was still crucial to God, though it would have new meaning under the New Covenant. I wanted to know what that was. I heed warnings from people who know God. Like the Hebrews of old, we have a promised life waiting for us, just as they had a promised land. We are offered a new life to be lived in God's grace and favor, a life which will be defined by knowing the Living God and being adopted into His family as brothers and sisters of the firstborn, Jesus Christ.

Their Promised Land — Our Promised Life

Once God brought the Hebrews out of their bondage in Egypt, He entered covenant with them, then led them on a journey to what Moses called their place of rest: the Promised Land. There all of God's promises for their new life were to be fulfilled, because of a covenant made on their behalf between God and Abraham long before they were born. But when the time came for them go to in and possess the land, they refused when they saw they would have to fight giants and dislodge the current inhabitants in order to take possession of it.

They panicked, certain that God was callously sending them out to let them and their children die. [1] So not only did they break their covenant promise to obey God, they completely

---

[1] Numbers 13:26 – 14:4

maligned God's character! How could they think so badly of Him who had done so much to set them free from their slavery?

The truth is that in spite of all His amazing power displays in Egypt, God was essentially a stranger to them. They had heard of Him while in their slavery, the old stories of their ancestors Abraham, Isaac and Jacob; but they had never personally experienced His presence. When He came for them and forced Pharoah to release them through fierce and terrible acts, it was wonderful and terrible all at once; wonderful because He set them free; terrible because slaves don't know what to do with their freedom. Plus, when you're following a fierce God you barely know, a familiar pot of stew and one's own bed in slavery can look much more inviting than manna, a desert, and giants you've never faced before.

As a result, the Hebrews ended up living in a kind of "no man's land" the rest of their days; free, but not enjoying the life they had been set free to live. They wandered around (in their salvation) for 40 years, not going back to their former bondage, still having God's presence to protect and provide; but in very limited measure compared to what they would have had. They had boring manna when they could have had fruit, vegetables, meat and honey. Their shoes never wore out, but they could have lived a settled life in fine homes instead of living as nomads in tents.

The same Spirit who tried to lead the Hebrews to their Promised Land must be allowed to lead us into our promised life.

Their fear of the giants and the work required to possess their land is like our fear of living in total dependence upon a God we barely know, and the work of learning a new way of life. Faith brings us into covenant with God, but the same Spirit who tried to lead the Hebrews to their Promised Land must also be allowed to lead us all the way into our promised life of knowing God.

Rest: A Portrait Of Covenant Life

As I pondered the plea in the book of Hebrews to enter God's rest, I thought of how often I had encountered language about "rest" in the Old Testament. In light of the warning in Hebrews, I decided it would be valuable to assemble all the major references about rest in one place and see what emerged. I discovered a rich treasure trove of truth that described the quality my life had taken on as I had pursued knowing God! I was pretty amazed. Having practiced my grand experiment of knowing God these many years, *rest* is exactly how life with God has felt to me since I received the gift of God's Spirit.

***Rest* is exactly how life with God has felt since I received the gift of God's Spirit.**

Sabbath Rest: Peace With God

The Hebrew word for sabbath is *shabbaton*, which means to cease working and rest. Though the Sabbath command appears to be all about what God expected His people to do, the reciprocal nature of covenant reminds us it was a two-sided coin. By this I mean that in giving this command God also affirmed His commitment to be as holy to His people as He was asking them to be to Him. Their way of being holy to Him was to call Him their God and worship Him alone. His way of being holy to them was to set His love and attention upon them, blessing them uniquely, covering them in His protective power. In sabbathing together God honored the descendants of Abraham in the world's eyes as being their God, completely dedicated to them, and the enemy of anyone who might want to harm them.

Thus the Sabbath rest was holy because it was a day set apart just for God and His people to share, to strengthen their relationship, as well as provide refreshment and renewal. I don't think we realize how very extraordinary it is to be invited to rest with God. The so-called "gods" of other religions offered no such rest; only sacrifices, offerings and rituals by which people had to earn their blessings. In stark contrast, the God of the Hebrews said, "Come rest with me," signaling His value for relationship over rituals.

For all these reasons, Jesus said in Mark 2:27 that the Sabbath was meant to be a gift to man, not a burden! The Jews kept the law of the Sabbath, but unfortunately ended up focusing on the legal observance of it more than focusing on the One who offered them true rest in His covenant love.

Rest: A Sign Of Our Oneness With God

The Sabbath rest wasn't just a mini-vacation. God declared in Exodus 31:17 that the Sabbath was to be a sign to the world that a covenant of peace existed between Him and His people. The Sabbath testified, *"These are my people, and I am their God. We are at peace with one another, therefore we rest together."* In this context, being at peace with God is a reference to the covenant oneness we share, which we learned about in Chapter Six.

The Sabbath rest was a sign of peace with God in the Old Covenant, but *in the New Covenant we are given true rest in the*

The God of the Hebrews said *Come rest with me*, signaling His value for relationship over rituals.

Presence of the Holy Spirit, the one who joins us to God. In fact, the Greek word *eiro* — translated "peace" in the New

Testament — has the root meaning "to join." To say we are at peace with God is a reference to our covenant union with Him.

Because we are joined to Him through the New Covenant of Christ, and one with Him in spirit,[2] an eternal peace now exists between us. He affirms this by calling us to rest with Him as a permanent member of His family. We cannot lose God or His Spirit. His covenant promises ensure that we will always be forgiven when we ask; that we can know Him in personal experience; that His love and favor will never be removed from us. We can disappoint the Lord, grieve Him, or even make Him angry, but none of these will cost us His love or destroy our covenant of peace. We can rest now.

Rest describes the nature and quality of new covenant life shared with God.

While the Covenant seals us together with the Lord in a new life, rest describes the nature and quality of that shared life. Rest is God's own word to describe the fullness of life He offers His people through knowing Him.

Koinonia: The Privilege Of Fellowship With God

The Sabbath rest was also given as *koinonia,* or fellowship, which is the privilege of all who are joined in covenant relationship. And even though we do not live under the *law* of Sabbath, the wisdom of setting aside times of physical rest with the Lord remains. Today more than ever, we dearly need to rest from work to renew strength and life. In sharing our rest with the Lord we strengthen our connection, nourish ourselves more deeply in His Word, and take time to honor Him with thanksgiving.

I believe the Lord loves this time, much like every parent who waits for grown children to come home for a visit. It was

[2] 1 Corinthians 6:17

meant to be less of an obligation than a privilege of intimacy, like family Thanksgivings. Going home to reconnect, eat food, share life and play games is an obligation of love for your family, but its larger value is in the intimate knowing of one another that people outside your family don't have. In covenant, you get to hang out with the Lord.

Congregating with other believers in church is wonderful, but a sabbath does not imply spending hours in a service once a week. Sometimes a lot of church activity actually wears one out instead of refreshing, especially if you're a worker bee there. Working and supporting your local church is fine, but may offer nothing to give you a true time of rest with the Lord, and you need that on a regular basis, built somewhere into your life.

The Spirit has taught me that a sabbath can be any time I step aside from life as usual to rest and refresh with the Lord. It can be a walk with the Lord in the cool of the day; it can be fasting and prayer to recharge body, soul and spirit; it includes play and recreation. In fact, I've found that God is big on recreation rest, as long as you don't leave Him out of it.

The Family Meal

In the covenant under Moses, God called for various offerings, each of which served a special purpose in maintaining the health of one's relationship to Him. Some offerings were for acknowledging and atoning for sin, in order to restore justice and good standing. One offering expressed total consecration to the Lord. Another was prescribed just for celebrating the relationship, called the Peace or Fellowship offering. The latter reminds me of our American Thanksgiving, since the worshipper used it to express his gratitude for God's blessings.

In each case, the worshipper brought an animal to the priest, who killed it, poured out its blood at the altar, and burned some of its fat on the altar as God's share. Then, except for a breast portion given to the priest, the rest of the meat was given to the family to roast and eat in the presence of the Lord, *with joy.* (An interesting note: the sin offering for a priest was burned entirely, with the skin on, so the stink of it wafted towards heaven and among one's community. But the worship and celebration offerings were burned *without* the skin, and God called these *a pleasing aroma.* He could tell just by the smell whether His child was repenting of sin or preparing to celebrate their relationship with a barbecue. Smile.)

The Lord's Covenant Meal

God likes family meals, and you belong at His table. Our communion meal, our celebration of the supper of the Lamb, is a remembrance and thanksgiving for all Christ has done for us. It is our peace and fellowship meal. Of course, it is always right to examine oneself before partaking of it, to consider our faithfulness to the Lord and His people. If we are in need of forgiveness from the Lord or another, we take care of that first; then we go joyfully to the table of the Lord, celebrating the relationship of great grace we share with Him and the Body. The Spirit of Christ is the living host at this table. His table and His meal serve to remind us that He is our faithful God and we are His beloved people.

How do we enter God's rest? By believing in our covenant with the Lord Jesus Christ, and sharing all of life with the Holy Spirit. He alone can bring us into and keep us in the rest God offers through knowing Him.

A Home For The Heart

The Hebrews had another word for rest which they used to refer to the security of covenant oneness and belonging: *me'nuah.* It meant "to be settled down in a permanent home."

Moses used *me'nuah* to refer to the Promised Land in Deuteronomy 12:9 as "the resting place" that God was giving His people, where they would settle down and end their days as desert nomads. Naomi used the word *me'nuah* to refer to the security of covenant love when she said to her daughters-in-law:

> *May the Lord grant that each of you will find rest in the home of another husband. (Ruth 1:9)*

Most of us aren't nomads, but before I came to Christ, my heart was a chronic wanderer. I like to think of *me'nuah* as finding a home for the heart. The value of doing a word study on the Hebrew and Greek words is discovering how the original writers used those words. For instance, David used *me'nuah* in Psalm 116:7 when he wrote, *"Be at rest once more, O my soul, for the Lord has been good to you."* David was instructing his soul to return to its confidence that God's committed love would not fail him in whatever he was facing.

David's life reveals many reasons for his faith to be tested, as he was no stranger to danger, war, and betrayal — especially at the hands of the very people he loved and served. His faith in God's faithfulness was an anchor for his soul in the storms of life, but that faith didn't come out of nowhere. It came from a life of knowing God as the Spirit revealed Him, in his shepherd hills and on the battlefield. I have borrowed David's prayer occasionally when my faith has been hammered by storms of life, letting it carry me past the focus on my problems to the remembrance of how often God has already been faithful to me.

When the author of Hebrews wrote of entering God's rest, He quoted Psalm 95:11 where "rest" is *me'nuah*. Both authors used rest to invoke the picture of a heart that is secure in belonging to and being faithfully loved by the covenant Friend. Regardless of what is going on *outside*, rest is what should be

Regardless of what is going on *outside*, rest is what should be going *inside*, where God is known in the heart of His child.

going *inside*, where God is known in the heart of His child. This is what it feels like to me as I know God these days.

My Heart Is Secure In God's Love

Incredibly, I feel my preciousness to God every day. I am easily on the "least of these" end of the scale, [3] but that's okay! It is enough that I am His and He is mine, forever. I believe. I don't just believe in God, I believe in His personal love for me. Through the Spirit's guidance, I have become rooted and established in this love. I never doubt that God is near and is pleased for me to lean against Him intimately; I never doubt that He will receive me after I've failed Him.

I feel my place in the family. I feel watched over. I feel hopeful in His helpful presence, as if I can face anything because He's there. We are comfortable in here together. In our shared life of intimate connection, it is far from perfect on my part. I am constantly aware of and grateful for His graciousness to let me grow into what He created me to be.

The Presence of the Lord has healed all my shame and sense of unworthiness.

As I have come to know God, fear and anxiety over my imperfections have faded away. When the Spirit disturbs our restful life together to reveal what He is ready to change in me, I know it will probably be uncomfortable or even hurt a bit, but I'm not afraid. I know now what life looks like on the other side of pruning and refining. [4]

The Presence of the Lord has healed all my shame and sense of unworthiness. Though in fact I am not worthy of the Lord living in me, that is not the point. The point is He honors

---

[3] Hebrews 8:11

[4] John 15:1-2; Hebrews 12:5-11

me with His Presence anyway, which has caused my sense of worth to rise. I am not referring to having more self-esteem, which is the worth I assign to myself; I am talking about *identity.* I am and forever will be a beloved daughter of the Most High God.

Your Heart Is God's Chosen Resting Place

Isaiah used *me'nuah* to describe the dwelling place of Jesus:

> *"...for the earth will be filled with the knowledge of the Lord as the waters cover the sea. In that day the Root of Jesse will stand as a banner for the peoples; the nations will rally to Him, and His resting place will be glorious. (Isaiah 11:9b-10).*

Now remember what Jesus said about His faithful disciples:

> *Anyone who loves me will obey my teaching. My Father will love them, and we will come to them and make our home with them. (John 14:23)*

Jesus spoke passionately and clearly in John Chapters 14 and 15 about His abiding in you, and your abiding in Him. You are His chosen resting place, His permanent home on earth, sealed by a covenant promise. Where Jesus abides — and where He is free to live and move and have His being — His glory is meant to be revealed. And it will be revealed as we live our lives responding obediently to His Presence.

As I have written, rest not only refers to the security of a covenant, it also describes the quality of life within that relationship. While I have written of what it is like for you to know God, it is good to also consider what it might be like for God to know you, sharing life in that heart of yours.

Can God Rest In You?

The Lord is also looking for rest in knowing you. In other words, He seeks restfulness in relating to you, as any person would; rest as opposed to wrestling, disciplining or grieving. The Apostle Paul refers to this dynamic in Ephesians:

> *And do not grieve the Holy Spirit of God, with whom you were sealed for the day of redemption. Get rid of all bitterness, rage and anger, brawling and slander, along with every form of malice. Be kind and compassionate to one another, forgiving each other, just as in Christ God forgave you. (Ephesians 4:30-32)*

Let me be clear: when I speak of the Lord being able to rest in you, I am not referring to whether He is *with you* or not; His covenant Presence is never in question. Nor am I implying that anything you do could cause a change in God. His Word assures us He is immutable (unchanging) in His nature. [5]

To say God is not at rest within you simply means His experience of you and His response to you must be different than when all is well with your soul, and between you and the Lord. Think of a parent whose child puts them in a position to discipline or be grieved over them, instead of being able to enjoy the quiet peace, joy and goodness that we experience when all is right between us. It doesn't change who they are or how the parent loves the child, it changes their experience of the child.

God is at rest with you when His Spirit is not contending with barriers of doubt and fear — and thus able to love and bless you freely. He can rest with you when there are no rivals for your devotion. When the Lord finds faith and faithfulness in our hearts, He can rest with us because He is not having to witness us walk in rebellion, deception, unforgiveness or bitterness. Consider the command and warning from the Lord that you must forgive others — and that as long as you do not forgive, the Lord will not forgive you. Think of the position you put the Lord in when you do not forgive.

The Lord's love for us will never waver, and His abiding in us is a covenant promise and fact. Yet His Spirit cannot rest

---

[5] See Hebrews 13:8 and James 1:17.

with us when the heart of His child is consumed by anger or wrong judgments about others. When we live in fear or anxiety, the Spirit surely grieves in some measure until we turn to Him for truth and healing. Until we do, we demonstrate little faith that He can and will make a difference in our heart condition. God rests best with us when He sees that we truly trust Him, are enjoying His love and grace, and behaving like His Son.

As I have shared life with God, the Spirit has made me aware of this dynamic as I have increasingly known Him as a Person. As a result I have purposed to make my heart a place of real rest for the Lord. As He lives in me I want Him to know me as one who yields, not fighting with Him; trusting, not questioning His motives; taking private thoughts captive and making them obedient to Him when they are unwise, untrue or unkind. I believe these goals have accelerated the process of knowing Him.

God rests best with us when we truly trust Him, are enjoying His love and grace, and behaving like His Son.

In short, you can give God grief, or you can give Him joy. You can delight Him, [6] and give His soul rest in knowing you. That's what I'm going for.

The study of God's rest is too vast to teach here, but I wanted you to understand why Hebrews begs us to enter into God's rest without fail, and how rest relates to our New Covenant. I hope with all my heart you will enter God's rest as you know Him in your own unique life, and enjoy the fullness of God's covenant grace.

---

[6] See Psalm 35:27; Zephaniah 3:17; Matthew 12:18.

16 Removing Barriers To Entering God's Rest

Therefore, since the promise of entering His rest still stands, let us be careful that none of you be found to have fallen short of it. (Hebrews 4:1)

So what is it that we can fall short of? Surely you can guess by now: we can fall short of entering into the full covenant life made possible through Christ. I wrote this book because I now share the passion of the author of Hebrews for making sure Christians don't settle for anything less than the fullness of covenant grace offered to them. There is more to learn from Hebrews about why some struggle.

Symptoms of restlessness: not knowing God's ways, never being sure what He wants of us, or how to respond to the challenges of life.

Obstacles To Entering God's Life

Hebrews 3:7-11 describes why people do not find rest — or enjoy the life God is offering:

So, as the Holy Spirit says: "Today, if you hear His voice, do not harden your hearts as you did in the rebellion, during the time of testing in the wilderness, where your ancestors tested and tried me, though for forty years they

> *saw what I did. That is why I was angry with that generation; I said, 'Their hearts are always going astray, and they have not known my ways.' So I declared on oath in my anger, 'They shall never enter my rest.'" (Hebrews 3:7-11)*

We are first warned to not allow our hearts to become hard. A hard heart is one that is insensitive or resistant to God. A hard heart develops for many reasons: unbelief; wounds of the heart; unforgiveness; chronic disappointment with life, God or other people. It is human nature to build a wall around our hearts to make ourselves feel safe — even from God.

Another problem is a heart that goes astray of God. A heart going astray is a heart turned aside to its own agenda or pursuits, not valuing or believing God. A heart gone astray may simply be off doing Christianity its own way, not heeding God's voice and guidance. God wants to lead us by His voice, as the author of Hebrews makes clear. He repeats three times in short order, *"Today, if you hear His voice, do not harden your hearts..."*

When we do not hear God's voice, we easily succumb to insecurity about His love. Our hearts wander off looking for life, love and satisfaction in all the wrong places. This is what leads to the ultimate symptoms of restlessness: not knowing God's ways, never being sure what He wants of us or how to respond to the challenges of life. We may well belong to God, but we are certainly not walking *with* God towards our promised life. Such a life is marked by uncertainty, confusion, even darkness.

It Begins With Unbelief

Hebrews 3:19 reveals the main issue standing between us and our promised life when it says *they were not able to enter, because of their unbelief.* The issue was not whether the Hebrews under Moses believed in God, for clearly they did; they saw His mighty works and heard His voice thundering from the mountain on fire. The unbelief that blocked their way was this:

not believing God would be faithful to bring them to a safe and complete possession of their Promised Land. When God declared in His anger, *"they will never enter my rest,"* He wasn't just judging them for failing to obey; He was angry because their disbelief was an accusation against His character.

It is important to point out that the Greek word translated as *disobeyed* in these verses is also translated as *disbelief.* Because this word is translated just as often either way, most Bibles include a footnote showing the reader the alternative. The Greek word being translated is *apeitheo*, which my favorite Greek dictionary defines as *"Not to believe, implying disobedience also. To disobey as through unbelief."*[1] The very definition of the word shows the relationship between disobedience and disbelief. They go hand in hand: disbelief leads to disobedience, and disobedience reveals an unbelieving heart.

For those who belong to God, the issue will always be about God's character and His Word. Distrust and unbelief reveal insecurity about God's motives and a complete lack of faith in His character. Remember, the Hebrews didn't just rebel, they accused God of sending them to their death when the Spirit tried to lead them to their Promised Land — thus accusing God of the height of covenant unfaithfulness.

In spite of seeing the greatest wonders any living people have ever seen, their fear and accusations revealed that the Hebrews did not truly know the heart of their God. We cannot follow someone we do not know and trust. It was true for them; it is true for us. When we don't know and believe the truth about God, we will always struggle with trusting and obeying Him. In order to avoid their mistake we need to repent of our lack of faith in God's faithfulness. As long as we struggle with believing God, we will never enter His rest. *True faith is rest.*

There is one more important issue to consider, and that is the object of your faith.

---

[1] Page 1807, The Hebrew-Greek Key Word Study Bible, New American Standard Bible, ©1984 and 1990 by AMG International, Inc.

Misplaced Faith

The Hebrews had faith, but it was focused on the wrong thing: the assumption that God would establish them in the Promised Land without them having to fight for it. Their faith was not in God's character and Word, *it was in their own idea* of how it should play out according to their desires.

The focus of our faith is meant to be God Himself, not a certain result. This is a primary point made in Hebrews Chapter 11, where the heroes of faith are praised because they trusted in God wholeheartedly in spite of some promises not being fulfilled in their lifetimes.

Rest comes when one ceases to grasp at his own desire and accepts God's will instead.

You need two things to enter God's rest: faith in God, and a heart surrendered to Him in full trust. It begins as one ceases to grasp at His own desire and accepts God's will instead. In this, the soul rests, ceasing all scheming, figuring, conniving, planning and obsessing involved in bringing oneself the life desired. This surrender is what Jesus described when He said:

> *Whoever wants to be my disciple must deny themselves and take up their cross and follow me. For whoever wants to save their life will lose it, but whoever loses their life for me will find it. (Matthew 16:24-25)*

Surrender is burying the seed of "self" so it can grow into the life Christ offers.

Repentance And Rest

I've been sharing with you the wonderful changes in my life through knowing God, but it has not all been joyful. While my life is far from perfect, it has a quality above anything I ever imagined. Yet like the Hebrew people, I've had battles to fight in order to possess the life promised to me by the Lord. However, the enemies blocking my promised land were not giant people, they were the former residents who ruled my heart.

For a long season in those first years, life with God became a continual exchange of my truth and ways for His. In God's grace and mercy, I didn't have to face these things all at once; but day by day, the Spirit led me towards unclaimed territory, and there is yet more to conquer. Looking back, I am amazed at the process; how wise, gentle, and effective the Spirit has been in helping me overcome the things which stood between me and the life He holds out. I don't need to enumerate them for you, but I will say that they all lead back to one thing: ignorance or lack of faith in who God truly is. And I'm quite sure that my experience is the same which the Hebrew people faced before they could enter God's rest: the thing they had to overcome was self. The giants in the land didn't change; the people facing them did.

Repentance From Sin Brings Us To Rest

The longer I share life with Christ, the more clearly I see the vast difference between my character and life before Christ, and after. The day I gave my heart to the Lord I came to Him as a woman completely broken by the mess I had made of my life. My eyes were open, I thought, to how my own choices had been the source of everything gone wrong in my life. I later realized God had graciously refrained from revealing some of the uglier truths about my character and choices until a time when I was more mature and could bear them.

Each revelation deepened my thankfulness and love for this God who loved me and pursued me while I still lived in shades of sin and shame more awful than I ever realized. As He showed me the truth, I could seek His forgiveness with a greater accountability for the injustice I had committed against my

Lord. As I acknowledged and asked forgiveness in each matter, God received justice, and my guilt and shame were washed away in His forgiveness. This gave us rest on each side of our relationship. In fact, this is what happens when transgressions are acknowledged and forgiveness is asked and given in *any* relationship.

When forgiveness is given, rest and peace is restored between us as the hunger for justice is quieted. Guilt and shame are removed, and if we have been hiding from the one we wronged — as Adam did God — we no longer have to do so.

The rest which comes from confession and forgiveness permeates the soul in a way few things do.

The rest which comes from confession and forgiveness permeates the soul in a way few things do. This rest only comes through humbling oneself, admitting without excuse, *"I have wronged you. I am in need of your forgiveness."* Humbling oneself is never easy, but once you have tasted the profound and satisfying peace that comes as a result, it is easier to go there the next time, and the next. Once I know I am in the wrong, I want to go quickly "to the place of justice," because guilt and hiding (in any way) from our relationship is more uncomfortable to me than the humility of confession. I've learned that humility is the shortcut to restoration of the relationships I cherish, whether with God or others.

> *This is what the Sovereign Lord, the Holy One of Israel, says: "In repentance and rest is your salvation, in quietness and trust is your strength, but you would have none of it." (Isaiah 30:15)*

Here the Hebrew word for "rest" means to *descend or sink down into stillness;* the perfect picture of a man humbling himself. In this instance the Lord has just given a list of grievances against His people, then warned them that the life they have constructed in their sin will collapse around them someday. When that happens, the Lord said, just *come back to me* (His consistent solution!) with repentance and humility, and you will be saved from what you have done; your strength will be restored through quietness and trust in me. My experience confirms this is true; and if there are consequences to my bad choices, God walks with me through them to help me make the most of it. That's just who He is, always.

God Already Knows, And He Still Offers Mercy

There is an amazing glimpse of the Lord's pre-packaged mercy when He knows His people will sin against Him repeatedly. As the Hebrews were preparing to go into the Promised Land, God warned them they would be unfaithful to Him there, and told them just what He would do about it:

> *There you will worship man-made gods of wood and stone, which cannot see or hear or eat or smell. But if from there you seek the Lord your God, you will find Him if you seek Him with all your heart and with all your soul.*
>
> *When you are in distress and all these things have happened to you, then in later days you will return to the Lord your God and obey Him.*
>
> *For the Lord your God is a merciful God; He will not abandon or destroy you or forget the covenant with your ancestors, which He confirmed to them by oath. (Deuteronomy 4:28-31)*

God's mercy is often an act of faithfulness to His covenant oath, as He said here: *He will not forget the covenant with your ancestors.* God doesn't rescue and save us because we deserve it; God saves because He keeps His covenant promise to extend all grace to those who are in His Son.

There are even places in Scripture where God says He will rescue someone *for the sake of His Name* — His reputation as a faithful God.[2] This is good news for us, and should shut the mouth of the liar who whispers in your ear that what you've done is too bad to forgive, or that you are too hopeless to change. Even if all that were true, it wouldn't alter the faithfulness of God; He will *always* be found by those who return to Him in this covenant of grace in which we now stand.

"Come To Me, For I Am Gentle"

Acknowledging our sin and repenting to God does not come easy at first; but once you experience God's gentle and humble response, it becomes easier to face Him. I've learned firsthand that sincere sorrow and repentance immediately open the door back into the arms of God. You will always find Him waiting and ready to restore you to rest with Him. We cannot manufacture this rest; it comes only through going to Jesus:

> *Come to me, all you who are weary and burdened, and I will give you rest. Take my yoke upon you and learn from me, for I am gentle and humble in heart, and you will find rest for your souls. For my yoke is easy and my burden is light. (Matthew 11:28-30)*

Matthew uses the Greek word *anapauo* to describe the rest Jesus offers. P*auo* means *"to pause and rest,"* but *ana* is a prefix that indicates repetition and/or intensity. Jesus is telling us to come to Him for rest continually — as a lifestyle!

It is like the manna God provided His people in the wilderness. The exact amount they needed for each day fell from heaven, and if they tried to store some for the next day, it always rotted overnight. They had to trust God for fresh bread from heaven each new day. Jesus said, *"I am the living bread that came down from heaven."* (John 6:51)

In beckoning us to come to Him, Jesus also reveals that rest comes to our souls from being yoked with Him. I think of Jesus

---

[2] See especially Ezekiel 36:16-22, as God refers to the salvation to come in the new covenant.

teaching His disciples in John Chapter 15, the night before He was crucified:

> *Now remain in my love. If you keep my commands, you will remain in my love, just as I have kept my Father's commands and remain in His love. I have told you this so that my joy may be in you and that your joy may be complete. (John 15:9-11)*

Rest comes when you turn to the Lord repeatedly with a trusting, yielded and obedient heart, because a great deal of what makes us weary and burdened is doing things our way. When I begin living from something other than a yielded heart I throw off His yoke, acting like I can do life better on my own and love myself better than He will. In this I am making Eve's choice all over again, eating from the tree of knowledge, which represents all we reach for to give ourselves life (as opposed to what God provides).

The way I have experienced God's yoke will not be the same as yours. I am a tender-hearted woman, childlike at heart; I have been the bruised reed God would not break and the smoldering wick He would not snuff out. [3] My husband experiences God different, because He is not at all like me. Yet no matter who you are, the shortcut to the gentle mercy of God is surrender.

Somewhere along the way I became so used to enjoying the peace and goodness between the Lord and me that it became unbearable to have that disturbed. I've become increasingly sensitive to the things that disappoint Him, such as when I make unkind comments or entertain unkind thoughts about someone. He rarely has to say a word to me, because I sense His displeasure instantly. I repent quick, and He forgives quick. We don't like a disturbance in the force.

---

[3] Matthew 12:20

The Veil That Still Separates

In His bestselling classic *The Pursuit of God,* A.W. Tozer ponders the question of what prevents us from experiencing God now that the veil which separated us from His presence was torn down when Jesus died on Calvary. Tozer offers that a veil remains, but this one is in our own hearts:

> *"A veil not taken away as the first veil was, but which remains there still shutting out the light and hiding the face of God from us. It is the veil of our fleshly, fallen nature living on, unjudged within us, uncrucified and unrepudiated. It is woven of the fine threads of the self-life... self-righteousness, self-pity, self-confidence, self-sufficiency, self-admiration, self-love, and a host of others like them."* [4]

Tozer's solution: there must be a work of God to destroy this veil, a bringing of self-sins to the cross for judgment. However, he warns us against *"tinkering with our inner life"* in an attempt to rend this veil ourselves! *"God must do everything for us. Our part is to yield and trust."* [5]

I no longer wrestle with self-judgment, though I used to self-examine all the time as to how I might be letting God down. This actually got in the way of knowing Him and the life He wanted to share with me. I live at rest now in His love and grace, trusting He will bring to light what is hidden in my heart when we are both ready. I have adopted the attitude of the Apostle Paul, who wrote in 1 Corinthians 4:3-5:

> *... indeed, I do not even judge myself. My conscience is clear, but that does not make me innocent. It is the Lord who judges me. Therefore judge nothing before the appointed time; wait until the Lord comes. He will bring*

---

[4] Pages 41-42, The Pursuit of God by A.W. Tozer, ©1982 Wingspread Publishers.

[5] Ibid, Page 44

to light what is hidden in darkness and will expose the motives of the heart.

I no longer self-examine all the time, or as Tozer put it, tinker with my soul. I leave it all up to the Lord, knowing I'm not innocent, but living unfettered by anxiety until God shines light on something He wants to change or heal.

To the degree I have trusted and yielded to Jesus, He has brought me into my promised life. And Tozer was right, tinkering with your soul, trying to die to self on your own, leaves self very much in charge. I'm telling you, it can be ugly. When you step up to really know God, the Spirit will lead you on a journey of challenges to your tendency towards self-preservation, self-reliance, self-confidence — all that "self" stuff.

To the degree I have trusted and yielded to Jesus, He has brought me into my promised life.

As I determined to live yielded to Christ, I felt genuine grief as I gave up parts of my self, things that made me, me. My old "self" died in moments of quiet decision and occasional tears of real grief. Frankly, it hurts; but the same one who leads you through this painful process is also the Comforter who heals you. As I followed the Spirit in knowing God, I decided I could trust Him, taking Jesus at His word in Matthew 16:25 that *"whoever loses their life for me will find it."*

I'm shouting back from the other side of that faith challenge, *"It's true!"* You don't just survive the process, you are born anew in a hundred little ways. I have found it to be true: whatever bits of self I give up or die to, become new life in His hands. One day while walking with the Lord in the garden of your life, you find something beautiful growing where you buried that seed of selfishness. I'm not just stringing together pretty words here. I have lived it, and I cannot find enough words to describe the treasure of possessing a new kind of life God has grown in me. You now belong to a king who — as you lay down your life to love Him and His people — will give you the life you never dreamed of having.

Yielding To The Spirit

The Lord says in Psalm 46:10, *"Be still, and know that I am God."* The Hebrew word for "still" refers to the stillness that results from *disconnecting from our own strength*, letting oneself go limp. In this verse God is telling us to stop relying on our own strength, know Him and receive His strength.

This is yet another way the Lord transforms us into the image of His son, who boasted that His great ministry works were never done on His own; that He only did and said what He saw His Father say and do.[6] Jesus set the example for us in living a life of complete dependence upon the Holy Spirit and the Father. In living a life yielded to the Lord you will find yourself in situations that thrust you entirely upon His faithfulness. I'll just say, it really worked for Jesus!

One of the biggest works God had to do in me was get me to let go of managing my own life. God asks you to submit to Him and disconnect from your own strength in order to receive His strength, wisdom, and values. As you gradually let go of all that stuff you were so sure was right, trust in yourself fades into a complete confidence in the Lord. As you know and walk with God, you become wiser, stronger and more faithful than you ever could be on your own.

You can keep trying to give yourself life, or let Him do it. God is passionate about us entering His rest so we can experience the fullness of His grace in the life He's holding out. Surrender sets you on the journey towards that life; and satisfaction of heart is waiting for you when you arrive.

---

[6] John 12:49-50; John 14: 31.

17 The Rest Of A Satisfied Heart

As a new student of the Bible, my hungry soul was thrilled when I saw again and again in Scripture that God is willing and able to satisfy the hunger of every living thing. Two of the many verses one finds:

You open your hand and satisfy the desires of every living thing. (Psalm 145:16)

...for He satisfies the thirsty and fills the hungry with good things. (Psalm 107:9)

Reading such things, we want them to be true. Yet for multitudes one of the great struggles of faith is the question: "*Can God really satisfy me?*" Even while believing in God, in His resurrection power, in the promise of heaven, somehow faith breaks at the idea that God can truly satisfy us in any real way we can experience. From this distance it is easy to judge Eve for the choice she made in Eden, but today, we still face the same choice she did. Will we run after abundant life on our own; or will we trust God entirely to give us our best life?

We're still making Eve's choice.

The tree of knowledge of good and evil[1] represents all that we reach for to satisfy ourselves, yet which ultimately robs us of life. We were designed to be nourished and satisfied by the Tree of Life, which represents all

[1] See Genesis 2:16-17.

the Lord offers us in sharing life together. Man was separated from the Tree of Life when he was banished from Eden, but it has been restored to us through Jesus Christ. This is another means by which we enter God's rest. In this sense, rest is the absence of any striving by the soul to meet its own needs.

Rest is the absence of any striving by the soul to meet its own needs.

Yet we need to examine why we are even tempted to go to that other tree, as Eve did.

The Origin Of Bad Choices

In pondering Eve's story in Genesis Chapter 3, it is easy to see what led to her choice: a combination of discontentment and failure to trust God. Both of these make us vulnerable to the offerings of the devil, which is why Paul said that godliness with contentment is a great thing for us to achieve. [2]

You would think that Eve, of all human beings, should have been content with the life she had — a perfect husband, no chickens to pluck, no need to diet. Perhaps she was content until the serpent planted the suspicion in her mind that God was holding out on her, that she needed something more than what He offered.

I've always been deeply aware of my hunger, and came to the Lord as a very needy soul. I craved what most people do: a great life, love, prosperity, and fulfillment. I had fiercely protected my independence, especially from God, whom I thought would stomp all over my big appetite for life. I figured no one would love me like I could and was, as they say, "looking out for number one." I was horribly wrong. Not only did I do a terrible job of giving myself life, I used my freedom to make choices that ultimately robbed myself and those who

[2] 1 Timothy 6:6

shared life with me: parents, husband, children and friends. All the while I told myself I was a good person, but it kept getting harder to believe. In trying to satisfy myself, I became a woman I hated. Grief at who I had become sank me into a deep depression. That's when the Lord came for me. I was ready.

As I began to share life with Him, the Lord only deepened the awareness of my heart hungers. He opened my eyes to what I was truly hungry for under the surface — a sense of purpose, a feeling of value, a fulfilling life punctuated with some joy. I already knew I didn't know how to give myself those things, but little by little, I began to see these very things building in me.

Along the way, I kept reading scriptures that promise God will satisfy His people. I was especially struck by Jesus' words in John's gospel, promising to be bread to His people, satisfying the hunger of all who offered it to Him:

> *Jesus declared, "I am the bread of life. Whoever comes to me will never go hungry, and whoever believes in me will never be thirsty. But as I told you, you have seen me and still you do not believe." (John 6:35-36)*

At first, I supposed this to be poetic language, and I didn't take it at face value. But when I asked for the gift of the Holy Spirit, and received His presence filling me, He gave me faith to see and believe that Jesus was serious, and He meant exactly what He said. Then the Spirit lead me through a process of personally testing this. It began when God asked for my cigarettes.

Can God Really Satisfy Me?

I was terribly addicted to cigarettes, even after I became a Christian. I knew I needed to quit for several reasons, but He Lord didn't force the issue in our first few years together. I suppose He was waiting and hoping I would take the initiative to give them up. But I failed every time I tried to quit, and His graciousness with me lulled me into putting it off for another day. But one day the Lord challenged me, asking me to think about all the reasons why I smoked. This I did, for a while paying attention to why I reached for every cigarette.

What I learned is that I was using cigarettes like a friend to help me through all the moments of life. I used them to calm me when I was stressed; to stimulate me when I was tired or bored; to calm hunger when I couldn't eat yet, and to cap off a good meal. Yes, I was addicted to the nicotine, but these were all the psychological hooks that kept me there.

When I met with the Lord over what I'd learned, He said to me, *"I want to be the one you reach for. I am jealous of your need for these cigarettes. I want to be the one you reach for when you're upset, the one you enjoy coffee with, the one who calms your nerves."*

He said to me, *"I want to be the one you reach for."*

Like most smokers, I'd tried to quit dozens of times in 18 years of a love-hate relationship with cigarettes. I was terribly addicted, and didn't know how to live without them. Now the Lord had made it personal, and I wanted with all my heart to give Him what He desired. It wasn't about cigarettes anymore; God had made it about us. So, I gave them up. I'd seen all the pictures of people with black lungs; I knew they might slowly kill me and end my life prematurely, as they ultimately did my mother; yet none of that had moved me enough to quit.

It wasn't easy; in fact, I cried and really grieved over losing what felt like a friend. But it was a false friend, I knew, robbing my life; while my true Friend wanted to give me life. During a difficult two weeks, every time I wanted to smoke, I turned to the Spirit with my desire, giving Him the opportunity to satisfy me, and amazingly, He did! I tested His word fully, asking Him to even satisfy the physical cravings as well as my mental and emotional need for this old "friend."

One night as I crawled into bed about three weeks later, I suddenly realized I had not thought about a cigarette a single time that day. I was free at last! I worshipped the Lord as I lay there in my new freedom, and cried for joy. I had given up on ever being able to quit smoking, so I was overjoyed. But a greater source of joy — and frankly, amazement — was discovering God's ability to satisfy me, in real ways I could experience. God's patience with me those five years was surely rooted in the wisdom of waiting for my faith and devotion to be ready for us to walk through that together.

Believing in the all-sufficiency of Christ for all we need requires strong faith in God's will for you, and in His power to carry it out. Most need to grow into this kind of faith. It was a journey for me, but like most journeys into the unknown, the hardest part was taking the first few steps. After that, you know what is waiting on the other side, the unknown becomes known, and you have answers to your questions. Today, a few steps down the road, I have answers. I have tested the Lord, and my answer is, *"Yes, God really satisfies my hungry heart!"*

Knowing God begins in earnest when you abandon the tree of knowledge and reach for God Himself — your Tree of Life. Today I believe one major difference between myself and those who struggle in knowing God, is what the Spirit has taught me to do with my hunger.

Hunger: What Do You Do With Yours?

Whoever or whatever we offer our hunger to ultimately determines our quality of life.

We often turn to other people or things with the neediness of our souls, instead of offering the Lord our hunger. Whoever or whatever we offer our hunger to ultimately determines our quality of life. This truth is seen tragically in those addicted to things like cigarettes, drugs or pornography; who hunger for a few moments of ecstasy that ends up robbing them of life. People experience all kinds of bondage because of where they take their hunger. The Lord describes what happens when His people use their free will to satisfy themselves:

> *I am the Lord your God, who brought you up out of Egypt. Open wide your mouth and I will fill it. But my people would not listen to me; Israel would not submit to me. So I gave them over to their stubborn hearts to follow their own devices. (Psalm 81:10-12)*

The Lord has an interesting response to those who refuse what He offers — He lets them have what they want. When we go off looking for love and satisfaction in all the wrong places, God doesn't have to punish us; He just lets us have what we really want, knowing our choices will punish us. He hates it, but allows it in hopes that we will return to Him:

> *If my people would only listen to me, if Israel would only follow my ways, how quickly I would subdue their enemies and turn my hand against their foes! Those who hate the Lord would cringe before Him, and their punishment would last forever. But you would be fed with the finest of wheat; with honey from the rock I would satisfy you. (Psalm 81:13-16)*

You can hear the longing in His voice: *"If only you would give your hunger to me, I would satisfy you with the best!"* God wants to be the one who satisfies us. He is jealous over anything or anyone else we reach for to satisfy our hearts.

A dissatisfied heart is prone to wander. God knows this, knows we have needy and independent hearts. Our efforts to fill ourselves up is what makes us fickle and unfaithful, and makes us vulnerable to deceitful bread. In tender love, God always waits for us to find our way back after our choices have let us down and left us hungrier still.

As a counselor, I see the effect neediness and discontent has on people. It drives them into addictions, toxic relationships, and all manner of temptations. It opened Eve to the serpent's deception, made it easy to believe his lie that just maybe God was withholding something she needed for abundant life. The liar fuels this discontent by convincing us that we need more than God can or will give us. His lie has persisted through the ages: that with the Lord, seeking satisfaction is forbidden. But the Spirit knows better; He said to us in Proverbs 13:12: *"A longing fulfilled is a tree of life."* The truth is that through Christ, we have been restored to the garden, to the Lord Himself, who is our Tree of Life. Longings are not wrong. They just need to be offered to God.

"A longing fulfilled is a tree of life."

Being satisfied by God begins with believing that God *wants* to satisfy you. One day in 2015 I asked Him, *"Lord, how can I love you today?"* The answer came: "*Lean on me. Acknowledge me. Need me.*" His answer surprised me in its sweetness and fatherly love. Having raised two children, I could relate.

The contentment God brings has become a great key to freedom for me. It brings rest to our soul, and saves us from the deceptive bread the world offers. It saves us from abusive, toxic or unhealthy co-dependent relationships that develop because we put hope in others to satisfy and heal our hungry hearts. Though it is God's design for us to love others so well that we do satisfy one another's hearts, it is not His way for us to demand it from them.

David the shepherd boy, warrior and king, left a message for us as he strengthened himself in the Lord:

> *Praise the Lord, my soul, and forget not all His benefits — who forgives all your sins and heals all your diseases, who redeems your life from the pit and crowns you with love and compassion, who satisfies your desires with good things*

so that your youth is renewed like the eagle's (Psalms 103:2-5)

Only God's love can satisfy you in the deepest way possible. His love heals you. This is one of the great blessings of sharing life with God, who loves you deeply, perfectly, faithfully, just as you need.

In knowing the Father, Son and Spirit, I have found for the first time a deep and abiding contentment. This is not some mystical state of nirvana, and I assure you I'm not ignoring my real needs or denying what is going on in life — I've never been capable of that. The Lord has met me in my deepest longings and brings my heart to rest in and through all that life brings or fails to bring. In all the places where people leave me hungry, the Lord satisfies me. Because people are no longer my primary source of joy, worth and satisfaction, I am free to love others the way God loves me. This removes the temptation to get others to be what I need, so that any trace of manipulation is removed from our relationship.

God Especially Satisfies The Hunger He Creates

Being satisfied by God is one of the great keys to living a life of steadfast obedience. Why do I say this? Because life with God has taught me that saying "no" to yourself in order to love and obey the Lord can take you to a place of self-denial that is so tough it hurts, at least for a little while. Sometimes, God Himself takes you to a place that leaves you empty.

I used to wonder why the Scriptures say we are called to suffer for Christ,[3] while at the same time promising abundant life.[4] My simple mind had trouble reconciling those two truths at first. After walking through life with the Holy Spirit a few years, I began to understand. Though some will face physical

---

[3] See Philippians 1:29; 1 Peter 3:14 and 17; 1 Peter 4:16 and 19, to name a few verses.

[4] John 10:10, NASB

suffering for their faith as they take the gospel to the world, for the great majority of us who remain at home in our ordinary lives, the kind of suffering we experience comes when we must say "no" to ourselves in order to say "yes" to God and His ways. For instance, one's soul may suffer at times in order to give love and forgiveness to someone who has wronged you.

Obeying Jesus' command to love your enemies will often cost you something, whether it be pride or comfort or justice. While these moments always feel like "the enemy" (or what they are doing) is the issue, you will realize at some point that *for a Christian, Jesus is always the issue*. I say this because when Jesus reveals His righteous way and asks you to walk in it, the issue of whether you will obey Him trumps all other issues. It doesn't matter what someone else is doing, it only matters what Jesus is asking of you.

Obeying the Lord often requires the denial of something I am craving. It might be peace and quiet, or freedom from demands on my energy or time; it could be giving away the money I was saving for something I wanted. More commonly, it is denying the need to defend my position or show how right I am in a disagreement. While this kind of suffering is a far cry from the suffering of torture, martyrdom and deprivation some face for Christ, it is a type of real suffering nonetheless, especially in today's culture of "You Can and Must Have It All." The fact that people reach for anything and everything *now*, even if they must go into debt, even it if will kill them in the end, testifies to our society's great reluctance to suffer even a little with "No." As members of this society, we're not immune to this mindset just because we're Christians.

The Hunger For Righteousness And Justice

Having experienced God's ability to satisfy his soul, David reminded himself to wait on God whenever his heart was hungry for something:

> *My soul, wait in silence for God only, for my hope is from Him (Psalms 62:5 NASB)*

Here David uses the Hebrew word *damam*, a word that pictures the quiet state of a heart that is not agitated or restless. It literally means *"to be silent, be still, or wait."* David and other Biblical writers use *damam* to refer to waiting on the Lord as opposed to striving and working to satisfy one's need — especially the need for justice. David was well acquainted with being mistreated by others, in particular those whom he loved and had served faithfully, like Saul, who tried to kill him out of jealousy. David wrote in Psalm 37:7:

> *Be still before the Lord and wait patiently for Him; do not fret when men succeed in their ways, when they carry out their wicked schemes.*

Experience with the Lord had clearly taught David that whatever his need was, the best thing to do was wait for the Lord to fill it — either by giving him actual justice, or by restoring a sense of wellbeing to his soul while he waited for it.

The hunger for justice — to be treated righteously by others — is a huge issue for the human heart. The Lord, in whose image we are made, understands this fully; and Jesus addressed this need in the Sermon on the Mountain when he said: *Blessed are those who hunger and thirst for righteousness, for they will be filled.* (Matthew 5:6)

This verse is usually taken as a reference to God's promise to credit us with the righteousness of Christ, and/or give us the ability to become righteous in ourselves as we are filled with His Spirit. Both are true. Yet the Spirit has shown me another layer of truth: Jesus was also referring to our need to be treated right

The hunger for justice — to be treated righteously by others — is a huge issue for the human heart.

by others, and His ability to fill or satisfy us when people leave us hungry.

We all hunger to be treated rightly, to be loved faithfully, to be dealt with justly. We long for tenderness and understanding. We hunger for connection, and long to know goodness at the hands of others. Righteousness encompasses all that is due between two people in a relationship, especially a covenant relationship. When righteousness is given and received, God calls it justice.

God loves righteousness and justice. Since we are made in His image, we also crave this; it is part of our God-given DNA. This need will never diminish in us; yet God demands that we forgive, knowing that doing so requires us to lay down our need to seek justice when we are wronged. This is especially difficult when the desire for vengeance is righteous (a right reaction to a real injustice). Anger at injustice is a godly emotion; God experiences it all the time. We become hungry for righteousness when people do not treat us — or the ones we love — right; when things don't happen as they should.

I hunger for righteousness and justice more now than I did before I knew Christ. As I have come to know God, experiencing His just and good ways of being with me, I crave kindness and goodness more from those around me, and register the lack of it more deeply. I enjoy a steady diet of how these look and feel as I relate to God; they are healing, restful and nurturing. The opportunities to be offended or disappointed in people have actually increased since the Lord lives in me, and I know what righteous treatment feels like. The good news is that this same Righteous One comforts me when I don't receive righteousness from people. He also helps me forgive quickly.

Jesus promises us that He can and will administer justice in His time, *and* satisfy your hunger to have been treated right in the first place. It seems mysterious and sounds improbable, but I testify from personal experience that His word is true. I have tested the Lord in this many years now. When my heart registers an injustice at the hands of another, I take my hunger for righteousness to the Lord, and ask Him to satisfy it. But I do this right *after* I obey Him by choosing to forgive the offender.

Forgiveness is a great test of the Lord's ability to satisfy the soul. We find it hard to forgive others, fearing that if we do, they will get away with what they have done. We want justice. Yet God demands that we do forgive, unconditionally, as often as we are wounded, even if by the same person many times![5] If we do not forgive others, Jesus assures us in Matthew 6:15 that our Father will refuse to forgive us of any trespass on our part until we do! We need to take this seriously.

Forgiveness is a great test of the Lord's ability to satisfy the soul.

Releasing people from your own judgment restores your rest with the Lord, because as long as you stand in judgment of others (against God's will) His Spirit does not rest with you. In choosing to forgive, your rest returns and all is well between you and the Lord. It's a pretty great transaction, enabling me to forgive quickly and truly, without lingering resentment.

Forgiveness is an act of faith, because often you will not witness the justice which the Lord promises. But forgiveness is also an act of faithfulness to your covenant Lord. When you make the choice to forgive, the Lord will give you the ability to rest in it, as He does with all things He requires of you. This is how I pray:

"God, I longed for righteousness from this person, and they did not give it. They betrayed me, but I choose to forgive them and release all judgment to you. Please satisfy my hunger for righteousness and justice in this, and give me rest, in Jesus' name."

---

[5] Matthew 18:21-22 and Luke 17:4-5. Note that immediately after Jesus describes how they should forgive, they cried, *"Lord, increase our faith!"*

I believe the Lord will faithfully give me justice when I faithfully obey Him in forgiving; in this we mutually honor our covenant obligations. I am happy to say that because of our history together in this, my heart now recovers quickly from the wounds of others, and I don't live in fear of being hurt.

While my life is far from perfect or ideal, inside where I share life with God, I continually feel as if I live by a stream of living water, with satisfying food always at hand. In other words, the normal state of my heart is being satisfied. My thirst for anything — righteousness, companionship, justice, peace, direction, rest — is satisfied whenever I turn to the Lord and offer my need to Him. A heart that knows God is not a needy heart. The only unquenchable hunger and thirst a Christian should experience is that which the Spirit creates in us.

God Wants To Nourish Us

The Lord continually invites us to His table, a feast for His beloved, and invites us to eat freely. My heart breaks over the multitudes who make their own pitiful sack lunches and eat them on the outskirts of God's place. Such ones may be fearful of presumption, or intimidated by the very idea of personally knowing God, or simply ignorant about God's desire. Whatever the reason, these do not yet have permission, in their minds, to know God in intimate ways.

A heart that knows God is not a needy heart.

A problem with most Christians is not that they aren't spiritual enough, it is that they are not nourished enough by the Spirit of the Lord. The children who know they belong at His table are the ones I think of as true believers, who not only put faith in Christ's atonement, but accept His invitation to share life here and now. They have come to believe that they can hear

His voice, feel His love, and be satisfied by His presence and personality.

Everything the heart longs for, everything we are made and destined for in relationship to God and others, can be summed up in the word *rest.* In entering God's rest we experience the fullness of His covenant grace: all is well with my soul; all is right between myself and others; all is right between myself and my creator. In knowing the Lord I become fruitful, peaceful, joyful and strong. My life says to the world, *Jesus can be trusted.*

The only time your rest should be disturbed is when you feel a stirring of the Holy Spirit to do something you have not carried out for the Lord. Unrest in your spirit is a signal to pay attention to something the Lord wants you to do for Him. Those who continually seek to know God will be called upon often to express His love and goodness to others. Rest comes from obedience. Having tended to the matter on the Lord's heart, we can return to rest in regard to that matter, because we have been faithful to our covenant Friend.

My life says to the world, *Jesus can be trusted.*

I leave you with a Scripture the Spirit imprinted on my spirit years ago — a prayer of Moses that became part of my daily prayers:

> *Satisfy us in the morning with your unfailing love, that we may sing for joy and be glad all our days. (Psalm 90:14)*

18 All Things Are Fulfilled In Knowing God

I have learned that God's invitation to personal relationship, and my choice to respond, is the means by which every promise and purpose of the Lord is fulfilled. Peace, wisdom, and the soul's rest come and remain steadfast as we know God. The cleansing of a defiled heart and the healing of a broken one are most effectively received in the personal ministry of our true Friend. God's plan to nourish us on His living bread and streams of living water cannot happen from afar; we must be at His table. The establishing of Christ's kingdom and the overthrow of God's enemy (Satan) in my life, is a work we do together in partnership, not one-sided actions on the part of God. This is not only necessary because of the free will He gives us, it is His plan; after all, His goal is relationship, not mere rulership of a people. We were created to know God.

All things come to fulfillment through the Trinity's relationship to one another, our relationship to them, and our relationship to each other. This is how God produces abundant life in us and how we become fruitful. As Colossians 3:10 says, knowing God in personal experience is how we ***"put on the new self, which is being renewed in knowledge in the image of its Creator."***

Becoming Recognizable Children Of God

Knowing God is the only way we can be mentored in becoming authentic, recognizable children of the Lord. It is the Spirit's main task in leading us:

For those who are led by the Spirit of God are the sons of God. (Romans 8:14)

Paul speaks in other instances of our being "the children of God," in which he uses the Greek word *teknon,* which refers to a child born to a father. But here Paul uses the word *huios,* which refers to a mature son, fully apprenticed, recognizable as a son of his father, displaying his character and way of life. Paul uses the same word when he goes on to say:

For the creation waits in eager expectation for the sons of God to be revealed. For the creation was subjected to frustration, not by its own choice, but by the will of the one who subjected it, in hope that the creation itself will be liberated from its bondage to decay and brought into the freedom and glory of the children of God. (Romans 8:18-21)

The children of God are destined not only for freedom, but to also share in the glory of their Father. I could not have imagined this 30 years ago; now my heart burns with the desire for it. Knowing God in even the small way that I do, I feel that I can do anything for Him, and I want to do everything. I want to heal everyone I see. I want to touch the broken-hearted with God's own love and compassion, and release the captives to begin their own journey to their promised life. I do a measure of these things now, but far less than I believe is possible with God.

The children of God are destined not only for freedom, but to share in their Father's glory.

Paul thrills me when he writes of the Lord's *"incomparably great power for us who believe."* (Ephesians 1:15). God's divine power enables all of this for us, but as Peter made clear, we only experience this power through knowing God the Holy Spirit.

His presence in you enables the Father to re-parent you and nurture you; to heal your soul, your spirit, even your body.

The Spirit does all this to help you become mature sons and daughters of God who have a covenant heart like your heavenly Father's. His plan is that through knowing Him you will learn to love like He does, so you can reveal His powerful goodness to the people He loves. You cannot come to full maturity in the image of Christ by your own effort; you need all that the Spirit teaches and establishes in you as you walk with Him.

Righteousness, Peace And Joy In The Holy Spirit

For the kingdom of God is not a matter of eating and drinking, but of righteousness, peace and joy in the Holy Spirit... (Romans 14:18)

The Apostle Paul wrote these words to correct people who continued to make legalistic judgments about how and what God's people should eat or drink. They still had an Old Covenant mindset, and assumed God was focused on such things as He measured their righteousness. Once among the most legalistic men in his world, Paul has been re-educated by the Spirit of Christ. He now understands what truly matters to God, and it is not perfect obedience to rules about exterior things! God is looking into the hearts of His people for evidence of an interior life full of righteousness, peace and joy. These qualities only develop in our hearts through knowing God the Holy Spirit.

Righteousness forms in us as we know and yield to the Spirit of righteousness in daily life. As we allow Him to direct not only our actions but our thoughts and judgments, we walk in the same righteousness Jesus did. We will know the right thing to do in every matter, as Jesus did. He demonstrated this when confronted with the woman caught in the act of adultery, a story told in John Chapter 8. The law of Moses — given by His own Father God! — required such a woman be stoned to death. The Pharisees threw this woman before Jesus to test His commitment to God's law, expecting Him to begin the stoning. Instead, He said, *"Let any one of you who is without sin be the first to throw a stone at her."* Jesus was the only one present qualified to throw that stone — and He did not! He explained later that He never judged anything on His own, but always sought the Father's mind and judgment on a matter. [1] As a flesh and blood man, he would have done this by the same means we can: communicating with the Father through the Holy Spirit.

Jesus knew the Father loved justice, and loved His people; that He would always show Him the righteous response to every matter. Jesus wanted to please His Father, not just assume He knew the right thing because He had memorized the laws of God. God doesn't change, so it wasn't that the Father no longer cared about judging adultery. But apparently perfect justice in that moment was to judge the sin of all the self-righteous Pharisees so ready to execute judgment. Facing their own guilt, they could not hurl their stones. So God didn't wink at the woman's sin, He revealed a kind of righteous justice that cannot come from mere words written on stone, but only from a living heart. For the first time, a human being indwelled by God's own Spirit had access to that living justice, and a heart to dispense it, which resulted in mercy for the woman.

If our Lord Jesus lived in such total dependence upon the Spirit, how much more should we!

Only God knows the righteous thing to do in any situation, knowing every heart and all motives involved. If our Lord Jesus lived in such total dependence upon the Spirit, how much more should we! This is righteous behavior in the eyes of God, a combination of access, humility and submission, and love of truth.

---

[1] John 8:15-16, 28-29

We have access to the same Spirit Christ did when He lived on the earth. On our own, we cannot possibly know how to judge all things. If we try to do this on our own, we risk making wrong judgments which may actually pervert the justice and righteousness of God. When we follow the Spirit, knowing the thoughts and ways of God, we can walk in the same righteousness Christ did.

As a Jew, Jesus was raised on the words of the prophets, so His soul was surely permeated with these words from Isaiah:

> *And now the Sovereign Lord has sent me, with his Spirit. This is what the Lord says — your Redeemer, the Holy One of Israel: "I am the Lord your God, who teaches you what is best for you, who directs you in the way you should go. If only you had paid attention to my commands, your peace would have been like a river, your well- being like the waves of the sea." (Isaiah 48:16-18)*

I believe this was the backdrop in Jesus' mind as He learned to know His heavenly Father — as a human man like us — and prepared to step into public ministry.

Peace In The Holy Spirit

I've found that real peace only comes from knowing God. You can quiet yourself, think good thoughts, wrestle down your worries, focus on the positive, and employ every mind discipline man can teach, but you cannot manufacture true peace. Any peace you achieve by such efforts will have to be maintained by those same efforts. That is a lot of hard work, and ultimately leaves you with YOU as the only thing standing between yourself and quiet desperation or anxiety.

I can tell when I have wandered too far from from the Spirit's influence, because joy and peace erode or even vanish. Confusion often comes when the sense of knowing what is needed in my life situations seems out of reach. My peace is entirely connected to His Presence and sure guidance.

The Rest Of A Tranquil Mind

"...whoever listens to me will live in safety and be at ease, without fear of harm." (Proverbs 1:33)

Scripture makes it clear there is a rest and peace we can enjoy only through hearing God's voice. In Proverbs 1:33 this rest is described by the Hebrew word *sha'an,* which simply means to be peaceful. It pictures a heart that is tranquil, quiet and at ease; free from fear, stress or anxiety. Frankly, people who don't even know God can achieve a tranquil state of mind through mental discipline. The difference is that our tranquility of mind doesn't come from the effort of controlling or emptying the mind of all stressful thoughts. It comes from being filled with the truth of God, dispensed to us through the Holy Spirit's wisdom. A tranquil mind is the reward of living with and trusting Him. Isaiah wrote:

There is a rest and peace we can enjoy only through hearing God's voice.

You will keep in perfect peace those whose minds are steadfast, because they trust in you. (Isaiah 26:3)

Knowing God connects me with a peace that is powerful and enduring; not won by striving. It comes from His presence and His counsel, which is truth. Like all humans, my own thoughts, judgments and agendas are the source of much of my anxiety. The Lord can blow all that away with the breath of His truth, the Spirit's counsel. I have found that it is as Jesus said; His truth will set you free[2] — of anxiety, stupidity, ignorance, and a host of other human afflictions.

I remember an occasion when someone very dear to me wanted to introduce me to a close friend of hers who happened

---

[2] John 8:31-32

to be a practicing psychic. Knowing I was a Christian, she assured me beforehand: *"Don't worry, she won't try to read your mind."* Frankly, I wasn't assured at all, because I knew practicing psychics can be adept at channeling the powers of unclean spirits. I found a private place to pray (the restroom) and asked the Lord how to guard my mind from any unclean spirits or demonic activity. He shocked me when He said, *"Don't worry about it. I want you to let her read your mind."*

Incredulous, I asked, *"Lord, is that you?"* The answer came, *"Yes! I want you to let her read your mind. And here's what I want her to read: that Jesus loves her and died for her!"* Wow. I would have never thought of that. Apparently, the Lord wasn't one bit intimidated by some spirit in her. Furthermore, He loved this woman, a fact which wouldn't have occurred to me in those less mature days.

During our meeting, I did hold these thoughts in my mind. We had quite a pleasant visit, certainly better than if I had been all guarded or judgmental. I truly felt the Lord's own compassion for her, which she surely sensed — in addition to whatever she read on my mind — because she actually questioned me about God and my faith in Him. I did not share the gospel with her other than as the Lord had instructed — I was too timid about that in those days, too — and I never saw her again. I don't know the end of her story, but I trust the Lord is still pursuing her heart if He hasn't won it already.

The point is, what would have been a source of anxiety for me was an opportunity for the Lord. His simple wisdom brought me tranquility and showed me how He thinks. As is often the case, regardless of how it worked out for her, God's truth changed me and taught me a valuable lesson.

I ask Him often now, *"Lord, tell me the truth about this."* Seeking God's truth is the best way to turn anxiety into tranquility. It's a great way to live. It is also the best way to know God together with others.

The Spirit's Wisdom Leads To Peace

One morning after getting instructions from the Spirit for my day, I joined my husband for coffee; but before I could share how the Spirit had directed me, Ron gave me a very different set of instructions for our day! I was in the season of learning to submit to my husband, so I didn't ask Ron if he had prayed about his plans, not wanting to challenge him when the Lord had me focused on trusting and honoring his leadership. I quietly returned to prayer, asking the Lord what to do — I could not obey two masters! The Lord's reply was simply, *"Trust Ron and do what he has planned today."*

Since I felt so confident in what I'd heard from the Spirit, this answer shocked me, because it seemed God was submitting to Ron, yielding to <u>his</u> will. So I tested what I had heard: *"Lord, please confirm this for me in your Word."* Immediately James 3:17 came to my mind. I turned there, and found these words:

> *But the wisdom that comes from heaven is first of all pure; then peace-loving, considerate, submissive, full of mercy and good fruit, impartial and sincere. Peacemakers who sow in peace reap a harvest of righteousness. (James 3:17-18)*

That was a wow! I realized God's highest priority in that moment wasn't accomplishing certain tasks that day, it was teaching me the right way to honor both Him and my husband. As a result of God's counsel I had peace, Ron had peace, and there was no conflict. God's wisdom does promote peace. It is considerate of all the human hearts He is guiding; and yes, God can be submissive in working with His children. This was the beginning of my lessons on how the Spirit guides us together with others who also follow the Lord.

"You're In The Ark With Me"

We were once facing a season of major transition in our lives that would change everything. We knew our work would have to change in some ways, but most significantly we would have to relocate our home, leaving our home town, church and friends of 20 years. It was hard to imagine how everything would turn out because of many variables, including the choices other people would be making. In spite of a steadfast trust in the Lord, I was becoming anxious about it all as I kept turning over all the possibilities in my mind. Finally I asked the Lord to tell me what I needed to know. This is what He said:

"Yes, your life is about to change in a big way. But you are in the ark with Me and you are safe. That's all you need to know. When the ark lands, life will be very different for you, but you will be fine, because you are with Me."

As usual, His counsel gave me great peace. In fact, it is still giving me peace, because that ark hasn't landed yet! But every step of the way in this prolonged season of change has been attended by the faithfulness and blessing of the Lord. I knew it would be this way, yet in my human weakness I needed to hear something from Him to hold onto, something more personal than an inspirational scripture to stick on the front of my refrigerator.

Knowing the Lord means I still have life and peace in the midst of a crisis.

There is nothing like hearing God's voice and His personal wisdom for your own situation. Being a Christian doesn't guarantee you will never go through bad or unsettling things. In fact, Jesus said we would encounter trouble in this world. But experience has shown me that through knowing the Lord I will still have life and peace in the midst of a crisis. It is a life that God guarantees and sustains.

Peace also comes through the order my Spirit Friend brings to my life. As I have learned to respond to His gentle, quiet guidance, He makes all things timely for me. I am prepared for what will meet me on the path ahead. I experienced this the first time soon after beginning to believe I could hear the Lord's voice.

I've always been an early riser, and dedicated to spending an hour each morning in prayer and Bible study before our family day began. I guarded the 5:30 to 7:00 a.m. slot as my time with the Lord. My husband was pastoring a church in South Texas; I was still new at being a pastor's wife, and had a lot to learn.

One morning as I went to pray and study, I had a strong desire to skip devotional time and go straight to getting ready for the day. So I prayed, and the Lord confirmed that dressing immediately would be wise. By 6:15 a.m. I was completely ready for the day. A few minutes later one of our church members called with a huge emergency and needed us immediately! I was amazed, and enjoyed the peace of being ready for the moment. As spoken of earlier, this began as a desire or urge which turned out to be the Spirit. He uses such things to get your attention and communicates in various ways. The Spirit has frequently brought order to a day that could easily have become chaotic or unnecessarily complicated.

Rest: Safety In The Midst Of Trouble

There is a special rest that comes to those who know their God in the midst of trouble and terrible things. When God was forced to judge the world of chronic and pervasive evil, He chose to cleanse the earth with a great flood that would destroy all mankind. He did preserve one righteous man, Noah and his family. Noah's name in Hebrew actually means *rest*, and his story teaches us how God is able to give His righteous ones rest even while they are in the neighborhood where God is judging the world for its evil.

God's presence brings safety and peace of mind even in the presence of danger. We see it in Jesus, napping in the boat during a terrifying storm; in God setting a table for His beloved David in the presence of his enemies; in Daniel emerging from a den of ravenous lions without a scratch; in Shadrach, Meshach and Abednego surviving a fiery furnace without even the smell of smoke on them. The Spirit says:

> *Because he has loved Me, therefore I will deliver him; I will set him securely on high, because he has known My name. He will call upon Me, and I will answer him; I will be with him in trouble; I will rescue him and honor him. With a long life I will satisfy him and let him see My salvation. (Psalms 91:15-16 NASB)*

"Because He has loved me..." The Hebrew word translated as *loved* here does not refer to the emotion of love; it is the action of love in reaching for and clinging to the one you cherish. *It is love that will not let go of its beloved.* Bad things will happen, but you will never be destroyed by them if you know the Lord. People tend to blame God for every evil that happens, while ignoring their failure to live under the shadow of His wing, through obedience. God protects His children, but He also gives them free will. And when they use their freedom to their own harm, He will still heal, redeem and help them.

This will be no more crucial than on the Lord's day of destruction, when He returns to judge the earth for all sin and evil. You really need to know God on that day and be in the place of obedience.

In Psalm 91:16 above, the word "salvation" is *yeshua,* which is where the names Joshua, Hosea and Jesus come from. I hope you now see that salvation is not just about not going to hell. Salvation encompasses all God does to save me from the world and my ways, so I may enjoy His world and have abundant life. Salvation encompasses all the Lord does to elevate my being to His level of righteousness, peace, and joy.

Joy In The Holy Spirit

Joy is not something you manufacture on your own. You can choose to be optimistic or cheerful, but genuine joy is the natural response of your heart in experiencing someone or something wonderful. When you see a strikingly beautiful woman or handsome man, you don't make yourself admire them; admiration just comes. When you see injustice, you don't have to make yourself angry; it rises up in you involuntarily. Adorably cute animals and children bring delight without any effort on your part. Joy is meant to arrive the same way.

Well-meaning Christian teachers have taught people to "confess" their way into things God has promised such as joy, faith and hope. Of course you can raise your mood by focusing on positive things, but it is a labor, not a rest; and like peace, you will have sustain it against all the realities of life. The joy that makes you strong, and the faith that floats your boat in a storm, only comes through knowing the Spirit.

After years of personally experiencing the way God is — His wisdom, kindness, creativity and graciousness, I believe He brings forth the highest joy response the human soul can know. No doubt this is what caused David to write, *"In your presence is fullness of joy!"*[3]

Most people have had some taste of true joy. It comes when a child is born; when we win the championship; when the one we've come to love declares they love us too. God intended His creation to experience joy much more often than we do. Even science affirms this. Scientists have discovered the healthiest development of an infant or toddler's brain occurs as he experiences daily joy at being delighted in by his parents. Scientists say this kind of joy (their word!) is what "hardwires" the brain to respond to life in healthy ways in adult life. Considering the epic rise of autism, bipolar disorder, ADHD and other brain chemistry disorders, it is clear that not near enough joy is going on out there between

The Lord loves joy, and created us to thrive through experiencing it.

[3] Psalm 16:11, NASB

parents and their wee children. It saddens me to see people having to live on drugs (and endure their side effects) so they can function normally.

The Lord loves joy, and created us to thrive through experiencing it. This is why the Lord wants to re-parent us,[4] to become for us the Father whose delight in His child produces an abiding joy that heals him and makes him strong. This is exactly what knowing the Lord has given me. There are major moments of joy with the Lord, but I've come to love the quiet river of joy that flows through my heart these days in knowing Him. This little internal river of life nurtures everything in me, and over time it has watered what the Spirit calls our "waste places." I frequently find Isaiah to be especially good at putting words to how I experience the Lord:

> *The Lord will surely comfort (Tonia) and will look with compassion on all her ruins; He will make her deserts like Eden, her wastelands like the garden of the Lord. Joy and gladness will be found in her, thanksgiving and the sound of singing. (Isaiah 51:3)*

I've known depression and self-hatred; I've been deeply wounded by people I loved; I've carried the guilt and shame of hurting people I love. My heart and life are becoming a testimony to the Lord's ability to redeem my waste places — things ruined by myself or others — and turn them into a garden of delight. Joy and gladness are the norm in my heart, and I couldn't be more thankful.

Joy: The Root Of All Grace

The word *grace* in our New Testament is translated from the Greek word *charis.* Grace refers to any gift freely given to another out of generosity and the sheer joy of giving, as opposed to something owed or earned. The full grace of God that comes to us in the New Covenant flows out of His primary covenant

---

[4] 2 Corinthians 6:18

gift, which is God Himself. With His presence come His favor (good will), His wisdom, and His ability to do what we could never do without Him.

The parent word from which *charis* is derived is *chairo,* which means *joy* or *that which causes rejoicing.* This means that joy underlies all grace, all that God gives us! We need to see grace as the inseparable combination of gift + joy, because only together do they fully express the open hand of the Lord to us. If you separate one of these elements from the other, you miss God's point.

Grace is what we experience in a covenant relationship with someone vastly richer or greater than ourselves, who extends His hand to us full of His freely given riches — love, friendship, provision, protection — with each party having joy in the transaction. The giver has joy in giving, the receiver has joy in receiving.

Knowing God has convinced me that it wasn't just love motivating God in giving us a covenant of grace; God was going for the joy! From God's point of view, it is not just "I give myself to you." It is: *"It gives me joy to give myself to you! I want you to have joy in receiving me!"* The joy of the Lord is the foundation, flavor and fruit of all He has freely given us. For the joy set before Him, Christ endured the cross, according to Hebrews 12:2. When Jesus pleased His father by loving righteousness and hating evil, the Father's reward was to anoint Him with "the oil of joy," according to Hebrews 1:9. The same reward awaits all who follow Jesus into those same values.

I love one of the things the Lord whispered to Sarah Young's heart in private, now part of her devotional for May 4:

> *The more you give yourself to Me and My ways, the more I fill you with inexpressible, heavenly joy.* [5]

Having experienced this personally, I say yes and Amen.

---

[5] Page 131, "Jesus Calling" by Sarah Young ©2004, Thomas Nelson Publishers

Paul's letter to the Philippians is so full of joy references that he sounds like a broken record — a really happy one! *"Rejoice in the Lord always,"* he says in 4:4, and then again, as if he can't emphasize it enough. Paul is not just teaching a spiritual discipline; he knows his audience is facing the same struggle he once had in making the leap from law to grace. Paul knows the Holy Spirit wants to lead people on a journey that will challenge all they have known, as He introduces them to the God who wants to build strength in them through joy.

No man had ever known of a God with such a motivation! I think Paul is not commanding his audience so much as giving them permission to go for the joy in knowing God. He now knows the strength that comes from that joy. Paul's focus on joy is quite a testimony to God's grace, coming from a man who had lived a life of such brutal self-righteousness that it quenched any hint of true joy.

What made the difference in Paul? He had come to know his God instead of the law! In knowing Him Paul discovered such a fountain of life-giving joy and goodness and grace that he gushed, *"I consider everything a loss compared to the surpassing greatness of knowing Christ Jesus my Lord..."* (Philippians 3:8)

Since all this comes from the apostle who had not been personally discipled by Jesus, we see the total effectiveness of the Spirit in revealing the Person of God to someone. The Spirit led Paul on his own personal journey from being a joyless rule follower to finally receiving the birthright blessing that Moses imparted to his tribe centuries before — the tribe of Benjamin:

> *Let the beloved of the Lord rest secure in Him, for He shields him all day long. And the one the Lord loves rests between His shoulders. (Deuteronomy 33:12)*

Paul had come a long way in his journey. It began with the Lord striking him blind on his way to kill those who believed in Jesus. It ended with Paul awaiting his death in prison, after enduring incredible trials along the way; yet joyful in it all. One would have to conclude Paul was either out of his mind or actually had a quality of joy that had become the strength of his whole being. I'm going with the latter explanation, because I've tasted some of that myself.

I have suffered some in obeying the Lord, but I wouldn't dare compare it to the serious suffering that many Christians have known as they followed Christ, some even to death. As I have written of the joy I've found in knowing God, I don't mean to obscure or deny the cost of giving your all to the Lord. I hope one of your "take-aways" from this book is to understand how some Christians can sacrifice so much for the Lord. It is joy in their God and the grace given by the Spirit that carries martyrs to and through such places, because at the end of all suffering for the cause of Christ is the Lord Himself, waiting to take you in His arms. Let us not resign joy to a confession or a Christian duty. Let us go for the joy that comes in knowing the Lord, which gives us the strength to do anything with and for Him.

Go for the joy that comes in knowing the Lord, which gives us the strength to do anything with and for Him.

Knowing God Produces Real Worship

God is worthy of our worship, and the choice to celebrate Him and offer thanksgiving is always appropriate. But there is a higher form of worship, that comes naturally, rising up in you when something amazes your heart. This is the worship God treasures; a genuine and irrepressible response to what one has seen and known of Him. The worshipper can't help himself, being so blessed by their encounter or life with God that worship flows up and out of their soul and spirit like a fountain.

It is not unlike admiration from a husband. A man who has learned to compliment his wife occasionally and does so, blesses her. But when that wife walks into the room and hubby's eyes fill with wonder as he exclaims, "Wow, you're beautiful!" it feels totally different; and every woman knows the difference. So does the Lord — He calls this *"worshipping in spirit and in truth."* (John 4:23)

When I worship the Lord as a choice, I begin with the desire to express my love and thanksgiving to Him. Seeing my desire to honor the Lord, the Spirit helps me meet with Him, connecting us together more intimately than normal. Often in these times I am able to "behold the Lord" with the eyes of my spirit. This is worship in Spirit: worship enabled by the Spirit in a way that is not possible without Him. As I express my love to the Lord, His manifest (felt or perceived) Presence becomes stronger. Invariably, His Presence refreshes and nourishes me. So every time I enter into worship to give something to the Lord, I receive the greater gift!

The Lord also reveals Himself to me thru worship times in ways that don't happen when I study the Scriptures or talk with Him in prayer. Worship opens us to ways of knowing God not experienced any other time. It's not unlike marriage: you know your spouse one way at the breakfast table, another when you're parenting together, another when you go through a crisis, another when you're at play, and another way in sexual intimacy. Remove any of these ways and knowing is incomplete.

I believe that worshipping the Lord "in truth" has two meanings. First, it refers to the fact that you cannot truly worship a God you do not know on some level. Second, worship in truth refers to your walk matching your talk, or in this case the love songs you sing to Him. We worship God in truth and in deed when we obey God's Word and His will as we understand it.[6] One can go to church, sing songs, and even have spontaneous worship rise up out of the heart, and still walk away from that occasion with a heart not yielded to God's truth or His Spirit. The Lord pointed this out through Isaiah, and Jesus later quoted his words to the religious crowd of His day:

---

[6] Romans 12:1-2

These people honor me with their lips, but their hearts are far from me. They worship me in vain; their teachings are merely human rules. (Matthew 15:8-9)

Ultimately, worship is a permanent posture of the heart towards God that comes from true faith that He is Present and worthy of honor.

Ron and I often worship God at home, believing worship was never meant to be only a Sunday morning group activity. Occasionally one of us will find the other and say, *"Let's worship the Lord awhile."* Worship always creates an encounter with the Lord, even in small moments, such as times in the garden. There I am often struck by the beauty of God's amazing creation and my heart swells with adoration for Him. He always responds to my adoration by letting me feel His pleasure in it.

Ultimately, worship is a permanent posture of the heart towards God that comes from true faith that He is Present and worthy of honor.

Knowing God: How We Become Fruitful

God has called me to be a teacher and a writer, two things I had never done nor dreamed of doing before I knew Him. But knowing God has made me fruitful in both of these endeavors, and I love how it looks when we work together.

When I write, searching for just the right way to phrase a concept, my spirit/soul (I can't divide them out from one other) now reflexively reaches for the Lord, without saying a word, and He responds. I have asked Him so much for help in prayers uttered out loud that when He sees me sit to write, I think His attention just turns to me, ready to answer me with the help He knows I will seek in my habitual way. It is similar to how you are with your spouse. After years together you can just give them a look across the room and they know what you need, are thinking or feeling. My Spirit Friend and I know one another's ways and move with one another without having to say much.

So as I write, words come: lovely, wise, insightful thoughts that make me smile. I'm sure they were born deep in my spirit, where I know Him, because I know myself and how I think on my own... my thoughts are not that lovely, wise or insightful! We are a team now, as He takes all I've learned and weaves it together. It is pure joy to me.

I am not one who deflects compliments from those who hear me teach or read my books by saying, *"Oh, it's all the Lord,"* because it is not. Yes, He brings the inspired thoughts, but they don't come out of an empty place; He brings them up from the rich deposit of our shared life together. He does it by putting together something He whispered to me as I worshipped Him recently, with something He taught me five years ago, adding a Scripture written on my heart from years of study. It's like the baked cake that has become something wonderful and very different from the raw ingredients you stirred into that bowl. We're baking cakes in here together; He's the master chef, I'm the sous chef who preps the ingredients.

The point is, the Lord can write all the books He wants, but He doesn't do them without doing it through His people who learn, study and work at it. To my knowledge He has only written without using a man's hands a few times: twice on Moses' tablets and once on Belshazzer's wall. It is the Lord's design and pleasure to partner with us in the work of building His kingdom.

It is very daunting to think of writing a book, and I have to move past that feeling every time. But when I sit down with pen and paper (okay, and computer), the Lord always does the heavy lifting. I don't know where my talent and work begins and ends, or God's inspiration; I'm just left to enjoy and marvel at what He brings out. As we write books together, the Lord reveals even more of Himself and His truth. This is how He works with all of His children who work with Him in their calling, using His gifts. God gave me a gift of teaching, and as I step into exercising that gift, He increases it in me.

The Lord has rewarded my faithful studies and devotion by making me fruitful, full of His wisdom and armed with a pen. (This is not a boast in me, it is a boast in Him. I don't want to steal His glory, I say these things to give Him more glory, and hopefully inspire you to let Him glorify Himself in little old you, too.) No doubt there are more professional or scholarly books out there, but I ceased comparing long ago, because I've learned that God has a heart-target for my books, and I write for Him to give Him a tool to touch those hearts.

I can live all this far easier than I can explain it, which is a good thing. Instead, I'll borrow David's words, which sum up the way I feel most of the time as a beloved child of God:

> *My heart is not proud, Lord, my eyes are not haughty; I do not concern myself with great matters or things too wonderful for me. But I have calmed and quieted myself, I am like a weaned child with its mother; like a weaned child I am content. (Psalm 131:1-2)*

I hope you're already experiencing this in the things the Spirit is stirring in you. If not, please press in! Say "yes" to all the ways and places God is calling you to work with Him. Don't look at how impossible it seems; find out just how willing and able the Spirit is, and discover the joy of working with Him.

The Holy Spirit is not some impersonal spiritual power of God, He is your Friend and Helper, the one who is alongside you every day, leading you to the life God promises. Everything will be fulfilled as you know and follow Him.

19 The Goal Of Covenant: A Kingdom

The Lord invokes many motifs with us. We have explored knowing Him as Savior, Father, Teacher, and Friend. You've learned how God cares for you in His covenant faithfulness; now you need to understand your calling as His covenant friend, who supports Him in His passion: the Kingdom. We need to talk about knowing Jesus as King and what it means to be a citizen of His kingdom.

At some point in your growth the Spirit will begin to draw your attention to the Lord's goal of establishing a kingdom of citizens who share His moral character and ways. After reading Ephesians for those six months straight, it is written on my heart that God the Father has set the agenda of the universe upon Jesus His Son. He is now King of all His redeemed ones, and will be enthroned as King over all at the end of days.

The Covenant To Establish God's Kingdom

God made a special covenant with King David whose primary purpose was to establish an everlasting kingdom through David's family line:

> *I have made a covenant with my chosen one, I have sworn to David my servant, "I will establish your line forever and make your throne firm through all generations." (Psalms 89:3-4)*

God kept this promise through Jesus Christ, a direct descendant of David's earthly line through both Mary and

Joseph, his surrogate father. In His three and a half years of public ministry, Jesus continually taught about the kingdom, revealing its laws and values, and underscoring its vital importance, saying *"I must proclaim the good news of the kingdom of God ... because that is why I was sent."* (Luke 4:43)

The kingdom should matter to us because Jesus taught that it is the treasure we should be willing to sacrifice everything for:

> *The kingdom of heaven is like treasure hidden in a field. When a man found it, he hid it again, and then in his joy went and sold all he had and bought that field. (Matthew 13:44)*

The kingdom should matter to us because Jesus taught that it is the treasure we should be willing to sacrifice everything for.

Jesus bought that field. He sacrificed His earthly life, dying to purchase the "field" called earth that would yield a kingdom of precious souls for His beloved Father. After His resurrection, He charged His disciples to tend to the business of nurturing and caring for this budding kingdom as their highest priority, asking them to teach believers all He had taught them. Thus Jesus began the work of preparing a people to take their place in the kingdom and live faithful to their King. After He returned to heaven, the Spirit took up His work in each redeemed soul.

Through the direction of Christ, the Spirit equips team workers to build up the kingdom. Evangelists broadcast the good news and summon people into the kingdom; teachers and pastors prepare the people for kingdom life and work; apostles and prophets govern and direct this body of kingdom citizens. [1]

[1] Ephesians 4:11-13

Teachers, pastors, parents and youth leaders: your job is to disciple people in how to know the Lord and take their place in His kingdom. Please teach them about their need of the Holy Spirit, and nurture them in becoming mature sons and daughters of God. Show them how to hear and respond to their invisible but very present Lord Jesus Christ — Emmanuel, God (Still) With Us. This is the object of all faith towards God and the responsibility of every teacher and mentor.

The Ways And Values Of Our King

Jesus' teaching on the kingdom is especially well organized and concentrated in what is known as the Sermon on the Mount. Among other things, He revealed that in His kingdom, hypocrisy and pride are not welcome. He taught that religious expression at the expense of loving people will not be tolerated. He said the King of this kingdom will identify so closely with His people that He will treat every good or evil act done to them, as if done to Him as well. In other words, our King is totally committed to overseeing the faithfulness, righteousness and justice of His kingdom, as Isaiah prophesied He would be:

> *In love a throne will be established; in faithfulness a man will sit on it— one from the house of David — one who in judging seeks justice and speeds the cause of righteousness. (Isaiah 16:5)*

Those who share and live by the king's values are called faithful, and those who neglect them are considered unfaithful — even wicked. Jesus used a parable to reveal how the citizens of His kingdom will be judged on the day when He sits on His throne and assembles all before Him. His parable ended with this:

> *Truly I tell you, whatever you did for one of the least of these brothers and sisters of mine, you did for me. (Matthew 25:40)*

Jesus drove this point home even further, teaching His followers they should spend themselves to take care of others; promising that as they did, their King would take care of them:

> *But seek His kingdom, and these things will be given to you as well. Do not be afraid, little flock, for your Father has been pleased to give you the kingdom. Sell your possessions and give to the poor. Provide purses for yourselves that will not wear out, a treasure in heaven that will never fail, where no thief comes near and no moth destroys. For where your treasure is, there your heart will be also. (Luke 12:31-34)*

To seek the Father's kingdom means to live by His values and walk in His ways. There is only one way to store up treasure in heaven: that is by sending it ahead of you, deposited in the hearts of those you have faithfully loved on earth.

As Jesus made clear, you've been given a kingdom and entrusted with authority and responsibility to nurture it under Christ your King. You are asked to care for it as the King would, by bringing His Presence, values and power to your personal world. As I have grown in knowing God, I have become increasingly aware of my role in His kingdom.

God's Kingdom Is Here And Now

If you are joined with Christ in covenant, you already live in this kingdom now, under the government of your Sovereign Lord. You are expected to know and uphold His righteous laws, referred to in the New Testament collectively as "the royal law." This is the law of love, which Jesus gave us in two parts. The first and greatest part of the law is to love the Lord with all your heart, soul, mind and strength (Matthew 12:30), which has been God's law from the beginning of time.

The second part came as a new commandment Jesus instituted the night before He went to the cross. It requires His faithful ones to love others the way He loves them (John 13:34), which is radically different than the old command to love others as yourself. It is a much higher law to live by, but not too hard to do because we have the Presence and power of the Spirit to help us carry it out.

At the end of earth's days, when Jesus returns, you will be judged by these laws. Jesus will cleanse the world of all evil. He will create a new heaven and a new earth, free of evil, where His faithful ones will live and share in His revealed kingdom. You will answer to your King on that day primarily for how you responded to His incredible gift of Himself, and for your stewardship of His gracious gifts, the special abilities given you to minister to others for Him.

The minute you were born again, the seed of His kingdom was implanted in you:

> *The kingdom of heaven is like a mustard seed, which a man took and planted in His field. Though it is the smallest of all seeds, yet when it grows, it is the largest of garden plants and becomes a tree, so that the birds come and perch in its branches."* (Matthew 13:31-32)

When I was first saved, I knew nothing except that God loved me and Jesus gave His life to save me. Today, I am a productive citizen of the kingdom, knowing my place and my responsibility. Since 1979 I have steadily learned and grown in knowing God by faith, so that the mustard seed of God's kingdom has become a tree of life not only to me, but to others who taste of God through my life. This is His desire in all who bear His Name and carry His ability and authority to bless.

The Lord has made me fruitful as I have trusted in the Spirit and His gifts of grace at work in me.

The Lord has made me fruitful as I have trusted in the Spirit and His gifts of grace at work in me. By the Spirit's guidance and power I've had the joy of seeing people healed when I prayed for them. I've seen blind eyes open, pain disappear, many barren women conceive, and watched a leg six inches too short grow out before my eyes. I've witnessed people become free of depression, addictions and all kinds of affliction. By faith I've shared the counsel of the Spirit that resulted in lives being changed and hearts being healed. All this is by the Spirit's power, and in the name of Jesus; all this with a woman whom the Lord found as a captive to sin, who once had a selfish, immoral and unfaithful heart!

Miracles don't happen every time I pray, but they happen often. As I grow in faith and faithfulness, I believe His power will be more effectively released when I pray. I don't believe we grieve the Spirit by making mistakes in using His gifts as much as we do when we don't even try. I've learned to relax about not being a perfect instrument, to focus instead on being a faithful steward, available to God to express Himself as He desires.

As members of God's family, we participate fully His kingdom, and like all family members, we have responsibilities. He has asked us to take good care of His people and reveal Him to them. God has given us spiritual gifts, and asks us to use them in faith, trusting the Spirit to make us effective as we do. This is how we confirm to the Lord that He made a good choice in us, as the Apostle Peter says:

> *Therefore, my brothers and sisters, make every effort to confirm your calling and election. For if you do these things, you will never stumble, and you will receive a rich welcome into the eternal kingdom of our Lord and Savior Jesus Christ. (2 Peter 1:10-11)*

Your Role In God's "House"

The Apostle Peter writes about what the Lord is building as the Spirit connects one redeemed soul to another through Christ's new covenant:

"...you also, like living stones, are being built into a spiritual house to be a holy priesthood, offering spiritual sacrifices acceptable to God through Jesus Christ... you are a chosen people, a royal priesthood, a holy nation, God's special possession, that you may declare the praises of Him who called you out of darkness into His wonderful light. Once you were not a people, but now you are the people of God..." (1 Peter 2:5, 9)

We not just our own, getting by the best we can while we wait for heaven. We were made to become something together for God's glory and use. The Spirit has not been nurturing us just for our sake. He has been preparing us as God's holy nation, building us into a house full of spiritual priests who can connect God with the people He loves. We are called *living stones*, a reference that goes back to ancient covenant practices.

Remember the covenant paradigm: every covenant had its memorial, testifying publicly that a relationship of mutual unfailing love has been made between two parties. Often in Scripture we find reference to these memorials being etched on stones with the names of the two joined in covenant. As we each know God individually, we become those living stones: a testimony to His glory as a relational God, Faithful and True. We were made for the praise of His glory, raised to be sons and daughters of His faithfulness and goodness.

As I carry the Lord's name and host His Presence, I will add to or subtract from His glory by my life. We give God glory by letting Him live and move and have His being in us, so that His power and goodness are revealed. This was the example set by the firstborn of this holy nation, our brother Jesus. Jesus emptied Himself so the Father could live through Him and be revealed to His world. This task is now ours. As a priesthood, we are mediators — a meeting place between people and the Living God. Each of us is now God's mercy seat on earth, where His Presence dwells and moves among the wilderness of lost souls He longs to save and lead to life.

Faithfulness Is Praying For Those On The King's Heart

Faithfulness includes praying for people, situations, and governments on earth, especially in your own community, state and country. Our prayers are powerful to help establish the King's justice and righteousness for all. Our intercession is meant to bring the Lord's healing and freedom to those who are sick and oppressed. Faithfulness to the Lord means interceding for His people to fully come into their destiny — His design for them. We all need help to become all we can be in the Lord.

Each of us is now God's mercy seat on earth.

You have access to His throne 24/7, which is not just a privilege for your concerns. This access comes with the responsibility to act as God's spiritual priesthood, mediators who seek to know God's will and pray for it to become reality on the earth. Jesus taught us to pray: *"Thy kingdom come, thy will be done on earth as it is in heaven."* As those who stand between God and people, we have been entrusted with the name and authority of Jesus to release God's will, justice and blessing to our world.

The Apostle Paul reminded us to be alert and stand together against spiritual forces of evil:

> *Put on the full armor of God, so that you can take your stand against the devil's schemes. For our struggle is not against flesh and blood, but against the rulers, against the authorities, against the powers of this dark world and against the spiritual forces of evil in the heavenly realms (Ephesians 6:11-12)*

He went on to say in verse 18, *"And pray in the Spirit on all occasions with all kinds of prayers and requests. With this in mind, be alert and always keep on praying for all the Lord's people."*

Faithfulness on your part is asking the King each day what concerns are on His heart, and waiting on the Spirit to reveal His thoughts to you in these matters. Ask the Spirit to fill you with the Lord's own passion and compassion about them — as He will — and then faithfully pray out of that passion. There are some especially tasked with the ministry of intercession, but all of God's people are equipped and called to intercede as the Spirit stirs and interrupts our rest to tend to the King's business. The King who watches faithfully over every soul in His realm is counting on you to facilitate His provision through prayer.

Over the course of our 20 years living in Azle, Texas, the Lord gave us various prayer assignments. For instance, He told me to "prayer walk" our small downtown area for several weeks. I would walk down the blocks, praying for the peace and prosperity of every business and city office, while being attentive to any extra insight the Spirit shared with my mind to declare. When we moved to South Texas, the Lord asked me to pray for the school bus that comes by our home every school day. I declare blessing, safety, healing, and desire to know the Lord over everyone who rides, drives, or works on that bus. It is a holy charge entrusted to me by the Lord. I am confident that my prayers make a difference because He called me to them. I presume He has called other people to pray over their neighbors, school buses, businesses.

If all God's people do their part to pray as the Spirit directs, we will be doing our faithful part to help establish God's kingdom by releasing His will on earth. As the redeemed covenant people of God, we are not powerless, and we are not bystanders. We are children of the One who commanded the world into existence by His Words. We are not equal to God in such power, but we do have a measure, and we have His Words, and we can be sure that when we declare His words to our world, they carry His power and will change what He sends them to change. The Lord said as much in Isaiah 55:10-11:

> *As the rain and the snow come down from heaven, and do not return to it without watering the earth and making it bud and flourish, so that it yields seed for the sower and bread for the eater, so is my word that goes out from my mouth: it will not return to me empty, but will accomplish what I desire and achieve the purpose for which I sent it.*

You and I will face a judgment when we meet our King face-to-face. However, we will not be measured against the laws of the Old Covenant, the Ten Commandments given through Moses. Our judgment will be in the context of a family member who has enjoyed the grace of a covenant relationship. Our judge will be the Father who gave us all things, and Jesus our covenant friend and King, who gave His life so we could enjoy the highest privilege of life. Our King has two royal laws by which we will be judged: to love the Lord with all your heart, soul, mind and strength; and to love others as the Lord has loved you.[2] It's an open book test, and there is no excuse for failing.

Developing A Covenant Heart

Christianity is a covenant that establishes a kingdom, ruled by a king with a covenant heart. Even now, He is building that kingdom one soul at a time as each develops a heart after God. You have been called into fellowship with the Lord so you can be mentored in having a true covenant heart like His.

The highest value of a covenant heart is to honor the faith that others have placed in him; whether that "other" is a spouse, child, parent, or employer. A covenant heart guards every relationship against any enemy that could destroy it. An enemy can be a person, a passion, or your own selfishness. Faithfulness is the highest value of God's kingdom and the mark of a covenant heart. Solomon said it like this:

---

[2] Mark 12:30 and John 13:34.

Let love and faithfulness never leave you; bind them around your neck, write them on the tablet of your heart. (Prov. 3:3)

Remember, when God asks this of His children, He already lives like this. He is more pleased with faithfulness than a thousand offerings at church. God makes it clear in Scripture that He aligns Himself with everyone you relate to — saved or unsaved — so that a sin against them is a sin against Him. Those who live "in the fear of the Lord" are those who take this to heart and live by it, along with all other expressions of covenant faithfulness.

When we do not keep faithfulness in our relationship with Him and others, God calls it *breaking faith*. To *keep faith* is to be vigilant about your faithfulness.

Keeping Faith Vs. Breaking Faith

In a reciprocal covenant of love with the Lord, our lives are now judged by whether we keep faith or break faith with Him and others.

You keep faith with the Lord by obeying Him and yielding to His Spirit. You break faith by disobeying or ignoring what you know He requires of you.

You keep faith with the Lord by believing in and responding to Him. You break faith when you behave as if He is not present; neither obeying nor honoring His Presence.

You keep faith with the Lord by forgiving others and leaving all justice to Him. You break faith when you do not forgive, holding out for justice on your terms.

You keep faith by learning and revealing the truth about the Lord. You break faith by remaining ignorant and misrepresenting the truth about Him to others.

You keep faith with the Lord by seeking and walking in His truth and values. You break faith when *you* decide what is true, determining what is good or evil.

You keep faith with the Lord by treating others as you would Him; giving what is due the Lord to all made in His image: respect, honor, and what Paul calls "the continuing debt to love." [3] You break faith when you withhold these things, or by mistreating or abusing others in any way.

You keep faith with the Lord by using His gifts to serve your neighbor. You break faith by holding back when He wants to touch someone through you. [4]

These are not commandments from God, they are expressions of what covenant love and faithfulness look like. To break faith in these ways is to miss God's mark or standard of committed righteous relationship. By these definitions, we all break faith with God and others at times, finding ourselves in need of God's forgiveness and grace. The new covenant is an awesome gift, and these are our obligations in it. Thank God the new covenant guarantees we will be forgiven when we fail in them!

A covenant heart is kind and generous, extending favor and grace to all they share life with. A covenant heart is an accountable and devoted heart, and such a heart will change the world, hand in hand with God. The bottom line is this:

God is your faithful covenant Friend — will you live your life as His?

[3] Romans 13:8

[4] A printable chart of this section can be downloaded at www.shammah.org/presentations/free-resources/

20 Final Thoughts

My goal in this book has been to reveal the life of a single redeemed soul knowing God, and to show how that life fits into the greater plan of the Trinity. I wanted to show you how much difference your one life of knowing God can make in your family, your church, your city, and in God's kingdom. We have telescoped into the interior of my heart and all the way back out to the kingdom God is building, in hopes that you will be inspired to know God for yourself.

Spirit Life

I call this life with God *Spirit life* because it all happens through His Spirit living in me, joined to my human spirit. It has been my experience that knowing God happens organically and naturally, developing as any relationship would.

I have moved away from the church as my primary source of spiritual growth because my daily life and home have become that place. While you need to participate in the community of faith at times, Spirit life goes on 24/7. The role of the church is to support your growth, but it is not meant to be the only place you meet with God, or even the primary place you encounter Him. He is always with you; at your home, in your workplace, at your picnic. You don't go to church to meet with God, because you take Him with you.

God uses the dynamics of our relationships to parents, husband and children in teaching us how to relate to Him. Through the indwelling Spirit, the Trinity has been a team in raising me as a part of their divine covenant family, preparing me for citizenship in their kingdom. The Father has especially "re-parented" me in every way that my dear but flawed parents didn't know how.

I love the promise in Psalm 33:18 which says, "*...the eyes of the Lord are on those who fear Him, on those whose hope is in His unfailing love...*" because I am one of those. I have full hope in God's love for me and I love knowing He is watching for ways to reward my hope.

There are some who see my life and say, "Wow, I want what you have!" I'm so glad, because I feel incredibly rich and blessed. This is why I write books, teach and mentor. But please understand that even though I am miles from where I began, it feels like I have just come to the part where I'm getting good at being God's child. I'm the Little One who fully trusts, is totally relaxed with Daddy, adores Him and believes I can grow up to be anything.

We Know God By Stages

The Spirit gave me something I needed very much as I began walking with Him: permission to be a child, accepting my complete helplessness to be anything but a foundling. Looking back over my own experience, I now believe this is one of the most crucial aspects of beginning to know God.

As you come to God you must be as a little child with Him, and grow in how you know Him.

As you come to God, newly saved or newly aware of His Spirit in you, you must be as a little child with Him, and grow from there in how you know Him, just as we do with our human parents. So at first it will be all about receiving the Father's love and being established in your identity as His beloved child. This is the season when you fill up on Father's delight in you, letting it heal and nurture you.

This will be the hardest part for those who come from a religious history like the Apostle Paul. The gentleness of the Lord is disorienting after the scales come off that blinded you to His tender love. This is a season that should not be rushed. Linger at the Lord's pace and fully discover Abba Father, the one Jesus wanted you to know so badly that He suffered torture so you could! When you begin to rest in your spirit about the Father's love, He will take you on to the next stages of knowing Him.

As a child grows up he gradually comes to know his parents in new ways, relating to them on increasingly mature levels. He begins to understand more about who they are as individual personalities, not just as Mom and Dad. He learns their values and is entrusted with new levels of responsibility. Somewhere along the way he learns to love and honor his parents instead of only being on the receiving end of all that love. His parents help him discover who he is meant to be when he grows up.

Likewise, the Spirit will increase your understanding and test your faith in new ways. More will be required of you and entrusted to you as you step out with the Lord in uncharted waters. You will begin to see what you are meant to be when you "grow up" in your salvation. In fact, you will be surprised by desires and dreams of doing things that you once would have thought totally improbable, if not impossible.

It is exciting as the Lord's passion and plans develop in you; yet scary as you consider your human flaws and limitations. You will have a moment just like Moses did when God told him to go set His people free from Pharaoh's mighty hand. Moses asked the same question you will: *"Who am I that I should go?"* [1] And you will get the same answer from God that Moses got: *"I will be with you."* At some point you will realize your flaws and limitations are not an issue to God; He will carry you through them or even use them.

---

[1] Exodus 3:11

Your flaws and limitations are not an issue to God.

I felt just like Moses when the Spirit began to send me out as a public teacher and speaker — totally inadequate! I studied for hours, wrote very detailed outlines many pages long, and relied heavily on them to deliver a message. As I grew at speaking the anxiety subsided and I became more relaxed as I saw that the Spirit really carried me in those times. Somewhere along the way all those pages of notes actually began to get in the way of flowing with the Spirit, who seemed to quietly download streams of inspiration as I spoke.

Recently I spoke at an ecumenical gathering of Christians in our community. Though I still do the usual preparation and study, I now go with a single page of the major points I believe the Lord wants to share. On this occasion a powerful message came out that felt nearly effortless — it was fun and joyful to me. As I sat drinking my tea with the Lord the next morning, He said to me: *"You are the daughter of my strength."* I felt His joy and fatherly pride, and I still carry this latest "Daddy compliment" in my heart as well as in my journal. The Father who does this for me will surely do the same for you as you step out and obey Him in the work He created you to do.

As you know God in new ways through each new season of your life, confidence grows, both in Him and in yourself, that together you are a team that can change your world. By now you have been so thoroughly loved by God that you want others to know what it is like, and now you know how. Your heart will become full of compassion for people as God's own heart for them rises up out of that place where you are "one." You won't be able to walk through a mall without noticing people who need something from the Lord, and you'll want to heal them all. One day, you will actually do something about that, which is the beginning of a life of revealing your amazing God to the people in your world. This brings joy to you and the Lord together. There is nothing like it.

Even as you know God, life will still be hard, challenges will abound, people and life will continue to test you in every way; but you will be able to meet all with faith, not fear. You will not fear anything but grieving the Lord Himself. You will have courage because God is with you; not just as a faith promise in a little box, but in truth.

God Has Provided All We Need To Know Him

I have spoken to you of knowing God, out of the full conviction that you can know Him as much as you desire. I believe this with my whole heart. Naturally we shall know Him more fully in heaven than while we still lived in our skin suits. Yet we truly have no excuse for not knowing God in great measure here and now, as the Apostle Peter testifies:

> *His divine power has given us everything we need for a godly life through our knowledge of Him who called us by His own glory and goodness. (2 Peter 1:3)*

You will have courage because God is with you; not just as a faith promise in a little box, but in truth.

Peter makes it clear that God has provided — past tense, done deal — everything we need to become a mature son or daughter of God. We can and must become like Christ: possessing His character, walking in His ways and power, for the sake of all we encounter in life — especially those closest to us. Our first charge is to present Christ to our spouses, children and friends — not just sharing the gospel with them but revealing the Lord's goodness to them.

Where Will You Be?

I almost never see visions. But occasionally, the Lord lets me see one with the eyes of my spirit. In the most vivid one I've ever had, I saw Jesus standing with one arm outstretched, a sword in His hand, pointed menacingly at an unseen enemy. Under the Lord's other arm was a young girl — me. His arm was tenderly encircling me, holding me close to His heart, His embrace as tender as His gaze was ferocious towards whoever was at the end of His sword. Then He spoke the caption for the vision, a question for the people of the world:

> *"When I return, will you be under my arm, near my heart, or will you be at the end of my sword? These are the only two choices."*

I know where I'm going to be.

Appendix: The Roles Of The Holy Spirit

Romans 8:16: Reassures you are God's child, He is your Father.

Psalm 32:8: Teaches you, counsels you when you don't know what to do, revealing the thoughts of God (the mind of Christ) to you. 1 Corinthians 2:6-16. See also John 14:26; 16:5-15.

Isaiah 42:16: Leads you and lights the way when you're blind (walking in a dark place and can't see the way).

Isaiah 57:18: Heals your physical and emotional wounds. Restores comfort when you've been hurt. Gives new life, John 6:63. See also 2 Corinthians 1:3-4.

Isaiah 58:11: Satisfies all your needs, waters your thirsty soul.

Mark 13:11: Tells you what to say when needed. See Luke 12:12.

Luke 10:21: Gives you joy. Reveals the Father and Jesus even to little children (or those who trust Him in a childlike manner).

John 16:13-15: Connects you to your birthright inheritance as children of God.

John 16:13: Prepares you for what is ahead. See Acts 20:23.

Acts 9:31: Strengthens and encourages you when you're weak.

Romans 5:5: Reveals God's love to you and helps you love God.

Ephesians 3:17. Establishes you in God's love as the foundation of your relationship.

Romans 14:17: Gives you gifts. Gives you righteousness. Gives you peace. Gives you joy. See also 1 Thessalonians 1:6.

Romans 15:13: Fills you with hope.

Romans 15:16: Cleanses you when you "get dirty" (do something offensive, violating God's holiness and purity). See also Titus 3:5.

Romans 8:26-27: Teaches you to pray, helps you be effective.

2 Corinthians 1:21-22: Helps you stand firm in Christ.

Philippians 2:13: Energizes, empowers and motivates you to do God's will.

Appendix: My Sheep Listen To My Voice

John 10:27: "My sheep listen to my voice; I know them, and they follow me."

Hebrews 8:10-11: In the New Covenant of Jesus, God promises we will all be taught by God and will know Him.

John 16:13: Jesus described the Spirit's role. "But when He, the Spirit of truth, comes, He will guide you into all truth. He will not speak on His own; He will speak only what He hears, and He will tell you what is yet to come."

Isaiah 50:4: "The Sovereign Lord has given me an instructed tongue, to know the word that sustains the weary. He wakens me morning by morning, wakens my ear to listen like one being taught."

Psalm 32:8: The Lord said to David: "I will instruct you and teach you in the way you should go; I will counsel you and watch over you." The Lord is called Wonderful Counselor, Isaiah 9:6. See also John Chapters 14 and 15.

Ephesians 5:10: We are told, "find out what pleases the Lord," and "understand what the Lord's will is." (Ephesians 5:17)

Colossians 2:3: Jesus is the one "in whom are hidden all the treasures of wisdom and knowledge." It is His voice of wisdom saying to us in Proverbs 1:23 and 33: "If you had responded to my rebuke, I would have poured out my heart to you and made my thoughts known to you," and "whoever listens to me will live in safety and be at ease, without fear of harm."

Proverbs 8:32-36: "Now then, my sons, listen to me; blessed are those who keep my ways. Listen to my instruction and be wise; do not ignore it. Blessed is the man who listens to me, watching daily at my doors, waiting at my doorway. For whoever finds me finds life and receives favor from the Lord. But whoever fails to find me harms himself; all who hate me love death."

Mark 4:23-25, Jesus says: "If anyone has ears to hear, let him hear. Consider carefully what you hear," he continued. "With the measure you use, it will be measured to you — and even more. Whoever has will be given more; whoever does not have, even what he has will be taken from him."

James 1:5-7: "If any of you lacks wisdom, he should ask God, who gives generously to all without finding fault, and it will be given to him."

Moses said to the Hebrews at Mount Sinai: "Now what I am commanding you today is not too difficult for you or beyond your reach. It is not up in heaven, so that you have to ask, 'Who will ascend into heaven to get it and proclaim it to us so that we may obey it?' Nor is it beyond the sea, so that you have to ask, 'Who will cross the sea to get it and proclaim it to us so that we may obey it?' No, the word is very near you; it is in your mouth and in your heart so that you may obey it... that you may love the Lord your God, listen to his voice, and hold fast to him. For the Lord is your life..." (Deuteronomy 30:11-14 and 20)

Appendix: Every Instance Of Hesed In The OT

Hebrew word "*hesed*" (Strong's #02617) is the unfailing love and kindness pledged in covenant. KJV, NAS, RSV and NKJV render it kindness, mercy, or lovingkindness; NIV renders it "unfailing love."

Genesis: 19:19 20:13 21:23 24:12,14,27,49 32:10 39:21 40:14 47:29 Exodus 15:13 20:6 34:6,7 Leviticus 20:17 Numbers 14:18,19 Deuteronomy 5:10 7:9,12 Joshua 2:12,14 Judges 1:24 8:35 Ruth 1:8 2:20 3:10 1 Samuel 15:6 20:8,14,15 2 Samuel 2:5,6 3:8 7:15 9:1,3,7 10:2 15:20 16:17 22:51 1 Kings 2:7 3:6 8:23 20:31 1 Chronicles 16:34,41 17:13 19:2 2 Chronicles 1:8 5:13 6:14,42 7:3,6 20:21 24:22 32:32 35:26 Ezra 3:11 7:28 9:9 Nehemiah 1:5 9:17,32 13:14,22 Esther 2:9,17 Job 6:14 10:12 37:13 Psalms 5:7 6:4 13:5 17:7 18:50 21:7 23:6 25:6,7,10 26:3 31:7,16,21 32:10 33:5,18,22 36:5,7,10 40:10,11 42:8 44:26 48:9 51:1 52:1,8 57:3,10 59:10,16,17 61:7 62:12 63:3 66:20 69:13,16 77:8 85:7,10 86:5,13,15 88:11 89:1,2,14,24,28,33,49 90:14 92:2 94:18 98:3 100:5 101:1 103:4,8,11,17 106:1,7,45 107:1,8,15,21,31,43 108:4 109:12,16,21,26 115:1 117:2 118:4,29 119:41,64,76, 88,124,149,159 130:7 136:1-26 138:2,8 141:5 143:8,12 144:2 145:8 147:11 Proverbs 3:3 11:17 14:22,34 16:6 19:22 20:6,28 21:21 31:26 Isaiah 16:5 40:6 54:8,10 55:3 57:1 63:7 Jeremiah 2:2 9:24 16:5 31:3 32:18 33:11 Lamentations 3:22,32 Daniel 1:9 9:4 Hosea 2:19 4:1 6:4,6 10:12 12:6 Joel 2:13 Jonah 2:8 4:2 Micah 6:8 7:18,20 Zechariah 7:9

About The Author

Tonia Woolever is a an ordained minister of the Gospel, Bible teacher, speaker, counselor, mentor and author. She married Dr. Ron Woolever in 1981 and in 1990 they established Shammah Ministries, a teaching and equipping ministry to all denominations in the Body of Christ. Their particular calling and passion is to reveal the unfailing love of God offered in the New Covenant of Christ, and to help Christians learn to live as faithful covenant children of God who walk with the Holy Spirit and hear God's voice. Since 1995 they have traveled across the U.S. and in foreign countries teaching these and other vital Christian truths. They are the co-authors of *Can I Really Hear God?*

Tonia is the author of *The Woman God Designed*, used for women's personal and group study. She speaks at women's conferences and loves to meet with women in a retreat setting, where her transparent personal style helps women connect with Christ in the real places of their lives. Tonia writes books in a series called ScribeLife, each focusing on a particular aspect of growing into the life God wants to build in His children, for His joy and glory, and for theirs.

Tonia has many creative loves: cooking, gardening, knitting, and photography. She finds joy in exuberant worship, good food, great music and movies, playing games and laughing with her husband, family and friends.

Tonia and Ron live in Texas. They are available individually or as a team for conferences, retreats, leadership training and seminars. For more information on topics and resources, see their website, www.shammah.org. If you would like to have Tonia speak at your conference, retreat or other event, email her at tonia@shammah.org.

ADDITIONAL RESOURCES

The following and additional products from Shammah Ministries, plus free downloadable resources, are available at their website, www.shammah.org:

BOOKS

The Woman God Designed

Leader's Group Study Guide for The Woman God Designed

SCRIBELIFE SERIES

Can I Really Hear God?

Rooted & Established In Love

They Will All Know Me

TEACHING ON DVD

Covenant: God's Principles of Committed Love

TEACHING ON CD

Covenant: God's Principles of Committed Love

Spirit Life: Walking in God's Abundant Life

Hearing God

Entering God's Rest

What Kind of Woman Will I Be?

CPSIA information can be obtained
at www.ICGtesting.com
Printed in the USA
LVOW08s0422031116
511422LV00012B/127/P